From Guernica
to Guardiola

From Guernica to Guardiola

HOW THE SPANISH CONQUERED ENGLISH FOOTBALL

Adam Crafton

**SIMON &
SCHUSTER**

London · New York · Sydney · Toronto · New Delhi

A CBS COMPANY

First published in Great Britain by Simon & Schuster UK Ltd, 2018
A CBS COMPANY

Copyright © 2018 by Adam Crafton

1 3 5 7 9 10 8 6 4 2

Simon & Schuster UK Ltd
1st Floor
222 Gray's Inn Road
London WC1X 8HB

www.simonandschuster.co.uk

Simon & Schuster Australia, Sydney
Simon & Schuster India, New Delhi

The author and publishers have made all reasonable efforts to contact
copyright-holders for permission, and apologise for any omissions or errors in
the form of credits given. Corrections may be made to future printings.

A CIP catalogue record for this book
is available from the British Library.

ISBN: 978-1-4711-5713-4
Ebook ISBN: 978-1-4711-5715-8

Typeset and designed in the UK by M Rules
Printed and bound by CPI Group (UK) Ltd, Croydon, CR0 4YY

MIX
Paper from
responsible sources
FSC® C020471

Simon & Schuster UK Ltd are committed to sourcing paper that is
made from wood grown in sustainable forests and support the Forest
Stewardship Council, the leading international forest certification organisation.
Our books displaying the FSC logo are printed on FSC certified paper.

CONTENTS

To my grandfather, Martin Glyn

PROLOGUE

In the arts, it is often said that the darkest times can spawn the greatest beauty and, when it comes to Spaniards in English football, it feels rather fitting. When we think about the Spanish influence of the modern era, it is the close control, it is the geometric precision of their passing, it is the one-twos, the back-heels and the nutmegs. It is those days when Manchester City's David Silva passes the ball like there is a computer chip in his boots, when Arsenal's Santi Cazorla dazzles amid a blur of passing and movement at pinball speed, when Manchester United's David De Gea gives the impression that he will happily play until midnight and his opponent still won't score a goal. It is Manchester City manager Pep Guardiola taking a sledge-hammer to the conventions of English football and thrilling supporters with the shortest team in the Premier League.

In the 2016-17 season, the Premier League featured 36 Spaniards, a figure higher than any other nationality except for English players. There were over three times as many Spaniards as Germans, more than double the number of Welsh or Scottish players and over a dozen more Spaniards than Dutch or Belgian players. By November of the 2017-18 campaign, 28 Spaniards had made Premier League appearances. Those players' current sides spent a total of £343.9m to sign them and they have a combined Twitter following of over 50 million. Big talent, big money.

We have come a long way since Dave Whelan and his 'three amigos' at Wigan Athletic in the old Division Three during the mid-1990s. Posing in sombreros for photographs, sharing a Ford Escort and living in a run-down semi-detached house, Roberto Martinez, Jesus Seba and Isidro Diaz barely spoke a word of English between them. Martinez, of course, would go on to win the FA Cup as the club's manager. Alex Calvo Garcia arrived at Scunthorpe as the only Spaniard and he became the first from his country to score at Wembley for an English club, striking the winning goal in a play-off final in 1999. Indeed, he has even written a book – *Scunthorpe hasta la muerte* (*Scunthorpe Until I Die*) – which must, surely, be the only foreign language book whose title includes the town of Scunthorpe.

Yet consider this statistic: by the time Chelsea made Albert Ferrer the first Premier League signing of a Spaniard in 1998, top-flight English clubs had purchased players from 51 other countries on six continents. Indeed, it was quite some time before Spanish players landed *en masse* in English football, notwithstanding the arrival of Nayim in the late 1980s. So, just how do we explain the absence of Spaniards in the top echelons of the English game between the 1950s and the late 1990s? In an era when Spanish football welcomed Brits such as Terry Venables, Gary Lineker, Sir Bobby Robson and Laurie Cunningham, to mention just a few, why were the Spaniards so reticent to swap the Iberian Peninsula for the English game? Or, indeed, why were English teams so reluctant to invest in the Spanish?

This is a book about football but it will also look at the political and historical context. Spanish football is inseparable from the politics that fuels its character and any attempts to understand the success or failure of its representatives abroad must be underpinned by in-depth analysis of an insular culture that is still coming to terms with its liberty.

The Spanish invasion is a modern phenomenon of the past 20 years and I hope this book explains the manner in which Spain's international success has impregnated England's national game, altering perceptions and changing attitudes. Yet for every sprinkling of quality that has arrived from Spain, there has been a liability waiting around the corner. We may talk about players such as Xabi Alonso, Alvaro Morata and Cesc Fabregas with the fondest regard, but Newcastle United followers will shudder upon hearing the names Albert Luque and Marcelino Elena, while Liverpool supporters may wince at the name Josemi and Arsenal fans remain underwhelmed by Jose Antonio Reyes. Some of my most enjoyable interviews for this book have been in the company of those who struggled to live up to their potential. I appreciated the honesty and self-deprecating humour of Marcelino and I was touched by the story of former Sunderland midfielder Arnau Riera, who captained Lionel Messi in Barcelona's B team but is now retired and working as a hotel receptionist.

In an age where Premier League access is ever more difficult, I am grateful to the many players from past and present who agreed to be extensively interviewed, including Mikel Arteta, Juan Mata, Cesar Azpilicueta, David De Gea, Ander Herrera, Pepe Reina, Fernando Hierro, Jose Antonio Reyes, Nayim, Alejandro Calvo Garcia, Marcelino Elena and Arnau Riera. Roberto Martinez, Aitor Karanka, Pepe Mel, Juande Ramos and Pep Clotet provided fascinating insights into management in England, while Xavi Valero and Pako Ayestaran, former lieutenants of Rafa Benitez, were equally instructive.

Stoke City chief executive Tony Scholes brought a different slant by explaining how his club has been influenced by Spanish ideas, while former Middlesbrough sporting director Victor Orta, now at Leeds, demonstrates how Spaniards have been entrusted with overseeing recruitment. Edu Rubio, the MK Dons head coach for the Under-23 and Under-18 teams, explains the Spanish influence filtering down to lower-league academies. I have also drawn on interviews I have carried out for the *Daily Mail* with Diego Costa, Alvaro Morata, Gus Poyet, Eric Abidal, Bojan Krkic, Gerard Deulofeu, Oriol Romeu and Quique Sanchez Flores.

Yet the story of Spaniards in English football has a deeper and richer backdrop. The year 2017 marked the 80th anniversary of the very first to arrive on our shores. My interest in this topic first stirred while studying Spanish at university. During a meeting with Amnesty International researcher Naomi Westland to discuss the Spanish Civil War, she informed me of the hidden stories of the first Spanish footballers to come to England.

In 1937, as General Franco linked up with Adolf Hitler to brutalise the Basque Country and ravage Guernica with an infamous aerial assault, 4,000 children boarded a rickety boat to England. In a battle for survival, they left their parents behind and embarked on a new life. Their personal and sporting stories are laced with triumph and tragedy, and some of these children, who began their careers at English clubs such as Southampton and Coventry, would go on to star for Real Madrid and Barcelona. One would score Real's first goal at the Bernabeu, another would be the first to conceptualise La Masia, the extraordinary Barça academy responsible for so many magnificent talents. These men would do so, however, having witnessed some of the most chilling scenes imaginable. The families of Emilio Aldecoa, Raimundo Perez Lezama, Sabino Barinaga and Jose and Antonio Gallego went above and beyond in their time and support for the project, bringing to life their relatives' most cherished memories and affording me access to all manner of cuttings, keepsakes and memorabilia.

There is, sadly, an unfortunate symmetry to then and now, as the Spain of 2018 finds itself embroiled in its gravest crisis since democracy returned following Franco's death in 1975. As the country comes to terms with an economic malaise and a Catalan breakaway movement, politics and culture are inextricably entwined in the football landscape once more. So this is a football story, but it is also a story about Spain – Spain as a country, and how its way of thinking translates into football. This is also a book about England, our feelings towards refugees, and is a reminder of how open and closed our culture can prove to be.

Through interviews with the biggest names and the forgotten heroes, this book hopes to be a celebration of the Spanish contribution to the English game. However, it will also throw light on the weird, wacky and woeful who have toiled without joy, thus exploring the challenges that Spaniards have faced upon arriving in England and how this reflected the state of the Spanish nation at certain periods of time.

CHAPTER 1

The Princes of Southampton

On 1 September 2013, Tottenham Hotspur's Gareth Bale became the world's most expensive footballer when he signed for Real Madrid for a fee reported to be worth £85.3 million. It was Southampton, however, where Bale began his career, joining the club as a child in 1999. Rod Ruddick, a scout at the south-coast club, spotted the Welsh youngster. It was an August bank holiday and the eight-year-old Bale was playing in a six-a-side tournament in Newport. Ruddick liked what he saw. He liked that firecracker of a left foot; he liked the pace that made Bale Wales' second fastest 50-metre sprinter by the age of 11, and he liked the unassuming manner in which the winger went about his work. Ruddick exchanged telephone numbers with the player's parents, Frank and Debbie, and a star was born.

At Southampton, there have been others. Theo Walcott, Alex Oxlade-Chamberlain, Adam Lallana and Luke Shaw form just a sample of the graduates who have most recently forged careers at Arsenal, Liverpool and Manchester United respectively. Yet Bale is different. Bale was signed by Real Madrid. It is normal for Manchester United and Arsenal to sign Britain's finest talents, but for a Southampton youth-teamer to breathe in the more rarefied air of Madrid? Well, that is something else entirely and it sets Bale apart from all those who have gone before him.

All except for one man – Sabino Barinaga. For Barinaga is the Southampton academy graduate whose name is eternally inscribed into Real Madrid folklore; the scorer of the club's very first goal at the Santiago Bernabeu and 92 more in a decade as a *madrileño*.

Sabino's story, which begins in the town of Durango, one of Biscay's major cities located south-east of Bilbao, is both heart-rending and uplifting. It is a tale in which the terrors of war in Spain intertwine with rare kindness from the British people, in which the artistic talents of Pablo Picasso and the generosity of Southampton Football Club converge as one.

Sabino was only 14 years old when the people of the Basque Country suffered the most traumatic episode of their proud history. The setting is the spring of 1937 and Spain finds itself in the midst of civil war. In the broadest terms, the Spanish Civil War can be described as a battle for supremacy between right-wing Nationalists and left-wing Republicans. The war began one year earlier, on 17 July 1936. The Spanish military, aided by right-wing Nationalists, launched a coup against the democratically elected government of Santiago Casares Quiroga. It sounded the starting pistol for three years of conflict as the warring forces struggled for the soul of Spain. General Franco's resultant dictatorship would endure for 36 more years beyond 1939.

As Franco's Nationalists advanced in March 1937, the autonomous Basque Republic – Euskadi – became embroiled in a struggle for its very existence. The Basque army eventually surrendered in August 1937, but the fate of the Basques should go down in the annals as a narrative of rare butchery. Writing in *The Times Literary Supplement* in 2007, Nicholas Rankin recorded that 7,000 had been killed in battle by the time of the surrender. Afterwards, some 6,000 were executed, 45,000 more imprisoned, while 150,000 went into exile for decades to come.

The Basque region of the Iberian Peninsula was arguably the site of the most vicious manifestation of tension between

Republicans and Nationalists. As the Basque resistance to Franco's forces intensified, the Nationalists became increasingly agitated as they sought a defining breakthrough. Matters soon came to a head. By this point, Franco and his generals were able to count on the collaboration of the Italian Fascist leader Benito Mussolini and his German counterpart Adolf Hitler. This alliance began in the Basque Country a sequence of events that would catastrophically alter the course of European history and set the tenor of global conflict for the rest of the century.

Their strategy was novel for its time: the aerial bombardment of a civilian population and using a tactic known in modern military parlance as 'shock and awe'. Nowadays, we are sadly familiar with this type of action, but in early 1937 it constituted a new mechanism of warfare in Europe and it was brutish in its conception. The strategy was to bomb targets of little or no military importance, the purpose being to terrify the civilian population and shatter morale. On the global stage, it was not completely new. The Italians, for instance, had employed such methods in their assaults on Abyssinia. However, the attacks on the Basque towns of Durango and Guernica in the spring of 1937 are accepted as being the first aerial bombings of civilian populations in Europe.

For Franco and the Nazis, the action represented a marriage of military convenience as well as a merging of shared ideological interests. Franco was able to utilise the full force of the German Condor Legion and then claim credit for its success, while the Germans were able to refine their craft and use the Basques as mere shooting practice for the aerial atrocities that would befall cities such as Rotterdam and Coventry during the Second World War.

Conversations began over the solution to Franco's Basque problem in the spring of 1937. Regular discussions took place between the commander of the Condor Legion, Hugo Sperrle, German Lieutenant Colonel Wolfram von Richthofen and

Spanish Nationalist commander Emilio Mola. Richthofen convinced the Spanish of the benefits of aerial bombings, but many accounts suggest Franco did not require much persuasion. Paul Preston, via German military historian Klaus Maier and access to Richthofen's diary entries, records that it was agreed at these meetings that attacks would 'proceed without taking into account the civilian population'. The first bombs dropped on the town of Durango on 31 March. Mola gave a radio broadcast and leaflets landed with a chilling warning: 'If your submission is not immediate, I will raze Vizcaya [Biscay] to the ground, beginning with the industries of war. I have ample means to do so.' A four-day assault followed. According to an initial investigation by the Basque government, the bombing killed 127 people immediately and a further 131 died as a result of their injuries.

These attacks came several weeks before the more publicised waves of terror that engulfed the town of Guernica but they were no less merciless. For Hitler, this would be the first time he ordered an aerial attack. In the market town of Durango, the opening bombs fell on the church, where villagers were attending Mass. A convent was obliterated, killing 14 nuns. Sabino Barinaga, future Southampton and Real Madrid striker, survived.

Seventy-eight years later, it is a spring afternoon in central Madrid and I meet with Sabino's daughter, Almudena, a smart and vivacious lady. Her father died in 1988 at the age of 66 but his story remains mostly untold to this day. Sitting in the sunshine in the Plaza de Chueca, puffing away on a cigarette and sipping an espresso, Almudena blows out her cheeks and grimaces when I ask how her father would describe those dark days.

'His hometown of Durango was obliterated during the bombings,' she says, shaking her head. 'He said the house was destroyed. It sounded horrendous. My father's voice would crack when he tried to explain the devastation of that period. He never told me too much, always the same story, an awful story. The planes were flying overhead and he was sprinting down the street. He looked back and there was a mother running too, holding her little girl by the hand. He carried on running. He hears an explosion, followed by a scream. He looks back again, only three or four seconds after he had previously. The mother is still holding her daughter by her hand, but the bomb blew the little girl's head off. We are talking here about the darkest moments of Spain's political history.'

Worse was to follow. As the Basque resistance continued, frustrations mounted for the Nationalists. A knockout blow was required. Richthofen's diaries detail the ambitions of the Nazis and Spanish fascists to reduce Bilbao to 'debris and ash'. On 25 April, another radio broadcast sounded. Another warning. 'Franco is about to deliver a mighty blow against which all resistance is useless. Basques! Surrender now and your lives will be spared!'

The terror arrived. On 26 April, market day in Guernica, the planes flew overhead. As the sun rose, it was an ordinary spring morning, a cloudless day, ideal weather for peasants coming in to buy their groceries but also, perversely, perfect conditions for warplanes to inflict maximum damage. The allies had realised that the greatest devastation could be dealt on market day, with an estimated 10,000 civilians expected to be in town. At 4.40pm, with the town full to the rafters, the church bells rang. Enemy planes were approaching.

In early 2017, I visited the town, catching a train from Bilbao, casting admiring glances at the countryside with its hills draped in green, and arriving into Guernica, the spiritual heartland of the Basque region. As I strolled around the main square, the town looked replenished and, 80 years on, there were few outward signs of the physical devastation. It is a stone-walled, medieval town, and the immediate impression is of a close-knit community. Yet Guernica still feels, primarily, like a place of memorials and memories. There is a park dedicated to reconciliation, an iconic assembly hall that remained untouched during the bombings and the Oak Tree of Guernica, under which the laws governing the Basque region were made in ancient times.

To this day, the elected head of the Basque autonomous government will travel to the Oak Tree in Guernica to swear an oath: 'Humble before God, standing on Basque soil, in remembrance of Basque ancestors, under the tree of Guernica.' There are tribute sculptures by the Englishman Henry Moore and Basque Eduardo Chillida. In the cafés and information centres, the locals know instinctively why a tourist would be in town.

At the Guernica Peace Museum, stark realities are laid bare. An exhibition records that the Condor Legion and the Italian *Aviazione Legionaria* dropped 'a mi...mum of 31 tonnes of bombs' on this historic town during three hours of sustained bombardment. It is claimed that one square kilometre of urban centre was wiped out and 85.22 per cent of buildings in the town were completely destroyed. The rest were at least partially affected as the fires kept burning for several days. The Euskadi government recorded 1,654 victims. According to the museum, there are 38 separate testimonials to corroborate these figures, even if the exact number remains disputed due to the attempts of the Franco regime to eliminate victims from the national historical memory.

The number of deaths is therefore a controversial and complex topic. The lowest Spanish count of the figure is 12, which many observers regard as insulting. The renowned South African journalist George Steer, whose coverage for *The Times* would awaken the world to the horrors of Guernica, did believe the deaths fell into the hundreds rather than thousands. Franco, for his part, went on the offensive, denying responsibility and claiming the Basques had torched their own city. Antonio Aguirre, president of the Euskadi government, said subsequently: 'Before God and the course of history that shall judge every one of us, I swear that for three and a half hours, the German planes viciously bombed the defenceless population of the historic town of Gernika, reducing it to ashes, pursuing women and children with the barrel of the machine gun. We have perished in great number, with many others fleeing hastily due to the fear and terror of it all.'

Franco, with all the transparency of a pint of Guinness, brazenly retorted: 'Aguirre is lying. We have respected Guernica, just as we respect all of Spain.' Franco was shameless, later anointing himself with the title of '*hijo adoptivo*' of the town of Guernica. It translates as 'adoptive son' but it is essentially the Spanish equivalent of the freedom of the city in the UK.

In an era in which Europe was governed by conservative minds and where irrational fears of Bolshevik conspiracies underpinned hostile perceptions of all matters Left, Franco's rebuttal might well have won the day. His propaganda machine went into overdrive. On Radio Berlin, the Germans blasted the 'lying Jewish press'. After his troops had cleaned up the town, Franco invited some international journalists for a stage-managed tour of Guernica, showing some petrol tins that he claimed underlined the guilt of the Basque government. However, this rapidly became a global public relations disaster and it was, in large part, due to some fearless journalism.

In April 1937, courage was to tell the truth in an age of lies and the international political community shuddered in collective horror when the authentic version of events was brought to light. Three journalists in particular played a starring role: the Australian Noel Monks of the *Daily Express*, the Scot Christopher Holme of Reuters and George Steer of *The Times*. Paul Preston, the outstanding historian of Spanish 20th-century history, tells the story of how the trio were eating together in Bilbao on the evening of the Guernica attacks. They drove to Guernica and Steer interviewed survivors, also smartly picking up a handful of bomb cases that were stamped with the German imperial eagle. This would later act as further proof of the attack.

In *The Times*, Steer wrote: 'At 2am today when I visited the town the whole of it was a horrible sight, flaming from end to end. The reflection of the flames could be seen in the clouds of smoke above the mountains from 10 miles away. Throughout the night houses were falling until the streets became long heaps of red impenetrable debris.'

He continued: 'In the form of its execution and the scale of the destruction it wrought, no less than in the selection of its objective, the raid on Guernica is unparalleled in military history. Guernica was not a military objective. A factory producing war material lay outside the town and was untouched. So were two barracks some distance from the town. The object of the bombardment was seemingly the demoralisation of the civil population and the destruction of the cradle of the Basque race. Every fact bears out this appreciation. The whole town of 7,000 inhabitants, plus 3,000 refugees, was slowly and systematically pounded to pieces.'

Steer's reportage stirred the national consciousness in Great Britain and the report was reproduced in the USA. Cabinet minutes from the meeting of the British government on 5 May 1937, chaired by Prime Minister Stanley Baldwin, emphasise the global sentiments. The Foreign Secretary Anthony Eden records a note from the US ambassador to say that the 'event had been received with the utmost horror in America, where it was regarded as a practice for the bombing of London and Paris'.

The American instinct would prove prescient. On 26 April 2007, at an event to mark the 70th anniversary of Guernica, the mayors of Hiroshima, Warsaw, Stalingrad, Pforzheim and more stood together with the Basque government to ignite a flame of remembrance. It was a reminder that after Guernica, shock and awe would be for evermore. The Basque writer Canon Alberto Onaindia described it as the 'first expression of total war'.

Meanwhile, Franco persisted with his imagined version of events. In *Guernica and Total War* by Ian Patterson, the author records a radio broadcast by Franco from Salamanca: '*Mentiras,*

mentiras, mentiras' ['Lies, lies, lies'],' Franco insisted. 'Aguirre lies! In the first place, there is no German or Spanish air force in Nationalist Spain . . . in the second place, we did not bomb Guernica. Franco's Spain does not set fires!'

Steer made further responses to Franco's denials in *The Times* on 6 and 15 May, while he also reported on the shooting-down of a German pilot in the Basque Provinces. Preston details how the pilot's logbook was found, which further proved the raid had taken place as it detailed his involvement. There is more evidence, in addition to the hundreds of witness accounts. Within the Guernica museum there resides a photograph of Hermann Goering congratulating and shaking the hands of the Condor Legion for the success of their operation. He would later admit at the Nuremberg trials in 1946 that this bombing was indeed intentional.

The name Guernica will for ever be associated with an act of supreme brutality. It is a name loaded with meaning, shorthand for terror. The town's plight was the inspiration behind Pablo Picasso's iconic *Guernica* painting. Picasso had read Steer's report while living in Paris, after the article had been reprinted in the French Communist newspaper *L'Humaniste*. Over the six weeks that followed, he developed his painting and immortalised the event in history. The portrait is used as a tapestry backdrop to the United Nation's New York debating chamber, serving as a constant, unsettling reminder to the world's diplomats of the perils of their decision-making. In Spain, it stirred the senses so much that Franco clamped down on those who owned a postcard of the picture.

It was a portrait that startled the world, making a rare global impact in the analogue age. It is one of the truisms of Europe's cultural heritage that the finest beauty can be extracted from the greatest evil. It calls to mind that wonderful quote by Orson Welles in the 1949 British film *The Third Man*. 'It's like the fella says,' muttered Welles' character, Harry Lime. 'Italy, in thirty years under the Borgias, they had terror, murder and bloodshed but they produced Michelangelo, Leonardo da Vinci and the Renaissance. In Switzerland, they had brotherly love, they had 500 years of democracy and peace. And what did they produce? The cuckoo clock.'

Picasso had his own sense of humour. Some years after publishing *Guernica*, he was living in Paris during the Nazi occupation of the Second World War. One day, a Gestapo officer stormed in, pointed at the mural on his wall and turned to the artist. 'Did you do that?' Picasso's reply was instant and disdainful: 'No, you did.'

The Franco lies continued for decades. Noel Monks, the *Daily Express* journalist present on the night, would later write in the *Daily Mail*: 'General Franco denied that the raid had ever taken place, and asserted that the Government forces had dynamited the town. Which made a colossal fibber of me, strained my relationship with my family in Australia and came near to having me excommunicated from my Church, for even the Pope supported Franco's denial.' In 1955, Adolf Galland, who served in Spain and was made a general by Hitler at the age of 29, brought out a book in which he admitted Guernica was a 'proving ground' for German air tactics and various explosive bombs and incendiary devices. 'Personally,' Monks wrote, 'I would like to hear what General Franco, who for 18 years has branded me a liar, has to say.'

Sixty years after the event, the Germans did finally acknowledge their complicity and guilt. In 1997, at a ceremony to commemorate the victims, the German ambassador to Spain, Henning Wegener, read out of a speech from his president, Roman Herzog. He said: 'I would like to confront the past and would like to explicitly admit to the culpable involvement of German pilots.' The *New York Times*, however, criticised the Germans for stopping short of a full apology. The German parliament had rejected a motion to discuss the raid, as the opposition to Helmut Kohl's coalition pushed for a whole-hearted and sincere apology. It was, nonetheless, vindication for Steer and Monks, who were fearless operators.

Nowadays, aerial bombing is ever more the norm, but owing to Picasso's painting, Guernica has become the byword for indiscriminate slaughter. As television pictures and newspaper front pages revealed the anguish of civilians in Aleppo in 2016, Guernica remained a frame of reference. In October 2016, the Conservative MP Andrew Mitchell said of the Russian air strikes in Syria: 'What they are doing to Aleppo is precisely what the Nazis did to Guernica in the Spanish Civil War.' The *Guardian*, *Daily Mail* and *The Times* were unusually unified, commending his words and courage in underlining the dangers of non-intervention. Peter Tatchell, the British human rights activist, hijacked a press conference led by Labour Party leader Jeremy Corbyn in December 2016 to decry the politician's failure to criticise 'a modern-day Guernica'. The Portuguese satirist and cartoonist Vasco Gargalo went one step further, superimposing the heads of Russian leader Vladimir Putin and the Syrian dictator Bashar al-Assad onto Picasso's portrait, in an image that went viral on social media.

Guernica was an event that shook the world and the consequences were extensive. As the Basque population grew fearful, it was by now no place for children. Children left because their parents were desperate. 'Child refugees go when there is no light left at the end of the tunnel,' wrote AA Gill, the late *Sunday Times* journalist, 'because the tunnel has by then been blown up.' Around 33,000 children were shipped out of the region. Evacuations became a daily occurrence. The vast majority went to France. Others went to the Soviet Union, Belgium, Denmark and Switzerland. The UK took just under 4,000, as Sabino and his two brothers were placed on the steamship *Habana* to Southampton. It was the beginning of an extraordinary tale of personal and sporting courage, trauma and tragedy giving way to triumph and trophies. And, as trivial as it may seem, it was also the beginning of the Spanish story in English football.

'By this time, my grandparents knew they had to get the kids out,' says Barinaga's daughter, Almudena, picking up the story. 'My grandfather was a supporter of Russia, a little bit of a Communist. He wanted my dad and his brothers to go to Russia. My grandmother didn't agree and she got them onto the boat to Britain instead. When my grandfather found out, he was running down to the port and trying to get onto the boat to pull them off! Thank goodness, it was too late. Without Britain, without Southampton, my father may never have fallen in love with football. He may never have scored 93 goals for Real Madrid.'

Sabino boarded the *Habana* with his two younger brothers, Iñaki and Jose Luis. After a perilous journey, they landed in Southampton on 23 May 1937. Speaking to the *Daily Mail* the following day, an eyewitness from the boat explained: 'Almost as soon as we left Bilbao harbour we ran into foul weather and it continued until we neared England. The children were bowled over like ninepins. They suffered terrible hardships and sickness.' The rickety engine warbled and choked its way northwards, a biblical human fish carrying the children to safety.

In Southampton, they were greeted kindly, as the report continued: 'The wild cries of delight as they caught packets of chocolate and other tit-bits which Southampton folk threw up to them as they passed through the streets in buses and vans testified to the suffering that had ended. Many of the little ones caused great surprise by asking for cigarettes. Woefully tired, very bewildered and thoroughly disinfected, the 4,000 Basque children who reached here today from Bilbao sleep tonight free from the terrors of hunger and war. Colourful, yet forlorn, young Juans, Juanitas, Miguels and Carmens made Southampton ring from dawn onwards today. Some of the older ones burst into tears but the younger refugees showed that they regard England as little short of paradise.'

Upon landing, Sabino and his siblings were grateful to be kept together at Nazareth House, an orphanage converted into a school and run by nuns. Wary of breaking the non-intervention agreement signed by 27 European countries in 1936, the British government did not contribute towards the upkeep of the Basque children for fear of being seen to take sides in the Spanish Civil War. In truth, the overriding feeling was that the British powerbrokers did not want the children in the country at all. Winston Churchill, for example, made a joke during one parliamentary session that the Conservatives should not put all their 'Basques in one exit'.

This, however, was a humanitarian crisis, not a diplomatic dilemma. These children were not economic migrants; they were stricken souls, running from rather than to. Thankfully, refugees do bring out the best in a good percentage of the civilian population, if not those in uniform. The government eventually succumbed to intense public pressure and allowed the children three-month visas; although Prime Minister Baldwin stressed that 'the climate would not suit them'.

The public mood was divided. At an Oxford Union debate, the motion 'This House maintains that Spain is no concern of ours' ended 50 in favour and 57 against, underlining the mixed feelings even among students. Ultimately, the children's maintenance was funded solely by the generosity of the private sector and the benevolence of the Great British public. The National Joint Committee for Spanish Relief headed up the operation, aided by organisations such as the Salvation Army, the Basque Children's Committee and the Save the Children Fund. Wealthy families around the country took the children into their homes; from the parents of Richard and David Attenborough to the Cadbury (chocolate) and the Clark (shoes) families. The children were housed at first on campsites before being moved on into colonies and family homes.

In his autobiography, *Entirely Up to You, Darling*, the legendary film director Richard Attenborough tells how his very first love as a 14-year-old adolescent was one of these young refugees. He recalls:

Rosa was one of fifty who came to Leicester. My mother was secretary of the committee formed to look after them and, of course, much more. She persuaded local families to sponsor the children by donating ten shillings a week, it was she who rented the abandoned mansion, which was to become their home, she who rolled up her sleeves and scrubbed the floors. Rosa helped with the little ones and took it all in her stride. I would cycle up to the Hall to spend hours holding her hand and gazing into those dark brown eyes. I can still see my first love now, waiting for me in the sunshine at Evington Hall. She can't have been more than fifteen; a small, perfectly proportioned, olive-skinned girl who always wore a rose tucked into her pitch-black hair. And for a few short months, she was my one and only for evermore. Had she but asked, I would gladly have laid down my life for her.

Back down at Southampton, Barinaga began to play football at Nazareth House, occupying his time in the evenings and the weekends. Another evacuee, Raimundo Perez Lezama, who fled the town of Baracaldo on the same *Habana* boat, joined him there. Lezama, a goalkeeper, would play in the same Southampton youth teams as Barinaga before returning to Spain and playing for Athletic Bilbao, where he won six Copa del Generalisimo medals and two La Liga trophies. He passed away in 2007 but his son Manuel welcomes me into his flat in Bilbao, only a stone's throw from the club's new San Mames stadium.

'My father is an authentic child of the war,' says Manuel, a moustachioed 60-something and former optician. 'He and Sabino were the first Spanish players in the English leagues but my father was older so he played first. When you see the invasion of Spaniards into the English game now, and particularly Basques, such as Ander Herrera and Mikel Arteta, I am very proud of this heritage. My dad was one of the oldest on the *Habana* ship. He was 15, going on 16. He went with his little brother, Luis, who was 11. My father always used to tell me how he had forgotten the taste and flavour of milk and bread during the Civil War in Spain and the first memory he had of England was this glass of fresh milk and white bread upon arrival. It was like paradise. At Nazareth House, they gave him food, clothes and an education. The English were so caring. Not once did I hear my father say a single word against the people of Southampton. Never. The treatment was extraordinary, a remarkable show of human decency and social consciousness.'

The benevolence displayed by the English public was far-reaching. 'One of the commanders in the RAF became like a second father to him. Remember, there weren't many young people around because so many were on the front fighting in the Second World War. My dad even lived with him for a while and became a driver in the RAF and drove for this commander. The officer was also a director at Southampton and he took him along for a trial. He had never played in goal before but they had too many outfield players and not enough goalkeepers. They trained him up and he began to distinguish himself.'

Barinaga's path was a little different. Southampton manager Tom Parker scouted him playing in the Nazareth House school teams. He was immediately taken by the young Spaniard's skill – Barinaga was naturally ambidextrous and confident with both feet – and he also noted his balance and powerful strike. Lezama and Barinaga played for the club's youngest nursery team, known as the 'B team'. Parker was keen to expand the club's youth system and allow more local youngsters an opportunity in sport. Southampton had, in fact, first clocked the Spanish duo in a car park not far from the stadium.

A *Daily Mirror* report from 17 March 1939 reads: 'Two Basque refugees were amusing themselves by kicking a ball about in a Southampton car park. They did the kicking so cleverly that a man strolled from over the way – out of the Southampton F.C. ground – to watch. What he saw made him rush in to manager Tom Parker. Tom came out, looked the boys over and took them under the club's wing. They've almost lived at the Dell since. Now Southampton have two of the most promising lads in this country.'

The Saints Supporters' Club financed the youth team and they entered into the Southampton Junior League. Their record is extraordinary. In the 1938-39 season, the team played 33 league and cup games. They won 31, drew one and lost one. Only Ferry Engine Company held them to a 1-1 draw in the league while the Fellowship of St Andrews beat them 2-1 in the Hants Junior Cup. They scored 277 goals and conceded only 17. Barinaga scored 62 of those goals. A *Daily Mirror* report adds: 'Barinaga has the makings of a brilliant forward, he got six out of eleven last Saturday, four of them with his head. The other lad, fifteen-year-old Raimundo Perez is a goalkeeper "as agile as a cat". Coach Parker said: "When this lad Sabino gets going there is no holding him and I regard him as one of the most brilliant youngsters I have ever seen. We're very anxious to keep him and if we can get a Home Office permit and his parents consent we shall do so." Barinaga said: "I would love to stay in England."'

Lezama's son takes out an old newspaper clipping that his father kept after returning from Southampton. Lezama also brought back three books on the Laws of the Game that were written before the turn of the 20th century. He would spend hours studying them in his dorm at Nazareth House, reading to improve his knowledge of the game and the quality of his English.

This particular clipping is an end-of-season review written by the local newspaper and the back-page headline reads: 'They may be some of the "stars" of the future.' It continues:

Probably the most outstanding was the 16-year-old Basque refugee Sabino Berinaga, one of the forwards since December. Previous to coming to England, Barinaga had never kicked a ball and his knowledge of the game was comparatively nil. His goal-scoring feats and natural aptitude for the game has shown that he, probably, is a great player in the making. Possessing height, Barinaga also has good ball control and distribution, and shots in both feet. He netted 62 goals in 18 matches, truly a remarkable performance in a first season of competitive football. Another refugee, Raimundo Perez, kept goal and made rapid strides in the game.

Manuel roots through his trunk, jam-packed with memorabilia, photos and information about those children evacuated from the Basque Country, and he reveals two glistening medallions. They are from his father's Southampton days; most probably the longest-surviving medals won by a Spaniard in English football. One is for winning the league title and the other from the Junior Challenge Cup. Encased in two black leather presentation boxes, etched with the words 'Southampton FA', he opens them up. The Birmingham-based goldsmiths, Vaughtons Medallists, produced the medals and they are wonderfully well maintained nearly 80 years on. 'These will be passed down my family for centuries,' he says, clenching the medals tightly in his grip.

Southampton wanted both players to remain but wartime had consumed England and they were now hankering for home. Barinaga missed his parents terribly and he felt a responsibility to his two little brothers, Iñaki and Jose Luis. The Home Office also deprived him of a licence to remain and on the day he returned home, Thursday, 21 March 1940, Tom Parker told the *Daily Mirror* that Barinaga was the 'best natural talent I have discovered'. Throughout his time in England, Sabino constantly wrote home, desperately hoping for a response, desperately hoping for some indication that his mum, dad and little sister were still alive. The outlook was bleak.

'Everyone in England told him that they had been killed but he refused to believe it,' his daughter says. 'He used to tell me that he had this feeling, deep down, almost like a special connection. He still believed that they were alive and he was convinced that he would find them. In early 1940, he returned to Bilbao with his brothers. There were lots of people returning at that point. It was still an anxious moment. Everyone knew Spain was dangerous. General Franco was in power and my family were Basques. My dad, though, he had a strong head on him; he was as stubborn as they come. If he wanted something, he got it. He decided he was going to find his mum, dad and sister and he stopped at nothing to do that. For a few months, he didn't find them. It transpired that they escaped to Barcelona. When they returned to Bilbao, they found each other where the house used to be in Durango. In 1940, they were together again. When you recall it this way, it almost sounds too miraculous to be true.'

Sabino was by now 17 and word of his goalscoring exploits had spread far and wide throughout Spain. He received an offer from Athletic Bilbao but Real Madrid came in at the last moment with a lucrative proposal. Some Basques might have resisted a move to Madrid, so often perceived – rightly or wrongly – as an extension of the Franco stronghold.

'This is easy to say in hindsight,' Almudena says. 'We all have 20/20 vision looking back. He'd had a difficult time. He was offered excellent money; it would take care of his family. You couldn't talk about politics at that time. It was too dangerous. So he didn't. He wasn't really a Basque nationalist. He didn't really like all that. We had conversations about this and he would say that he was neither a Basque national nor a Spanish national. He saw himself as a citizen of the world. He loved England; he later worked in South America and Mexico. He never understood the idea of nationalism. He just wanted to enjoy his life, to know and love people regardless of where they came from or what they looked like. Is that really so wrong?'

During 11 years at Real Madrid, Barinaga scored 93 goals in 182 official matches, winning two Copas del Generalisimo and one Copa Eva Duarte. 'He could play all over the pitch and this versatility led him to play in many different positions where he always stood out for his ability to attack and score goals,' reads the Real Madrid website.

'He scored a ton of goals,' Almudena adds. 'He was very lean, very ripped, with big, muscular thighs. He never smoked a cigarette in his life. He was an athlete. Well, he did eat a lot, actually. He was like a hoover. He also liked his wine . . . and his whisky . . . Like I say, an athlete! But this was a different era.'

His most famous goal came in 1947, when he scored Real Madrid's very first at the new Santiago Bernabeu stadium. It arrived in a 3-1 victory against Portuguese side Belenenses. His son, Sabino Jr, still has the pennant that Barinaga received in recognition. He also scored four goals in the infamous 11-1 victory over Barcelona in 1943. Almudena says: 'He loved playing for Real Madrid. He was paid very well indeed. In the end, he had a fallout with Santiago Bernabeu, the Real president at the time. An English manager came in called Michael Keeping. He didn't rate my father. My dad tried to speak to Bernabeu, who told him, "You are like a son to me, you will play." Nothing changed, though, so he asked to leave and he signed for Real Sociedad. From then on, Bernabeu saw him as some kind of traitor. My father's name was barely spoken about at this club. People would raise their eyebrows when it was mentioned. Bernabeu made it that way, my father believed. When he passed away, the club sent some flowers but that's it.

'In a way, he was fonder of Southampton. The manager Tom Parker treated him wonderfully. He started his path. He had other offers in England, from big teams in London, but he would never have signed for another English club. If he had stayed in England, he loved Southampton so much that he would have remained for ever. For many years, he continued to write to Sister May, one of his teachers at the school in Southampton. She still wanted to know how he was getting on and he cared deeply for them. He went back to Southampton a lot. We have a photo of him with the directors of Southampton in the 1970s.'

For the goalkeeper Lezama, leaving Southampton was also a wrench. 'He played three seasons in Southampton – 1937-38, 1938-39 and 1939-40,' his son Manuel explains. 'His brother returned to Bilbao in 1939 but my dad stayed. The final year he played with the first team. Many kids barely learned English because they were with Spanish friends all the time but my dad was now living with the commander. Eventually, he felt he had to go home. When he arrived in Baracaldo, his father asked him, "What are you going to do now? How are you going to live? What have you done in England?" He said he could speak English, which was of course useful, but then added that he had learned to play football as well. In post-Civil War Spain, the teams were looking for players. He went to a club called Arenas Getxo. My grandfather knew a director there. He had a trial and inside five minutes, the manager turned to the director and said, "Fuck, sign me this kid. This is my goalkeeper."

'I am perhaps biased but my father was an amazing goalkeeper. In Bilbao, they call him the father of modern of goalkeeping. You talk about Manuel Neuer? My dad was doing these things half a century before. He played out from the back, he was a sweeper-keeper, he anticipated danger, he had presence, and he caught crosses. Pep Guardiola would love him! He was a pioneer. This was long before Carmelo Cedrun, long before Andoni Zubizarreta. He brought in this new way of goalkeeping: to dominate the area, to rush out of goal. Three months after signing for Arenas, Bilbao had snapped him up. He played there for 16 years.'

The historian of Spanish football, Jose Ignacio Corcuera, wrote of Lezama: 'Far from receiving applause, some of his innovations were taken by the majority of the fans to be pure eccentricity. But these were revolutionary ideas for the age. For example, when he spoke about training on tennis courts but with a football and only using your head to keep the rally going, nobody took him seriously. Many years later, there are many highly rated coaches who are incorporating this as a method in training.'

In these parts, they know a good footballer when they see one. When a 38-year-old Ryan Giggs was substituted during Manchester United's Europa League defeat by Athletic Bilbao at the San Mames stadium in 2012, the entire ground rose to its feet. The locals were celebrating a player who played the game how they feel it should be played, with adventure, wit and flair. The United left-back Patrice Evra returned the applause from the field of play and Giggs was so touched by the ovation that he donated the shirt he had worn in the first leg, a 3-2 defeat at Old Trafford, to Athletic's San Mames museum. In 2015, the club launched an annual 'One Club Man Award' and presented the inaugural prize to Southampton legend Matt Le Tissier before their derby match against Real Sociedad. The club said of Le Tissier: 'Many great players have expressed their admiration about you. Pele, for instance, was quoted saying that if you had been Brazilian you would always have been among the starting XI.'

The Manchester United midfielder Ander Herrera played in both those Europa League ties for Athletic Bilbao. 'The ovation for Giggs – it was special,' he grins, perched on a bar stool in a hotel opposite Old Trafford. 'I remember being emotional on the pitch to see, hear and feel it. It is a very special characteristic of the club. They did the same for Real Madrid legend Raul when we played Schalke, too. They recognise greatness. The old San Mames was a special place.' Herrera puts his thumb and index finger together, raising them towards his nose and inhaling: 'You could smell the football. I can't put this into words. It's the memories, the culture, the shared sense of belonging and the feeling that sport has a greater meaning.'

Herrera is right. Bilbao is a special place to experience football. The weekend I visit Manuel he insists we meet on the Sunday, rather than the Saturday, so as not to clash with match day. It is only an end-of-season dead rubber against Villarreal but every game is an occasion here. The whole place buzzes in anticipation. The walk along the main road that leads to the

San Mames stadium – called the Poza Lizentziatuaren kalea – is invigorating. Red-and-white flags drape from the bars and the apartments above. In the traditional Basque *pintxos* bars, they serve Iberian ham, mini stuffed peppers, salted cod and fried anchovies. Stalls are set up selling hot Spanish tortilla sandwiches. Supporters drink the traditional Basque cocktail kalimotxo – a peculiar mix of red wine and Coca-Cola – and talk passionately about their football. They are hospitable hosts and Manchester United supporters still remember how Athletic fans lined up outside the stadium to applaud their away support following that 2012 Europa League tie.

The city is potty about football. In the many souvenir shops, you can buy Athletic bibs, slippers, lighters, aftershave, ties, wallets, watches and wine collections. You can even dabble in your very own Athletic lingerie. In the butchers, the little marble pigs at the entrance are draped in Athletic scarves. Inside the ground, stewards and supporters wear the traditional Basque *txapelas* – the original berets – and children wear masks of lions, referencing the club's nickname '*Los Leones*'. The locals call the San Mames '*La Catedral*', a national place of worship. It is a special ground in which to watch football, one of the most atmospheric in Europe, more Istanbul than Iberia in its intensity.

It is near-impossible to visit Bilbao and fail to fall for the charm of this football club. They operate a policy of using Basque players, protecting their fierce national identity. For football supporters, there is little more intoxicating than watching a group of home-grown talents succeed together. It is a feeling poignantly summed up by the Catalan Michelin-starred chef Ferran Adria, who reflected on the importance of local talent to Barcelona supporters. 'If we win the Champions League, it doesn't matter who was playing,' Adria said. 'But if we lose, then we will certainly be hearing that those who played weren't Catalans.'

Herrera tells me: 'To me, Bilbao is a perfect club. They create their players and look after us. When you arrive in Bilbao – you know you have to listen and learn. I remember ten years ago there was a very difficult moment for Bilbao and they were very close to relegation. There was a debate as to whether they should keep the philosophy or not. Even if they are relegated to the second division one day, they can't change this. Never. Never, ever. It's the one thing that makes Bilbao different from the rest of the world. Otherwise, you become just another club. And then what do you have? The dressing room is super-close. You will walk into the changing room and you can say, "I don't have plans after training today – who wants to do something?" Normally, you do that with your two or three close mates in a dressing room. In Bilbao, everyone mixes with everyone. It is a true family. Fantastic club, fantastic people.'

They have witnessed some wonderful players here. Throughout the generations, they have seen a cast of stars from 'Pichichi' and Telmo Zarra to Dani Ruiz and Jose Angel Iribar. Lezama, produced by Southampton, belongs in such company. Surrounding the club's new stadium, only three players have roads named in their honour. Rafael Moreno, better known as 'Pichichi' (the little duck), is the first. He was Athletic's great goalscorer in the 1910s and La Liga's Golden Boot is now named after him. Only five feet tall and eight stone in weight, he scored 77 goals in 89 Copa del Rey matches and 200 goals in 170 matches in total. In *La Roja: A Journey Through Spanish Football*, Jimmy Burns writes of Pichichi: 'A fitness fanatic, he used his pace and dribbling skills to get round the often brutal stratagems of Basque defenders much bigger and stronger than him, while proving himself a hugely effective striker of the ball. Local journalists branded him El Rey del Shoot, the Strike King.'

The second is Telmo Zarra, who played in the same Athletic teams as Lezama between 1941 and 1955, scoring 332 goals for the club. Only Lionel Messi and Cristiano Ronaldo have scored more league goals than Zarra's 251 in Spanish football history. His legacy is continued with the annual Zarra trophy, awarded to the highest-scoring Spanish player in La Liga. In 2015, Lezama joined the elite cast when the town hall unveiled

Paseo Raimundo Perez Lezama. One of those in attendance at the ceremony was the great Jose Angel Iribar, who grew up worshipping Lezama before embarking on his own 20-year reign in the Athletic goal.

Barinaga and Lezama remained good friends upon returning to Spain, but friendship morphed into rivalry in the summer of 1943. Now in the strips of Real Madrid and Athletic Bilbao, *los principes de Southampton* – the Princes of Southampton, as they were called by teammates – met each other in the Copa del Generalisimo final. Athletic won 1-0 and Lezama was the star. It was an occasion of great political significance: General Franco faced the embarrassment of personally handing over the trophy to the Basque people. 'Perhaps unlike Sabino, my dad was a fierce Basque nationalist but we are talking about Franco's Spain here. You had to be crazy to come out and say something. Your head would be blown off,' Manuel says, pointing two fingers at my head and mimicking the booming thunder of a gunshot. 'I think my dad's performance in this game was inspired by everything that had gone before, the terror that the Spanish Nationalists had inflicted on his family and friends.'

Manuel still has the official match report from the game: 'Madrid deserved the victory for the magnificent football that they played in the second half. The best player on the pitch was without question Lezama, who saved everything that the *madrileños* threw at him. Madrid were fighting against the magnificent performance by the Bilbao goalkeeper.'

Pouring a cup of coffee, Manuel breaks into a grin. 'I told you he was good.'

After retirement, Lezama did not enter into management but Barinaga did, managing 11 club and international teams between 1954 and 1978. In Spain, he coached Real Betis and Real Oviedo three times each, Osasuna, Malaga, Atletico Madrid, Valencia, Sevilla, Real Mallorca and Cadiz. He also had spells managing the Moroccan national team and Club America in Mexico.

In February 1966, he returned to England when he brought his Valencia team to play Leeds in the Inter-Cities Fairs Cup and the story is a classic for those who revere or revile the Don Revie era at Elland Road. The match was played on a freezing winter evening and Barinaga's Valencia were an elite European side. They had lifted the trophy in 1962 and 1963 and Barinaga, clearly having forgotten the harsh realities of an English winter, had his own idealistic view of how the beautiful game should be played. 'If you like to play good football, the ground should be dry with plenty of grass.' The surface at Leeds United's Elland Road, however, was wretched and skilled opponents would toil in alien conditions. Naturally, Don Revie described the pitch as 'perfect' on the eve of the game.

The match itself was a tinderbox that flared late on. The following day, the front pages of the national newspapers were splashed with pictures of policemen on the Elland Road pitch, wrestling with players to break up a brawl that had broken out. Ronald Crowther of the *Daily Mail* described it as a 'near bullfight'. The incident that sparked the furore involved Jack Charlton, who told the story in a biography of Billy Bremner. 'What had been a sizzling atmosphere became downright white hot, as we threw everything into an assault which, we hoped, would bring us a winner. Fifteen minutes to go, and I raced upfield to add my weight to one of our attacks. As I challenged an opponent in the Valencia penalty area, I was kicked. This angered me, of course – but before I knew where I was I found myself having to take much more . . . for one of my opponents slung a punch, which would have done credit to Cassius Clay.'

What followed was a chase scene that you could quite envisage with the Benny Hill theme tune played over the top, as Charlton sprinted around the pitch in pursuit of his Spanish antagonist. 'Right there and then my anger boiled over . . . I chased around that penalty area, intent upon only one thing – getting my own back. I had completely lost control of myself, after these diabolical fouls upon me, and neither the Spaniards nor the restraining hands of my team-mates could prevent my pursuit for vengeance. Suddenly players seemed to be pushing and jostling each other everywhere. Police appeared on the field to stop this game of football from degenerating into a running battle. And [referee] Leo Horn walked off with his linesmen, signalling to club officials of both teams to get their players off, too. I was still breathing fire when I reached the dressing room.' Billy Bremner acted as peacemaker and commented: 'I don't think the Spaniards could really understand an angry Scotsman.'

CHAPTER 2

Messi and the Midlander

On 25 November 2012, Barcelona realised a dream. Fourteen minutes into a La Liga fixture away at Levante, the Catalan defender Martin Montoya came on as a substitute to replace the Brazilian Dani Alves. In doing so, a wintry evening in Valencia became for ever enshrined in Barça's history, marking the first time that the entire first-team XI comprised only products of the club's iconic La Masia academy. Victor Valdes, who has spent the latter part of his career in England with Manchester United and Middlesbrough, was in goal. Montoya, Gerard Pique, Carles Puyol and Jordi Alba made up the defence. Sergio Busquets, Andres Iniesta and Xavi graced the midfield. Up front, Pedro Rodriguez, Lionel Messi and Cesc Fabregas completed the team.

Barcelona, managed that day by Tito Vilanova, himself a product of the academy, won 4–0 and went on to lift the league title. It was one of many peaks during a glorious recent past. In November 1998, Louis van Gaal, the former Barcelona coach, forecast this possibility in a meeting with Catalan journalists. After the match in Levante, the midfielder Xavi noted: 'Van Gaal said once that his dream was to see 11 academy players together on the pitch and today it became reality.'

Van Gaal, never slow on the uptake when the opportunity

presents itself to talk up his own credentials, spoke to *El Mundo Deportivo* during the following week. 'I feel exceptionally proud,' the Dutchman said. 'Ten years after I'm gone, Van Gaal's academy is still there. I gave debuts to Victor Valdes, Xavi, Andres Iniesta and Carles Puyol, who form the spine of the team. It is not only those players but also Gabri, Thiago Motta, Pepe Reina, who have spent years at the top of the game. Barcelona played an official game with 11 players from their academy and that's fantastic. I worked a huge amount with the academy and it is really beautiful for me. I am very proud that Xavi has made reference to me at such a special moment. He is a great boy and a great footballer and I am delighted things are going so well.'

The Dutchman, for all his success, is one of those erudite tacticians who bask in the praise when things are going well but does not particularly enjoy answering questions on his strategy when matters are heading in the opposite direction. This, rather sadly, was his more regular fate during a desperate spell in England at Manchester United. Van Gaal, who endured a fractious relationship with the Catalan media, ended on a mischievous note when asked about his La Masia legacy. 'I would like to send a wave to my friends in the media who covered my time in Barcelona.'

Certainly, Van Gaal's faith in young talent is impressive, but he also faced accusations of denaturalising Barça, recruiting excessively from his native Holland and sometimes favouring foreign talent. In November 1998, he ended a game against Real Mallorca with Carles Puyol as the only Spaniard on the pitch. During the season in question, Van Gaal's squad included over 15 players from outside Spain. Rather, the true kingmakers in Catalonia are more commonly acknowledged as being Oriol Tort and Johan Cruyff. It was they who did more than anybody else to turn the theory into reality, they who were the essential figures in the inauguration of La Masia in 1979.

In Spanish, '*La Masia*' translates as 'the farmhouse', even if it has come to be shorthand for a generation of footballers who treat the ball with a care and precision that eludes all others. The original Masia was built in 1702, beginning as a workstation for construction and architecture. In 1957, it became the club's headquarters, then, as Barça expanded, La Masia was remodelled once more, evolving into the academy centre on 20 October 1979, when former President Josep Lluis Nuñez accepted Cruyff's advice and Tort devoted his life to co-ordinating the youth network.

Tort is the lesser known of the two but his impact and track record are unrivalled. Born in 1929 in Hospitalet, he was on the Barcelona books as a youth player and then became a coach for the youth teams in the late 1950s. 'Tort finally became coordinator of the youth divisions in 1977,' wrote the Catalan journalist Genis Sinca. 'But it was under the leadership of Josep Lluís Núñez [1978–2000] that he was entrusted with the most special and secretive task – spotting new talents, forming a farm team of future stars framed within the symbol of La Masia, the eighteenth-century farmhouse that stands next to the Camp Nou. Oriol Tort became a talent spotter when this profession was still in its infancy.'

Tort was involved in the scouting process for Xavi Hernandez, Andres Iniesta, Ivan de la Pena, Cesc Fabregas and Victor Valdes. Perhaps most crucially, he found Pep Guardiola. Sinca continued: 'One day, just like any other, his eyes latched onto a small, somewhat puny child, who was playing in Gimnàstic Manresa, and who had an uncanny skill with the ball. He was just what he was looking for, and Tort knew it. The boy fitted in perfectly with the ethos of attacking football the club wanted to build from the ground up, the typically Dutch style introduced by Rinus Michels and Johan Cruyff. Intelligence, skill and speed would be the basis of the 90s Dream Team. That skinny boy would be the prototype model. Tort had just discovered Pep Guardiola. The legendary scout promptly brought another one of his great skills into play, one that was perhaps even more valuable. He talked to the parents. He convinced them to send their children to La Masia, where they would be brought up in the lower ranks of the club to play in the *juveniles* [youth categories], and where their schooling would not be neglected. Moreover, Tort told them that in La Masia the boys were brought up within a system of values based on respect and friendship. Never has a football club got so much out of a committed and sensitive employee like Oriol Tort for so long.'

Tort died in September 1999 but his life's work came to fruition in 2011. The proficiency of the Barcelona youth academy was underlined when a trio of La Masia graduates – Lionel Messi, Xavi Hernandez and Andres Iniesta – formed the three finalists for FIFA's Ballon d'Or at the awards ceremony in Zurich. And if the three men on the podium were not enough, La Masia graduate Guardiola was anointed coach of the year. 'Oriol Tort represents that anonymous, behind-the-scenes but essential character fundamental to so many clubs,' said Vicente del Bosque, the great Spanish World Cup-winning coach, at a press conference on the same day. On the red carpet at the ceremony, Barcelona youth technical director Albert Benaiges said: 'This Ballon d'Or is for Oriol Tort.'

La Masia, Catalonia's exceptional academy of arts, has produced the definitive blueprint for football success in the 21st century, inspiring the glory of the Spanish national team and nurturing a cohort of talent through an intoxicating brand of tiki-taka football. On the days it all comes together, it is a bewitching experience for Barça supporters and their global cast of neutral admirers. For opponents, it is grievous ordeal, an exercise in quite exquisite agony. Sir Alex Ferguson, the former Manchester United manager twice defeated by Pep Guardiola's Barcelona in Champions League finals, described the experience as akin to spinning on a carousel, leaving his players dizzied and disorientated. Theo Walcott, the former Arsenal winger, was left similarly bewildered after a Champions League encounter. Shaking his head, he told reporters: 'It was like someone was holding a PlayStation controller and moving the figures around.' In Spain, they call it *'ganar sin despeinarse'*, meaning to win without messing your hair up and, at times, they make it appear so easy that you could believe it all to be a choreographed show; so pinpoint are the passes, so rehearsed is the movement. But this is a style of football that merges art and graft, beauty and industry.

'In La Masia, it was a whole way of existence – and, of course, about how to play beautiful football,' wrote Jimmy Burns. 'La Masia was the icing on the cake of Barça's version of *fútbol base*, Spain's well-financed and impeccably organised national football training programme. The learning curve began to take shape in early kick-arounds on beaches, neighbourhood streets and waste grounds, but then became more focused as kids evolved through highly competitive football games at primary school and beyond, and teachers were contacted by club scouts, looking for those with real potential to be top-flight professionals in their late teens.'

Guardiola, who has subsequently transplanted this style into Bavaria with Bayern Munich and Mancunia with Manchester City, idolises Cruyff. 'I knew nothing about football before knowing Cruyff. A new world appeared in front of me. Before Cruyff, we had one Argentina coach who played an Argentinian style, then came a German coach who played a German style. But then Johan arrived and he said: "Guys, now we play this way." When I was there you see seven-year-old kids doing the same training session, with the same patterns, as the first team. He created something from nothing and to do that, you have to have a lot of charisma and personality.'

Yet Cruyff was not the first to suggest this. Indeed, Tort was not the first to suggest Barcelona professionalise their scouting process, house children and indelibly inscribe Barça into a child's mind and body. Rather, the concept of a Catalan academy with Barça principles was first outlined over 20 years before, precisely in 1957. And what's more, the original brainchild behind Barcelona's glorious potential was a Basque refugee, a child who boarded a ship to Southampton in 1937 and settled in the Midlands.

Emilio Aldecoa was 14 years old when his parents placed him on the *Habana* steamship to Southampton. It set sail from the Basque port of Santurtzi, and I drop by this quaint little town on a dozy June morning. With the khaki hills rising up out of the pale, bored, flat water, the sea could barely appear more innocent, belying the distress of that spring day in 1937, when it was choppy and strained, both on and off the boat. Emilio's son, John, had contributed to a short Spanish television documentary, called *Los Niños del* Habana (*The Children of the* Habana), and I had been passed his contact details by the research team.

The first time I call, however, John answers the phone with the guardedness of a beauty queen eyeing Donald Trump. He is not particularly keen to be contacted by strangers. Thankfully, he relents, content to tell his father's remarkable story, and he agrees to meet in the café area of a snug B&B in the Welsh town of Chepstow. Home to Britain's oldest stone castle, its walls chiselled and the views over the River Wye splendid, it's a marvellous spot. It was a military base for the Normans a thousand years ago and a tourist attraction for arty folk carrying sketchbooks in the 18th century. John sits down and begins to relax.

'We never, ever discussed it in depth,' John says of his father's journey. 'He was like a war veteran in that sense. The stuff that went on doesn't bear thinking about. I remember times when he went to visit family in Spain. He was always frightened or extremely wary of the Guardia Civil, with their funny hats and daft uniform. He never spoke about the boat journey. He spoke about the family that took him in at Stafford. He came into the campsite at Southampton and wound up in Stafford. A family took them in – I can't recall their name – but I have the family picture.'

In Stafford, Aldecoa began to play football in the games arranged specially to raise funds for the Basque boys. He was well into his teenage years and earned a job with English Electric, the industrial manufacturer formed in 1918. Following the beginning of the Second World War in 1939, the British workforce gradually became depleted and in Aldecoa they found a willing labourer. 'He started playing for the English Electric and one of the trainers contacted Wolves and they gave him a trial. They told him, "Get to the ground on Saturday and we will give you a runout."'

Work, however, took precedence. 'My father was on shift that day and didn't finish until 2pm. Then he had to make it to the game. They were playing Derby. Incredibly, the train was late from Derby so the Derby players themselves were late arriving. As such, everyone was late in the end and he subsequently managed to get there on time. He had good luck that day. He got the runout and was taken on as an amateur.'

Aldecoa signed up in 1943 and, at the age of 20, he made his professional debut against Crewe Alexandra. In doing so, he became the very first Spaniard to play a professional football match in English football. 'It's an amazing source of pride for me,' John beams. 'At Wolves, he played as a number 11.' John points to a match report from a local newspaper. He reads it aloud. 'Aldecoa could outpace all opposition and was always a potential match-winner.'

In the 1943-44 season, Aldecoa emerged as the club's most lethal weapon, scoring eight goals and finishing as the top scorer. By 1945, he had earned a move to Midlands rivals Coventry. 'He really did it for the love of the game,' John says. 'There wasn't much for him here in football in terms of cash, players weren't paid vast sums until Jimmy Hill came along and fought for their rights. It was £6-a-week in the summer and £8-a-week in the winter. When he played at Coventry, he'd work as a groundsman during the summer to earn extra money.'

Aldecoa could not afford his own home and lodged with a local family in Wyken. The Thompson family took Emilio in and Chris Thompson, who was six years old when the player arrived, recalled this period in an interview with the *Coventry Telegraph*. 'Even now, looking back, it doesn't seem particularly strange to me that I was living with a famous footballer. It was totally normal in those days – it was 1945, and throughout the Second World War we'd had a succession of young ladies staying with us from all over the country. They'd been sent to work in Coventry, and we were one of the houses that put them up. Emilio got married to a girl who used to come to visit him and stayed nearby on Sewall Highway when she came over. I remember thinking she looked more Spanish than he did. When they announced their wedding, it was war rationing at the time and everybody in the street turned up with a lot of dried fruit for the cake. We had to pool all our fruit to make it for him. I remember that when my dad was ill, Emilio spent days laying a patio in our garden so that my father wouldn't have to.'

Aldecoa was grateful to this country. He was among those children who sank onto stained mattresses and flattened cardboard upon landing in Southampton, kicking a ball around on the grass beside the tents that had been pitched up on local campsites. He was bereft – old enough at 14 to be aware of the horrors unfolding back home – and he never forgot. 'He was Basque,' John says firmly. 'His family, my grandmother, had a little café. His father was an electrician in the steelworks. He was injured when he severed a finger. When the troops came in and the Civil War finished, the café was confiscated. Some sergeant from the Guardia Civil stormed in and took it. My father was not forgiving towards the regime.'

Aldecoa was generous off the pitch but also developing into a star on the field. In 1946, Coventry defeated Chelsea 2-0 and the *Daily Mail* headline read: 'All-Spanish wing worried Chelsea', as Aldecoa and Jose Bilbao, another refugee from the

Basque Country, lined up on the left side. Jose Bilbao would play only six games for Coventry but Aldecoa was part of the furniture as football captured the imagination in the postwar era. 'It was a huge morale boost to have football back,' says Jim Brown, a historian of Coventry Football Club. 'He played a few reserve games and was given his first-team debut against Portsmouth in October and he scored. He was the first Spanish football player to sign as a professional in the English League.'

The Coventry supporter Tom Denrith told the *Los Niños del Habana* documentary: 'I only saw him on two occasions but what an impact he had on me. He was flamboyant; he was so upright and athletic. Also, his good looks. The old Coventry players were real bruisers and then he was this handsome, good-looking winger with thick black hair. He was like a matinée screen idol.'

After three campaigns in the second division, Aldecoa returned to Spain, signing for Athletic Bilbao and enjoying two impressive seasons. From the left wing, he scored nine goals in 48 games and then spent two seasons at Valladolid before attracting the attention of Barcelona. In Catalonia, Aldecoa joined a team that would go down in the annals of football history. Spearheaded by the legendary Hungarian Laszlo Kubala, Barça became the dominant force in Spanish football. They won three consecutive Copas del Generalisimo, in 1951, 1952 and 1953, as well as two La Liga titles, in '52 and '53. In that period, they also won the Copa Eva Duarte and the Copa Martini Rossi, and subsequently became known as '*Barça de las Cinco Copas*', for winning five trophies in the 1951-52 season after also adding the Copa Latina to their haul.

Aldecoa adored his time at Barcelona, John says. 'They played against Bilbao in his third game for Barcelona. It was crazy, even in those days. We have this idealised image of men in top hats going along merrily to watch the football. Wrong! All the Bilbao fans were shouting "Bastard!", "Traitor!" My mum said that day was awful for him. But no, really, he adored playing for

Barcelona; he was so proud of that achievement and particularly playing with his great friend Kubala.'

Kubala is one of the iconic figures of the Spanish game. Several books pay tribute to him. In 2012, Spanish journalist Frederic Porta wrote a biography entitled *Kubala! The Hero Who Changed Barça's History*, which includes a foreword by Marti Perarnau, the journalist Pep Guardiola trusts above all others. In Jimmy Burns' forensic account of Spanish football, a chapter is dedicated to 'Kubala and Other Hungarians'.

Kubala's journey to Spain was possibly even more dramatic than the ordeal endured by Aldecoa. It is perhaps why they became so close. Kubala's route included a hasty escape from military rule, stop-offs in three countries and a ferocious pursuit by the authoritarian Communist Hungarians. Somehow, someway, it also ended up with Kubala becoming the highest-paid player in the history of Barcelona. In January 1949, he took a gamble on his life when he fled Communist Hungary, attempting to earn a career as a footballer and escape the brutality of the Soviet-influenced regime in his homeland. He kitted himself out in military uniform, travelling through Austria and Italy, even settling in Rome in a refugee camp for a while, where he put together a football team. The refugee team, called Hungria, then headed to Spain to play against Real Madrid and the Spanish national team, and it was there that Kubala met Barcelona's sporting director, Pepe Samitier.

Burns recounts the farcical manner in which Kubala became a Barcelona player by recalling a conversation with Enrique Llaudet, who worked at the club at that time: 'Kubala came to Spain thinking he was going to be signed by Real Madrid, but because he was half-pissed he didn't really know whether he was coming or going. If Kubala had one weakness, it was that he drank too much – whisky, wine, whatever he got his hands on. Well, as things turned out there was real confusion on the train that took him from Madrid to Barcelona, with Kubala at one point turning to Samitier and saying, "Hey, we are going towards Madrid, aren't we?" and Samitier saying, "Sure we are," then Kubala insisting, "But the sign says Barcelona," which is when El Sami said, "Don't you worry. We are going to the club now." And that is how he brought us Kubala.'

Kubala was the Lionel Messi of his time, a byword for greatness. He didn't come cheap. Porta writes that Kubala received a three-year contract on 700,000 pesetas a year (equivalent to about £6,300, when the top rate in England was only £1,000) and the club also promised to ensure the safe arrival of his wife and children. Kubala's career at Barça was delayed, owing to a one-year international ban after the Hungarian FA reported him for being a defector. The Hungarian authorities also made several failed attempts to extradite him. Thank goodness they failed. In 11 years as a Barça player, he scored 280 goals in 345 games.

'Kubala was a genius,' Porta wrote. 'He was also the guy who first came up with "*paradinha*" [the little pause to deceive the goalkeeper] when taking a penalty. He only missed two spot kicks in his career! His shooting accuracy was fantastic, he shielded the ball with his body, he unlocked defences at will. Moreover, he instilled greater professionalism into his teammates, introducing warm-up exercises before games, a practice that was rare in those times.'

Aldecoa learned a huge amount from Kubala and the two families spent a great deal of time together. 'To his dying day, my dad wore a gold wristwatch that was a present from Kubala,' his son John says. 'My dad used to take me down to the training ground at Barcelona; I had a terrific right foot as a kid and I later worked for the British air force. Kubala would stand in the car park doing keepy-uppies and tricks like a modern-day freestyler and I'd sit there just fascinated watching him. He was a lovely fella, ever so nice. They were just nice people; the Spanish are family orientated and you felt part of it. At Christmas, the players' families would have a big festive dinner; they'd put a pantomime on for us. I was six, seven, eight years old. It was a different life, a community life; I can't imagine it's like this these days. I am not pretending it was all perfect. In Spain in the 1950s, you knew what was going on, you knew the atmosphere between Guardia Civil and the Catalan people, but people got on with their life. What was the alternative? I grew up speaking Spanish; Catalan was banned. I picked up a few Catalan words but my dad warned me never to be heard saying it. We knew it was forbidden.'

Aldecoa's career was not as glittering as that of Kubala and it is true that he is not among the most cherished of that era. He made a sole appearance for the Spanish national team, a home match against Ireland in May 1948. After the game, there was a dinner for both teams at the Hotel Ritz in Barcelona. John still has the menu. The two sets of players chewed the fat over wine, sherry and port, before sitting to dine over seafood and traditional Spanish tapas.

It was off the field, however, that Aldecoa's most impressive feat can be found. In 1957, he sent a proposal to the Barcelona hierarchy. It is a remarkable, progressive and pioneering piece of work that remains relevant to this day. It is, in essence, a prototype for La Masia. It pointedly highlights the concerns around Barcelona at the time, underlining their failure to recruit local talent from Catalonia. It then insists on the need for an organised scouting programme, the requirement for boys to be coached in the same manner at all age groups, the need for differentiation as players progress according to their mental and physical development, and Barcelona's obligation to house these children. If you scrub out Aldecoa's signature, you could quite easily believe it to have been a report written by the cele-brated visionaries of Barça's recent past, such as Tort, Cruyff or Guardiola. Perhaps most remarkably, however, the end of the report pays tribute to Manchester United and the Busby Babes, suggesting that Aldecoa may well have discovered his inspira-tion in the north-west of England.

Aldecoa writes: 'It is clear that in the region of Catalonia, there are a number of the best centres for young footballers in Spain. Just have a glance through the line-ups of the best clubs in the first and second divisions and we can see this clearly. We also know that many Catalan players have gained international fame by playing outside of our region. To ensure that this does not become the norm, Barcelona Football Club needs to develop and create an organisation of control, training and coaching with skilled trainers and people who put their enthusiasm for the club ahead of personal considerations. It is my modest opinion that Barcelona must develop this identity. Apart from technical and physical considerations, the boy must also want to enrol himself in Barcelona, this is important ABOVE ALL. He needs to have this feeling of loyalty and love for one's colours, the love for a club – we must encourage and support this feeling at every stage.'

Aldecoa goes on to express the importance of signing players at a young age, so as to mould them into the Barcelona way of life. 'A footballer can be born special, with some predispositions of quality. However, he also develops weaknesses and defects in his game. The elimination of these defects, the signalling of the right path, at an early age is the basic work of a coach. If a boy arrives into the hands of a trainer at 19 or 20 years old, there is little to nothing you can do by this stage; his vices or defects are so ingrained into him, the work becomes overly difficult and is rarely successful. Instead, that boy with natural talent, who is born with some innate quality, needs to be guided and moulded in his earlier age range, 14, 15, 16 years old, sometimes a little older perhaps, but rarely this is the case.'

He then sets out a plan to target and recruit young talent – a model that is essentially still the one followed by many academies to this day. 'So how do we find these boys? How and who do we want to train and coach the lads? The first thing to remember is we need to have patience with this kind of work.

We are dealing with human beings, not mannequins. But it is also crucial that the people integrated into our organisation are professionals, demonstrating the right moral values, and that they totally buy into what the club stands for. Let's never see these boys as just another source of income. Let's never hand a place to a kid because he's mates with whatshisname who runs the team or the cousin of someone else. Above all else, he must be there for the right reasons, to be a good and positive force for the club. So how do we find them? This becomes a simple task if first of all we put in place the correct system; the boys themselves are all here in front of our eyes, playing in this region. So I propose:

1. A central office within the club, dedicated exclusively to these needs, with eight to ten trainers who are under the orders of one main head. They should be expected to write technical reports and send them in for consideration. Alongside these reports and consultation with the trainers, we must make a plan of work every month. This will inform us as to the boys progressing more rapidly than the others. After that, some will go up and some will do varied work if they are finding certain facets more difficult [differentiation]. Reports from matches will give us an exact value of the player's ability in competitive game situations out on the field, in the noble fight with their opponents. We will learn about their leadership qualities, their strength of spirit in adversity, all these things. These moral, basic values that a good player must bring together and must never be forgotten, regardless of the level of technical or physical perfection that they may possess. We have a duty to prepare a player morally and technically so that he can adapt himself to any other field of life or, hopefully, for another football club, something we should never block if it is in the player's best interests and he can not compete at our level.

2. In every Province or important football region, we must have a scout, someone who the club trusts with its life. The scout will be obligated to go to games involving young players, on local park pitches, even street games. He must then send a comprehensive report about any kid who has impressed his expert eye. This kid should then be observed by another member of staff from the central office and then a decision can be made as to whether to take him on or not.

3. Every player included in the club's squad must be certain that he will have the opportunity to earn a position in the first team. I believe that personal contact and guidance is a crucial factor in assuring the confidence of the young boy, believing in him, the security that no matter where he plays, he is a BARCELONA player, and he is treated as such, with the very same consideration as the biggest superstar at the club.

4. At our great club, we have an opportunity to create a new training centre in the new stadium. We can bring in all the modern apparatus we need and as important as this, or perhaps even more, the creation of some living spaces for a number of young players of exceptional quality and potential, where they would be under our constant watch, offering them an education and way of life. We must never forget, I repeat, we are dealing with human beings and we must have a clear conscience in terms of the care and provision we provide for their future.

5. When it comes to any involvement in the life of a boy, it's very much necessary to consult with the parents and gain their full permission. We can never allow our own interests to overcome that, or compromise the happiness of a boy. Showing our goodwill and wishes, it is easy to arrive at a complete agreement that serves both the interests of the boy and the club.

6. The expense of this process is very small if we consider

the benefits it can and must bring. Manchester United, it must now be twelve years ago, saw their stadium in ruins after the aerial bombings [during the Second World War]. They had no team and had to play matches in the stadium of their neighbours, Manchester City, to whom they paid a rent. Today they have a magnificent stadium, having constructed a wonderful stand worth some £200,000 and they are one of the most powerful English clubs. Their team is magnificent and YOUNG. They've spent some £18,000 and we can follow their lead. They have won three league titles between 1946 and 1957, lifting the trophy in 1952, 1956 and 1957. They have finished second on four occasions, won the FA Cup in 1948, reached the final in 1957 and been in the semi-finals on three other occasions.'

Aldecoa's veneration of Matt Busby's youth model is all the more remarkable as this was written before the air crash in Feburary 1958, when the team's fable became eternally crystallised into football folklore. His report concludes: 'I don't claim to have any great authority or that my ideas should take precedence. Rather, I simply like to express ideas that I believe can give a great improvement to this club which I have represented for several years and with which I identify so much.'

It is the report of a visionary. And just think of the La Masia alumni who may owe Aldecoa a debt of gratitude: Pep Guardiola, Cesc Fabregas, Carles Puyol, Xavi Hernandez, Mikel Arteta, Gerard Pique, Lionel Messi, Ivan de la Pena, Sergi, Albert Ferrer, Hector Bellerin and Bojan Krkic are just a selection. Can it really be that Messi is indebted to an adopted Midlander? And can La Masia be deemed one of the greatest, unknown legacies of the tragic Busby Babes?

'Wow, can this really be?' asks Arteta, now the Manchester City assistant to Pep Guardiola, when we sit down at the club's training ground. 'I feel very proud that this man was the first Spaniard to play in England, he seems to represent all that we stand for.' There are certainly tantalising conclusions, but the extent to which Aldecoa's writing actually influenced Barcelona's direction remains unclear. Manel Tomas Belenguer, the historian who maintains Barcelona's archives, is unable to find any record of an official club response to Aldecoa's letter. It is therefore possible that this pioneering work fell on deaf ears. It may all be coincidence that Barcelona's academy was developed in this way when Cruyff and Tort assumed the reins of power.

There is, however, evidence to counter this. We do know that Aldecoa remained close to key figures at the club and, in the early 1970s, the president of Barcelona, Agusti Montal, made a concerted attempt to bring him into the club as a translator and aide to the English coach Vic Buckingham and his assistant Ted Drake. Aldecoa declined but always remained close to directors at his former club and particularly Kubala, who managed Barça between 1961 and 1963 and then again in 1980. We know that Kubala was a keen advocate of young talent, as Ferran Olivella, the Barça centre back between 1957 and 1969, found out as an 18-year-old. In the early 1950s Kubala was the jewel in Barcelona's crown but often took young players for one-on-one training sessions. 'I trained with him alone,' Olivella said. 'Nobody taught me quite like him. I've never seen anybody strike a ball as purely and cleanly as he did, it was like an intensive training course with a professor.'

Aldecoa and Kubala would exchange coaching manuals and John recalls how his father would fill exercise books with training notes and ideas for the evolution of young talent. Kubala, according to several accounts in the Catalan press, pushed for an organised academy system during the 1960s, but it only came to fruition when recommended by Cruyff in the late 1970s.

In 1960, Aldecoa returned to England, joining up with Birmingham City, where he was an assistant manager and youth scout for several years. 'I was born in Spain but had to be naturalised to join the RAF,' John explains. 'I came back at the age of nine with my mother to Stafford. My parents were still together but things were hard. You couldn't send money out of the country, there was no exchange rate between England and Spain. That changed late in the 1960s and early 1970s when the tourist trade began. Fortunately, my dad would send a 1,000-peseta note and the bank manager was a friend who could make it happen. There was nothing official, though. It was very, very difficult. My dad came back in 1960, when he was persuaded by Birmingham City directors.'

Where Aldecoa wandered, Kubala followed. In August 1960, the Hungarian-Spaniard flew over to Birmingham to visit his friend. A picture from the *Daily Mail* shows Kubala in conversation with Gil Merrick, the Birmingham manager, and Aldecoa. 'You can always learn in soccer – or so they say,' the *Mail* wrote. 'Barcelona star Laszlo Kubala is proving it by his visit to Britain to gather information in his plan to become one of Spain's top soccer coaches. And yesterday he talked tactics with Birmingham manager Gil Merrick and City coach Emilio Aldecoa.'

While at Birmingham, Aldecoa made more important interventions and, according to his son, he played an essential role in the scouting process behind the signing of Bob Latchford and Trevor Francis, two players who would eventually break British transfer records. In 1974, the forward Latchford was the subject of a £350,000 transfer from Birmingham to Everton. In 1979, Francis became the country's first £1 million footballer when he signed for Brian Clough's Nottingham Forest, again from Birmingham. Don Dorman was the Birmingham chief scout but, behind the scenes, Aldecoa was out on the fields, on the search for young talent.

'He began to help with the scouting and youth recruitment,' John says. 'He helped sign up the Latchford brothers, Bob and Peter, to Birmingham. Peter Latchford was only five-foot-ten or so and his brother would stick him up against a shed and kick the balls at him. He became a goalkeeper and had a great career with Celtic. As he left, they'd just begun courting Trevor Francis as a schoolboy. You weren't allowed to take on or court young players below 16. I believe they had begun talking to his parents by that stage after viewing some trials in St Albans and then for a Plymouth Schools team, where Francis scored a hat-trick apparently. I met the Latchford boys a few times and remember going round to their house. Their mum was ever so possessive. She'd have the little brown suitcase ready for them with socks and underwear all laid out. But they were nice, kind boys.'

Aldecoa had returned to Spain by the time Francis burst onto the scene as a teenager. When I contacted Trevor to verify the claims, he admitted he was not aware of Aldecoa's role in his recruitment. It is, however, unlikely that Aldecoa would have spoken to the player and family as Dorman took the lead in that regard, even buying Francis' parents a washing machine.

Back in Spain, Aldecoa was known as 'el inglés' – the English-man – and he became a commentator on English football in the newspapers.

On the eve of the 1966 World Cup, a regional Catalan news-paper devoted a spread to Aldecoa's story in English football. He spoke about his involvement in Birmingham's youth system, where he underlined his vision: 'My job here in England, where the professionalism is not so strident, is to instil the values of the club into young players. I coach the boys between the ages of 15 and 21 and thankfully, during the last few seasons, there are many players in the first team who I have brought on considerably during their younger years. At this moment in time, I can speak of the two fullbacks, the centre back, the left midfielder and the right winger. I can sense the change in English football. It is leaving behind its rigidity and the lack of imagination from which it had previously suffered. Clubs are starting to accept new systems, new ways of thinking and more contact from abroad.'

He predicted England would reach the World Cup final (they of course lifted the trophy) and also cast his verdict on each of the players. 'Bobby Moore of West Ham, a captain, strong, hard, more competent than brilliant. Norman Hunter of Leeds, a very tough player, a proper fighter, more inventive than Moore. Bobby Charlton, wow! A guy that possesses all the qualities of a great player, he is world class. On his day, there is quite simply nobody better. Geoff Hurst, rapid on the turn, brave in the penalty area, scores goals for West Ham. Jimmy Greaves, a brilliant forward, good technically and inventive. He is irresistible when the mood takes him. Since the age of 18 years old, he scored 30 or 40 every year for Spurs!'

Aldecoa, however, was not only the Basque refugee paying attention in 1966. In the east of England, in Cambridge, Sir Alf Ramsey's former shoeshine boy was cheering on his former mentor and this is where we meet the Gallego family and two brothers who left war-torn Spain behind for English football. Nearly 50 years on, in the gardens of Cambridge crematorium, a hundred or so people are gathered round, suited up in the spring sunshine. It's a solemn scene but there are warm smiles breaking out, old friends clasping hands, elderly gentlemen musing over their next golf outing, idle coffee morning chitter-chatter taking place among the ladies.

It is 21 May 2015 and a footballer is being laid to rest. Antonio Gallego lived a good life, passing away at the age of 90, and, amid the sadness, there is a desire to celebrate and treasure those fading, sepia-tinged memories. I have wound up here, just outside the university town of Cambridge, after meeting Naomi Westland, a researcher and activist for Amnesty International. A year earlier, she had written an article for *El País* in which she visited the Gallego family. Antonio and his brother Jose had boarded the *Habana* ship as child refugees, eventually becoming footballers for Norwich and Southampton. Naomi placed me in contact with Antonio's son, Paul, but the day I call him sadly transpires to be the week following his father's death.

Paul is patient beyond all reasonable expectations, insisting his father would want his story to be recalled. The tale to be told is that of two brothers who became footballers in the English game, crossing paths with the World Cup-winning manager Sir Alf Ramsey and serving the sport into their fifties. As such, he asks me to attend the ceremony and meet their family and their friends. So here I am, on a sweltering spring day, sitting inside a crematorium surrounded by them all, collecting anecdotes and memories.

Antonio arrived in England on the *Habana*, the same boat that brought Sabino Barinaga and Emilio Aldecoa to these shores. Unlike his two counterparts, he chose a different existence, deciding to remain in the UK for the rest of his life rather than return to his native Spain. The ship to Southampton was an escape route for the Gallego children, their portal to a happier existence. But it was also a great strain, a sudden loss of innocence, a life transformed without any warning, a family displaced and uprooted against their will.

The Civil War had removed their sense of normality in an instant, forcing their mother to make desperate decisions. Their father, a fiercely political man, was fighting for the left-wing forces and the family believe he was killed at Guernica. His body has never been recovered. The onus was on his wife Luisa to protect the family. To keep her children close was to take a gamble on their lives. To place them on a ship was to face the possibility of never seeing them again. She eventually chose the latter, after previously placing her children into an orphanage for shelter. Antonio was 12, joined by his brother Jose, who was 14, and three more siblings. Luisa kept her sixth child close, a baby daughter, as the pair sought refuge wherever possible amid the bombing. Tragically, her little girl fell ill and died.

Children on the ship wore a white hexagonal card around their necks, held up by a loose piece of white string. It read '*Expedición a Inglaterra*' and also contained an identification number. Antonio was number 4117 and he kept his card until his dying day. 'The journey was bloomin' rough,' Antonio told *El País* in 2012. 'José was the eldest; he looked after the younger ones the best he could but really that job fell to me because he was so shy. As long as I had my brother behind me I could stick up for myself. By then, our house in Spain had been ripped to bits, our dad had gone, fighting for the Republic and she [Luisa] wanted us to get in the clear.'

Arriving into Southampton, the five siblings were moved to a camp at Eastleigh before moving into a house on Station Road in Cambridge, just a stone's throw from the main railway station. The home, owned by Jesus College, one of the subsidiaries of the University of Cambridge, housed over 30 Basque refugee children. Jessie Stewart edited a book called *Recuerdos: The Basque Hostel at Cambridge*, which explains some of the locals' early impressions of the children. 'The most interesting record of their development in the first six months was a series of paintings. In the early days, few of these were without an airplane, a burning house or a battleship belching fire – but after a few weeks village and farm scenes and strange flower pictures appeared more and more frequently and it became rare to see any reminder of the war.'

As for the Gallego family, sport would be their outlet. The Basque boys in Cambridge set up a football team and charity games were played to raise donations to maintain the refugees. 'Football meant everything to us,' Gallego said. 'We got attached to Cambridge and made lots of friends here through playing football. If it hadn't been for football, we would have lived a very different life.'

In 2016, around 14 months after the funeral, Antonio's son Paul kindly invited me to his family home, where he lives with his mother and Antonio's wife, Joan. She is now into her nineties and a wheezing rattle punctuates her sentences. She hasn't quite been the same since her husband passed away, Paul reflects, but her mind is clear and her tongue remains sharp. 'Where's that nice photograph of your dad, Paul? No, not that one, you daft sod.'

The pair sit side by side on a sofa, reminiscing their way through a keepsake box. 'Well, I met him when he was just a boy,' Joan begins. 'Then they went into that big house near the train station and we were the same age. His birthday was June and mine was September the same year. We were only children, and the local school kids would donate one penny a week for the upkeep of the Basque children. We met before the big war, the Second World War. He learned English very quickly. He was a very gentle man.'

Paul explains: 'There was Joe, Tony and three sisters. They all stayed together and they were lucky. Their father had been killed in the Civil War, we know he was killed but that's as much as we know. We know he was a very political man. That's why their mother got them out of the country. As he got older, my dad felt real resentment towards Franco. Frankly, he hated him, hated his guts. He was always wary of going back and the dangers of the Guardia Civil. I went with him a couple of times. We knew that if we were in a bar, we were not to say too much. My dad was suspicious of people. We went in 1969 and 1982. We saw his mother's side in San Sebastian and his father's side near Valladolid.'

As the children settled into life in England, the ordeal continued for their mother Luisa. 'My dad did not see his mother for ten years,' Paul explains. 'They did keep in contact, somehow, possibly through the Red Cross. She was in Paris when the Nazis stormed France.' He shakes his head, asking his mother, 'How do you keep in touch during a war? It seems impossible now. Before all the smartphones and emails. It must have been letters. I suspect contact was very infrequent. There was certainly a point at which the mother didn't know if her babies were alive and well and the children didn't know if their mother was still alive. You can't really imagine that feeling, that uncertainty.' Joan interrupts: 'After Paris, then she was in Portugal and eventually she came to live here in England in the late 1940s. They got in touch with the local MP, who pulled the strings to organise it, from what I can recall.'

She moved to Cambridge in 1947, and by then her two sons Jose and Antonio were embarking on careers in football. They had both joined Cambridge Town, the local amateur team. Jose was the first to be scouted, joining Brentford in the first division, and Antonio then played for Norwich City. Neither had particularly thrilling careers. They did not possess the talents of Barinaga, Aldecoa or Lezama but Jose, in particular, was an impressive winger and he did have his own brush with footballing royalty. He signed for Southampton in 1948, where he rubbed shoulders with Alf Ramsey.

'This is a true story and it was Jose's party piece. They were at Southampton at the same time and obviously Jose was a new player and Ramsey was senior by that time. Ramsey took him under his wing, he was very kind, and, in return, Jose used to clean his boots every single day. It's true that both Jose and my dad felt more English than Spanish. I'll give you an example. During the World Cup in 1966, my dad and I went to nearly all the matches. It was less than £4 for a book of ten! It was ten shillings for the final and the rest was divided up. The day of the final was just fantastic. We drove up in the car from Cambridge. We had been to every England game, against Uruguay, Mexico, France, Argentina, Portugal, and then it was Germany. It's odd looking back. We expected to win it because England were at home. My dad was cheering England on, of course he was. He felt English; he'd support England if they were playing Spain. He was grateful to England, to the English people; this country saved his life and that is not being dramatic.'

Jose stayed for just over a year at Brentford before dropping down a division to Southampton. Injuries, however, took their toll after a particularly brutal tackle inflicted by a Barnsley player. In 1950, he joined Colchester United, spurning Exeter City, as he wanted to remain close to his family in Cambridge. Soon after, he returned to the non-leagues, playing for Cambridge United in the semi-professional leagues, while Antonio turned out for Cambridge Town. Antonio's short spell at Norwich was cut short when he was released in the summer of 1947. A letter from J. F. Wright, the Norwich chairman, read: 'I regret to have to inform you that your services are not being retained by this Club for Season 1947-48, and in consequence your name has been placed on the open Transfer List. The transfer fee required by the Club is FREE.'

Jose and Antonio both continued to play amateur football into their fifties, with Jose working as a gas inspector and Antonio as a salesman of cigarettes and sweets. Jose died in 2006, aged 82. 'Jose stopped playing football when he was 50; he had a heart attack after a game one day,' Paul says. He was, however, a natural sportsman, later taking up golf and winning the President's Cup at the age of 60 at the local Girton Golf Club. The local paper recorded a 'dazzling net 62 off a handicap of 15', only six years after Jose joined the club for health reasons. He told the *Cambridge Evening News* in July 1983: 'I was recommended to take up golf for therapy after a series of heart attacks. Most of the time I go round with just one club, the three iron, for the walk. But when it is a competition I like to go for it.'

Insisting that he had given away all his old trophies, his verdict on football is particularly enlightening. 'I am interested in reading about United, but I have lost touch with them and football. And I don't really understand the game now. They talk about 3-3-4s and 4-2-4s. I think they are very skilful, but I feel the game has lost a lot. It is not how good you are now, but how good you are at stopping the other man playing.'

As the service begins at the crematorium, friends share happy memories of their friend Tony (the anglicised version of his name Antonio, just as Jose was known as Joe by the locals). Cambridge United scarves adorn the room. The musical arrangements include *The Godfather* theme tune – 'He loved that film,' smiles one old friend, nudging his wife. Then comes 'Glory, Glory, Hallelujah!' – a tribute to the team he supported, Tottenham Hotspur. 'I tell you what,' says an old contemporary of Antonio's. 'He didn't do too bad for an immigrant, did he?'

CHAPTER 3

Golden Goal

Brian Moore, the doyen of ITV's football commentators, called it 'possibly the most extraordinary goal that has ever been scored in a European game, certainly in a European final'. Writing in the *Guardian*, David Lacey described it as 'an exquisite piece of Spanish-Moroccan impertinence'.

Over a slightly fuzzy phone line from his home in Ceuta, Nayim breaks into a giggle. Talk has turned to the goal that still has Tottenham Hotspur supporters singing his name from the terraces. 'No, I've never spoken to David Seaman since ... but I know what they sing!' He breaks into song. 'Nayim ... from the halfway line!'

Nayim, full name Mohamed Ali Amar, is the former Spurs forward whose name will always be inscribed into Lilywhite folklore. Rather peculiarly, his most memorable contribution to the Tottenham cause did not come in the white and blue colours of the north London club, but instead the white and blue of Real Zaragoza. His defining moment arrived in May 1995, two years after he left Tottenham behind following an impressive five-year spell with the club. The setting was the Cup Winners' Cup final, as Stewart Houston's Arsenal faced Real Zaragoza at the Parc des Princes in Paris.

It was a tight and tetchy contest that appeared set for penalty kicks when Arsenal's John Hartson cancelled out the Argentine Juan Esnaider's strike. In the dying embers of extra time, however, Nayim had other ideas. As Arsenal defender Tony Adams stooped to head the ball away from a Zaragoza goal kick, Nayim scurried towards the play and chested the ball down. He glanced up briefly, spotting Seaman off his line. Nayim set himself, allowing the ball to bounce twice before dispatching a stunning 50-yard up-and-under that sailed beyond the grasp of the tumbling Seaman and dropped in under the crossbar.

For Seaman, it was a moment of humiliation. He departed the field with his head bowed and his cheeks burning. His face would not appear so mortified until the Brazilian Ronaldinho left him similarly red-faced at the 2002 World Cup in Japan and South Korea. Ironically, Arsenal would not have made the final without Seaman's significant talents. The England goal-keeper had saved three penalty kicks in a shoot-out victory over Sampdoria in the semi-finals of the competition. Only minutes earlier in extra time in Paris, Seaman had made a stunning stop from Xavier Aguado, as his fingertips diverted a header against the post. Yet only the most ardent of Arsenal followers would recall these details from Seaman's 1994–95 season. This is the relentless and unforgiving existence of a goalkeeper, toiling in the endless and impossible quest for perfection.

Seaman's form recovered. He became the second best goal-keeper in English football as the 1990s progressed, behind only Manchester United's Peter Schmeichel. But memories of the Parc des Princes remained. Rival supporters taunted him, mimicking his dramatic fall by waving their hands and flopping their bodies backwards. 'Let's all do a Seaman,' they teased, singing en masse to the conga tune.

On the eve of Euro 96, Seaman said: 'When I realised Nayim's freak lob was going over my head I just thought: "Why me?" because prior to that I felt I had made a big contribution.' In an interview in 1998 with the *Daily Mail*, Seaman reflected: 'I always know I am one mistake away from trouble. The Parc des Princes, what a nightmare. I must admit that this reminded me of the pitfalls of the profession. I even had a funny feeling when I went back to that ground with England. It's hard to forget.'

They have not forgotten in Zaragoza either, where in 2006 a street in the suburb of Trasmoz was named in honour of the goal: *Calle Gol de Nayim*. Trasmoz was previously famous in Spain as the location of Dr Julio Iglesias Puga's kidnapping. Dr Julio was the father of Julio Iglesias, the Grammy Award-winning global superstar who has produced numerous platinum-selling albums. Iglesias actually began life as a footballer and a good one at that. He was a goalkeeper in the Real Madrid youth teams and the first choice in the reserve team when he suffered a near-fatal car accident at the age of 19. The crash compressed a nerve in his spine and he was bed-ridden for two years. While he was recuperating in hospital, a nurse bought him a guitar. Little did she know that her patient would become one of the world's most popular recording artists, with over 80 albums and 300 million records sold globally in 14 different languages. Dr Julio was also, of course, the grandfather of Enrique (of 'I can be your hero, baby' fame).

In Trasmoz, the Basque separatist group ETA held him captive for 20 days between December 1981 and January 1982. He was eventually released and Dr Julio, a gynaecologist, spawned two generations of heart-throbs. It may not, therefore, be overly surprising to learn that he was also cast as a womaniser in Spain, affectionately nicknamed '*Papuchi*' ('Little Daddy'). When he died at the age of 90 in 2005, his 42-year-old wife was expecting their second child in the space of two years.

Nayim laughs. 'I can't rival the Iglesias family for notoriety! But I know what you're going to ask. Did I mean it? Did I mean to score that night against Arsenal? Yes, yes, yes! Before the game, we had studied Arsenal's videos and we knew precisely that they play offside and that Seaman would take up very high positions. During the game, I remember one of my teammates,

Santiago Aragon, had already tried it and missed the goal. But it's not so easy to pull off. When the ball came to me, I saw it and thought, "Why not?" I'd actually done it before when I was growing up in Ceuta as a teenager. When I was at Tottenham, I'd stay behind after training and do long-distance crossbar challenges with Paul Gascoigne and Chris Waddle. This was obviously different. It was the last minute of the game. The intention was there but I was lucky that the goalkeeper messed up, too. I was surprised it went in. Seaman was the best goalkeeper in the world at that time. Well … actually … Peter Schmeichel was brilliant. But Seaman was up there. There was a certain prestige attached to his name, he was England's first choice. It was the defining moment in my career.'

Gus Poyet, the former Chelsea and Tottenham midfield player and a teammate of Nayim at Zaragoza, supports his version of events. Poyet says: 'He told Santi Aragon and I that Seaman is always off his line. After the final, we went back to Zaragoza's empty stadium and the three of us each took a ball and tried to repeat his trick. We hit 50 balls and some went into the goal but not with the same dip as Nayim's goal. I think Nayim should have some kind of plaque at the Parc des Princes – something that says "Nayim scored this goal in that final".'

Nayim is talking from his hometown of Ceuta, a Spanish enclave on the northern shores of Morocco's Mediterranean coastline. A meeting point for the Atlantic Ocean and the more tranquil Mediterranean Sea, this was one of the shorelines traversed by Homer's Odysseus on his mythical voyage home to Ithaca. Separated from the south of Spain by the Strait of Gibraltar, Ceuta was claimed by General Franco at the beginning of the Spanish Civil War, having previously been governed by Greeks, Romans, the Byzantine Empire, Muslim tribes and eventually the Portuguese. It has created a hodgepodge of an identity for the inhabitants, semi-African, semi-Spanish.

In our story, Nayim is an essential figure, as the first Spaniard to play in the Premier League. Perhaps surprisingly, he also brought an end to a wait of over 35 years, in which elite English football did not feature any Spanish players at all.

English football boasts a rich and deep heritage of overseas players. As early as 1892, the Canadian Walter Bowman became the first foreigner to play in the Football League upon signing for Accrington. In 1908, Tottenham signed the German Max Seeburg, the first European-born footballer to play in England. Nils Middelboe, Danish national team captain, signed for Chelsea on amateur terms in 1913. Egyptians, Frenchmen, Austrians and Dutchmen followed before the outbreak of the Second World War.

'By the early 1930s,' wrote Matthew Taylor, in *When Saturday Comes*, 'the progress of overseas football had convinced one or two British clubs that the signing of a foreign player might be worth the risk. What they didn't account for was the opposition of the Ministry of Labour. Arsenal had arranged a deal with the Austrian national goalkeeper Rudy Hiden, which included a job as a chef in addition to his football wage, but immigration officials refused him entry when he arrived at Dover. The Belgian centre-forward Raymond Braine, signed by Clapton Orient, actually made it into the country but was also forced to leave. To avoid such cases, the FA decided on a two-year residential qualification for players from outside the UK, a measure which effectively prohibited British clubs from signing foreign professionals.'

Political involvement in football was not unusual during this time. In the 1930s, when European governments were at best conservative and at worst Nazis, national identity and immigration control were matters of high concern. Fascist regimes employed sport as an arm of the totalitarian state to underline the strength of the nation. In Italy, Mussolini introduced the *Carta di Viareggio* blueprint for Italian football, limiting teams to two foreign players in 1926 and banning all non-Italians by 1928. At the 1934 World Cup, Italy decided to goad France in the second round of the tournament by turning out in black shirts, symbolic of Fascism. Fino Fini, the director of the Italian Football Museum, told a BBC documentary: 'The General Secretary Achille Starace suggested it would be a slap in the face to the French. Mussolini said, "OK, let's do it, let's do it."'

In England the stance of Whitehall and the Football Association with regard to foreign players endured beyond the Second World War. The two-year residency rule meant that recruitment of players from the continent was essentially outlawed in English football until 1978. There were some exceptions, though, and it did remain possible to secure overseas signings from the Commonwealth, although even this had its complications. Nonetheless, between 1951 and 1956, six consecutive FA Cup finals included a foreign player. In 1951, the Chilean George Robledo played for Newcastle and in 1952, when his brother Ted joined him on the field, he scored the winning goal in a Toon team that featured Jackie Milburn.

The pair had wound up in England after their mother, Elsie Oliver, from South Yorkshire, flew out to Argentina to become the governess to the children of an English mine worker. After the family were relocated to Chile, Elsie fell for Aristides Robledo, an accountant, and she gave birth to George in 1926 and Ted (Edward) in 1928. In 1932, Elsie returned to Yorkshire without her husband. The boys attended school in England and George signed terms with Barnsley as a 16-year-old. After 47 goals in 114 games for the Yorkshire club, Newcastle paid £26,500 to sign George. Brother Ted joined as part of the same deal.

George's form was so impressive that he was included as part of Chile's 1950 World Cup squad, in the same group as England and the USA in the infamous year when the Americans stunned England, the inventors of the game, and won by a 1-0 scoreline. The USA were 500/1 to beat England and their starting team was made up entirely of amateurs, including a postman, a painter-decorator, a dishwasher and a hearse driver. George's Chile lost to England and Spain but did beat the USA in a 5-2 victory in which he scored the opening goal.

After the two FA Cup finals, the brothers returned to Chile to play for Colo-Colo, but in 1970 tragedy befell Ted. Writing in the *Independent* in 1999, Richard Williams reported: 'A few days after returning to the Gulf from a visit to England, Ted went missing from a ship, the *Al Sahn*, sailing out of Dubai. There was said to have been a fight with the ship's captain, although no one who knew him believed that the introspective Ted could have provoked such a confrontation. The captain was charged with murder. [The third brother] Walter went twice to the Gulf to look for the truth, but his brother's body was never found and the circumstances of the death remain unresolved.' George was deeply affected by his brother's disappearance and he died at the age of 63 in 1989.

After the Robledo brothers' participation in the 1951 and 1952 FA Cup finals, South African-born Bill Perry scored the winning goal for Blackpool in the famous 'Matthews final'. The dazzling winger Stanley Matthews was making his third attempt to win the FA Cup after previous defeats in the 1948 and 1951 finals. He succeeded in 1953 in a 4–3 victory over Bolton. Perry scored the 92nd-minute winner.

Australian Joe Marston played for Preston in the 1954 FA Cup final, a 3–2 defeat by West Bromwich Albion. Marston was a friend of Duncan Edwards, the prodigiously gifted Busby Babe who died in tragic circumstances amid the wreckage of the Munich air crash in 1958. Marston shared a room with Edwards when he turned out at Hampden Park to represent an English League XI against a Scottish equivalent in March 1955. Marston's impact at Preston was highly significant, so much so that he received an MBE in 1980 and came fourth in a vote by Preston supporters as they declared the one hundred greatest players in the club's history. Future Aussie stars Craig Johnston, the former Liverpool winger, and Tim Cahill, the ex-Millwall and Everton midfielder, would describe Marston as a pioneer and inspiration.

Then, in 1955 and 1956, came the turn of the German Bert Trautmann. The goalkeeper was a rare example of a European arriving into English football at a time when strict restrictions were imposed by Parliament, the FA and even the Professional Footballers' Association, who deemed foreign players a threat to the work of home-grown talents. The PFA had been central to blocking the transfer of Austrian goalkeeper Rudolf Hiden in 1930.

The Manchester City goalkeeper Trautmann was a remarkable case. A former Luftwaffe paratrooper, he'd only been released from a prisoner-of-war camp in 1948. He was a member of the Hitler Youth and served in Russia during the Second World War. Trautmann was one of only 90 from his first regiment of over 1,000 who survived the war. He played football for POW teams in the north-west of England and was scouted as a replacement for Manchester City's long-serving goalkeeper Frank Swift.

Over 20,000 Manchester City supporters, a large Jewish contingent among them, protested upon Trautmann's signing. A local rabbi, Alexander Altmann, demonstrated remarkable compassion and forgiveness, urging his community to extend an olive branch to the former Nazi officer. 'Thanks to Altmann, after a month it was all forgotten,' Trautmann told the *Observer* in 2010. 'Later, I went to the Jewish community and tried to explain things. I tried to give them an understanding of the situation for people in Germany in the 1930s and their bad circumstances. I asked if they had been in the same position, under a dictatorship, how they would have reacted? By talking like that, people began to understand.'

As Manchester City goalkeeper, he entered FA Cup folklore when he played much of the second half of the 1956 final against Birmingham City with a broken neck after a collision with Peter Murphy. Surgeons subsequently told him he could have died or ended up paralysed. City won the game 3-1 and Trautmann's redemption in the eyes of the British public was complete when he was voted the Football Writers' Association Player of the Year.

There are some wonderful and colourful football careers and lives to be reflected upon among the foreign contingent in England during this period, but they remained very much in the minority: the 1964–65 *FA Yearbook* recorded only 15 non-British players in English football's top two divisions. Obstacles were placed in the way of foreign arrivals. West Ham, for instance, were unable to sign Israeli captain Mordechai Spiegler in 1970.

In his autobiography, former West Ham forward Trevor Brooking wrote: 'Spiegler, a technically gifted midfield player, was told quite bluntly by the Football League secretary, Alan Hardaker, that he was ineligible to play in England. Ron Greenwood had been impressed by him during the 1970 World Cup in Mexico and invited him to train with us. Mordechai had an encyclopaedic knowledge of English football and one day sat with Jimmy Greaves on the bus taking us to a pre-season training run. Sitting next to the great Greaves must have been a wonderful experience for Mordechai, who talked non-stop about English football all the way to training. Now for Jimmy, football was for playing, not for talking about. When he got off the bus he sidled up to Greenwood and said: "Don't let him sit next to me again – please!"' Mordechai instead signed for Paris Saint-Germain.

Until 1978, UEFA had been complicit in limiting the recruitment of foreign football players as national federations were concerned it would hinder the development of national teams. This attitude altered in 1978 when it was proved that the Treaty of Rome permitted freedom of movement within the European Community. This opened the door to European recruitment, while clubs could also sign two players from elsewhere across the world. This led to Tottenham signing Argentine duo Osvaldo Ardiles and Ricardo Villa, but there was frustration at the PFA when Sheffield United signed their compatriot Alex Sabella, who had not yet been capped by his nation.

Sheffield United, incredibly, signed Sabella after the club had failed in a bid for a 17-year-old Diego Maradona. The Blades manager Harry Haslam scouted Maradona while on a trip to Argentina and, as soon as the game finished, he sought to organise a £200,000 transfer. Second division Sheffield United, however, did not produce the cash quickly enough and instead had to settle for Sabella from River Plate in a £160,000 deal. Sabella's signing triggered a tightening of regulations by the PFA. It was decided that a panel of representatives would run the rule over prospective signings and that only 'established internationals' would be allowed to come to England.

During the late 1980s, the recruitment of foreign talent stalled once more as English clubs were banned from participating in European competitions following the Heysel disaster and accusations of hooliganism. This logically made England a less appealing option for the cream of the continent. In 1989, Arsenal became the last club to win the top-flight title by using only English players. Just a decade later, on Boxing Day 1999, Gianluca Vialli's Chelsea became the first to field a starting XI consisting only of foreign players. In 2005, Arsenal became the first in English League history to field an entire squad of overseas players. This rapid evolution can be partially attributed to the European Union's decision to scrap the quota on the number of footballers from one member state allowed to play within another EU nation. The other decisive factor was the Bosman ruling in 1995, as this further increased the movement of footballers within the European Union.

Yet, for all the relative progress of the 1980s and 1990s, it remains surprising that Nayim should be the only Spaniard in the top flight of English football until the arrival of Albert Ferrer in 1998. Ferrer, a steady fullback, became the first signing of a Spanish footballer by a Premier League club when he left Barcelona for Chelsea – Nayim had been signed in 1988, four years before the breakaway of the top flight from the old Football League in 1992. By the time Ferrer arrived, Premier League clubs had already recruited footballers from Argentina,

Australia, Austria, Barbados, Belgium, Bermuda, Bolivia, Brazil, Bulgaria, Canada, Colombia, Costa Rica, Croatia, Cyprus, Czech Republic, Denmark, Estonia, France, Georgia, Germany, Ghana, Greece, Hungary, Iceland, Israel, Italy, Jamaica, New Zealand, Nigeria, Norway, Poland, Portugal, Romania, Russia, Saint Kitts and Nevis, Senegal, Serbia, Slovakia, South Africa, Sweden, Switzerland, Trinidad and Tobago, Turkey, Ukraine, USA, Uruguay and Zimbabwe. So, why not Spain?

CHAPTER 4

Apertura

'In England, it is in our nature to travel,' commented the *Sunday Times* travel writer AA Gill. 'We all have a craving for some decent weather. But I do often wonder what exactly the Spanish are looking for when they go on holiday.' This, perhaps, provides a very simple answer to the question why English football waited so very long before hearing the patter of Spanish feet scurrying towards these shores once again. It rains a lot in England, the sun does not shine very often and the winter can be rotten. It is not the greatest compliment to English football that the only players who came here until 1988 were shoehorned onto a refugee boat on a life-saving mission to escape civil war as children in the Basque country.

Thankfully, there is more to it than this. For example, can we take it for granted that Spanish players were particularly appealing to English clubs during this time? Real Madrid maintained a rich heritage of success in European competition, but Spanish clubs did not captivate continental audiences in the latter half of the 20th century. Between 1966 and 1992, for instance, Spanish clubs went 26 years without winning the European Cup and their representatives made only three appearances in the European Cup final. Bayern Munich defeated Atletico Madrid in 1974, Liverpool beat Real

Madrid in 1981 and Steaua Bucharest saw off Barcelona in 1986. Barcelona did win the Cup Winners' Cup three times between 1979 and 1989, while Valencia also lifted the trophy, but Spanish clubs were not the dominant force that they now are in European competition.

On the international scene, Spain won the European Championship in 1964 but only reached one more final, in a defeat against France in 1984, before winning the competition again in 2008 and 2012. Spain, as a nation, has still only competed in one World Cup final and that was in 2010. 'It's easy to forget now,' Nayim says, 'but during that period, Spain was not at the summit of European football. Spanish football, in terms of the national team and reputation abroad, wasn't really big back then. Madrid and Barcelona were big names but it's when they started dominating the European scene that the invasion in the 1990s and 2000s of Spanish players began. When I was there, I was rare, the only one. I sensed opportunity but there was an insularity in Spain, too.'

Spanish footballers, traditionally, have not travelled too well. When the former Barcelona forward Bojan Krkic signed for AS Roma in the summer of 2011, Italian newspaper *Gazzetta dello Sport* wrote that, as the 33rd Spaniard to play in Italy, he would have to overcome a 'history of failure and disillusionment'. The Italian case study provides evidence of the Spanish struggle to adapt. Pep Guardiola lasted 13 games at Brescia in 2003. Ivan Helguera, the impressive defensive stalwart at Real Madrid, played eight games for Roma in the 1997–98 season. Gaizka Mendieta, voted the best central midfielder as a star of Rafa Benitez's Valencia's side in the 2001 Champions League campaign, played only 27 underwhelming games for Lazio before returning to Spain. The Real Madrid president Florentino Perez subsequently described Italy as a *trituradora* – a waste disposal unit – for Spanish footballers.

To find an exception, we have to return to 1961 when the iconic Luis Suarez, the only Spanish winner of the Ballon d'Or,

left Barcelona to join esteemed coach Hellenio Herrera and
starred for 12 years in Italy with Inter Milan and Sampdoria.
This is not to imply that the people of Spain possess something
peculiar or idiosyncratic in their cultural make-up that deter-
mines the behaviour of the region. What we can pinpoint,
however, are the socio-political implications of General Franco's
dictatorship that contributed to a sense of insularity.

Following the Second World War, Spain remained the pariah
of western Europe, and the Western democracies that had
fought so hard against fascism had little time for the extrem-
ists on the Iberian Peninsula. English football clubs would
not have been inclined to look towards Spain to do business.
Boris Nikolaj Liedtke, a historian of Spain's international relations, wrote: 'Worldwide public opinion was moving against
Franco. Canada publicly rebuffed Spain's attempts to establish
diplomatic relations. During spring 1946, six Communist, four
Latin American, three Commonwealth and four other states
severed diplomatic relations with Spain.' Poland then called
upon the United Nations to cut off relations and the organisation's Secretary General Trygve Lie echoed the demands. The
Belarussians also wanted an end to communication with Spain.

The UK, Australia and the US took the view that as Spain
did not constitute a threat, Spanish internal affairs were not a
matter of concern for the UN. They felt that rupturing relations with Spain would provoke more European convulsions.
Ultimately, Spain was condemned, excluded from the UN and
the organisation called for the immediate recall of ambassadors
from Madrid. Yet for Franco, it was not the worst setback, as
he was able to rally domestic support in the name of national
unity. 'Apart from prestige value,' Liedtke concluded, 'relations
continued unchanged. Diplomatic relations as such were never
ended. The US and Britain had recognised the Franco regime
since 1939 and continued to do so after 1946.'

Nevertheless, it remains true that Spain was met with suspicion. Javier Tusell, the Spanish historian, commented: 'The

image that foreign visitors had of Spain in the early years of Francoism was that of a country that had been condemned to irremediable poverty.' Pepe Mel, the former West Bromwich Albion manager who grew up in Spain in the 1960s, explains: 'Spain was a third-world country until 30 years ago. Many people were on the breadline or worse. People were scratching around just to put food on the table. Spain has grown a lot in the last 40 years and it is reflected in everything. Sporting success is one element but Spain has improved immeasurably in terms of public health and the field of medicine. Before, such progress had been unthinkable.'

Jimmy Burns writes of 1950s Spain as a period 'when Franco's nation struggled on account of its isolation from the rest of Europe. It was in the days before mass tourism, when Spain, and Madrid in particular, was still regarded by most foreigners as a sinister, backward and repressive place.'

This could be seen by the political infringement upon football. The Franco propaganda machine introduced the sports newspaper *Marca*, which came to be the nation's highest-selling daily, with over 350,000 copies sold per day. *Marca*'s very first front page had a photograph of a blonde girl raising her arm in a fascist salute. It was a message of unity and support to all Spanish sportsmen and sportswomen. Real Madrid became cast as a sporting arm of the Franco regime. It is true that Santiago Bernabeu, the former Real Madrid footballer and then long-serving president, worked in the treasury, while several cabinet ministers were also members of Real Madrid. Tusell records that every club was obliged to include at least two Falangists in their team, a ruling that remained in place until 1967. The vernacular of sports journalism was 'Castilianised' by the censor, meaning that English club names were outlawed. In 1941, Athletic Bilbao therefore changed its name to Atletico de Bilbao following a special decree by Franco.

Yet it is too simplistic to say that Spaniards did not arrive in English football purely because of the Franco regime, as this would overlook the dramatic change in Spanish international policy at the start of the 1960s. The dictator did not die until 1975. Following the collapse of the economy in 1959, Spanish borders opened up to foreign investment. The notion of 'apertura' (opening up) began in 1953, when an alliance was signed with the USA that allowed Spain to join the United Nations and UNESCO. This meant Spain began the shift from an agricultural nation towards an industrialised economy. It was part of a progressive mutation in Franco's Spain, as the introduction of foreign tourism and emigration went hand in hand with the liberalisation of trade and fewer economic regulations.

By 1959, it was necessary. Tusell describes a 'cataclysmic' situation, in which vital imports such as oil were on the verge of being suspended. The change worked and by the end of 1959, the Spanish Foreign Currency Institute balance moved from $58m in the red to $52m in credit. Tusell attributes the turnaround to foreign investment, emigration of Spaniards to Europe and tourism. In the early 1960s, Spain enjoyed an economic growth on a par with Italy, France and Germany. The rise in tourism reversed the trade deficit, with the numbers of visitors rising from 7 million in 1961 to 24 million by 1970. Between 1960 and 1973, only Japan's national economy grew faster.

Spanish people felt an everyday, tangible change. By 1975, nearly two-thirds of Spanish households had fridges, television sets and washing machines, and the family's food budget was on average 38 per cent whereas it had previously been 60 per cent. This laid the foundation for the invasion of consumerism and the number of television sets rose from 600 in 1956 to in excess of 2 million a decade later. A liberalisation of the economy shifted the cultural landscape of Spain. Free movement in the Common Market encouraged Spaniards to search for a better standard of living abroad. Spain did not join the EEC until 1986, but between 1960 and 1973 it is estimated that 1.5 million people left Spain for northern or western Europe to help fill vacancies in post-war industrial projects, at a rate of more than 100,000 emigrants per year. It was, therefore, very much possible for Spaniards to play football outside of their homeland.

Within Spain itself, a process of urbanisation took place, as a result of which the number of Spaniards living in big cities rose considerably. In the decade 1960-70, Tusell notes, the rural population decreased from 42 per cent to 25 per cent of the total population. This, in turn, opened Spanish eyes to a more globalised world. There remained work to do. It was only in 1970 that the government started to spend more on education than they invested in the army. The number of female workers grew – but only to 24 per cent of the overall working population. Clearly, though, Spain became a more open country between 1959 and the death of Franco in 1975, and it remains an oddity that as ever more continental players headed for English shores, the wait continued for a Spaniard to enter English football.

That player would be Nayim and it owed much to Terry Venables, the former England national team manager and coach of Barcelona. Venables arrived in Barcelona in the summer of 1984. On 26 May that year, the front page of *Mundo Deportivo*, the sports daily in Catalonia, read: 'Hello, Mr Venables!' The man nicknamed 'El Tel', a *Fawlty Towers*-esque nod to his Spanish sojourn, arrived at Barcelona after an impressive season at Queens Park Rangers. His predecessor Cesar Menotti commented: 'I wouldn't have this guy from England; they can't play football,' before predicting: 'He won't last longer than Christmas.' As it transpired, Venables won La Liga in his first season and almost won the European Cup in his second campaign, as Romanian outfit Steaua Bucharest defeated Barcelona in the final of the competition.

During that time, he signed three British forwards: Englishman Gary Lineker, Scotsman Steve Archibald and Welshman Mark Hughes. These were different times for British and Irish footballers, when the best money was to be found abroad rather than at home. Between the late 1950s and 1980s, headline acts in the British game, such as John Charles, Denis Law, Jimmy Greaves, Liam Brady, Kevin Keegan, Mark Hateley, Graeme Souness, Ray Wilkins, Luther Blissett, Ian Rush, Glenn Hoddle and Laurie Cunningham, all headed abroad. This, in itself, may go a long way to explaining the dearth of Spanish talent in England. The best players would be paid better in Spain, while the English PFA and FA were hostile at that time towards more foreign talents invading the English game.

In his 1989 autobiography, *Sparky*, Mark Hughes cuts to the crux of why British talent was lured to Spain, admitting that Barcelona were paying him in 'telephone numbers'. At Manchester United, Hughes had been earning only £200 a week, although this was a legacy of a contract signed as a teenager. 'No secrets . . . it was money,' Hughes said. 'Bundles of it. Nothing else would have booked me on the plane. So many British footballers, given the opportunity to play abroad, tell the world it's for all kinds of different reasons. They need a new challenge, they have built their dreams on playing in Europe, they want to develop their technique with the continentals. Maybe, but they're only half-truths. The real motivation is money. And that makes them football mercenaries just like me. There is no shame or disgrace in that – it's all about securing yourself and the family.'

More recently, Lineker echoed these sentiments, albeit in a more measured tone than Hughes. 'In my day, it was an opportunity to earn a lot more money, whereas nowadays the Premier League pays as well as anywhere so players don't need to go for financial reasons.'

The Argentine superstar Diego Maradona departed in the same summer that Venables arrived at Barcelona. The Scottish forward Steve Archibald was signed as his replacement. Archibald, a former car mechanic, was a fiery character. At Aberdeen, he had played under Alex Ferguson and the two had a memorable spat after Archibald scored a hat-trick in the quarter-finals of a Scottish Cup tie against Celtic. The tradition is for the hat-trick hero to keep the match ball but, on this occasion, Ferguson insisted Archibald was not to keep the ball as a souvenir and the forward defied his manager. In his biography of Ferguson's time at Aberdeen, Michael Grant describes how Ferguson hauled Archibald into his office to rebuke him and how, 'The following day he was sitting in the coaches' room with Pat Stanton and Teddy Scott, drinking tea and chatting, when the door burst open. Archibald shouted, "There's your fucking ball" and booted it hard into the small room. The three of them ducked and spilled tea over the floor as it ricocheted around.' At Aberdeen, Archibald was in Ferguson's office so often that the seat opposite the manager's desk became known as 'Archibald's chair'.

His success at Barcelona was particularly curious, as he did not, in fact, want to leave Tottenham for Spain. In truth, the Barcelona hierarchy did not want Archibald, either, much preferring the Mexican Hugo Sanchez, who would go on to sign for Real Madrid and become a legend of the Spanish game. 'I didn't want to go to Barcelona,' Archibald insisted, in an interview with journalist Graham Hunter in 2016. 'I'd never been to Spain on holiday, never wanted to go to Spain on holiday. I never wanted to leave Spurs, who wanted the money. Irving Scholar, the new Tottenham owner, was a young guy who thought he could run the world. Nobody at Spurs was saying, "Stay!" The deal was on and so I went. Even at the hotel where I was set to sign, Hugo Sanchez was upstairs because the club wanted him and Terry said, "No, no, I want Steve." It was going on for hours and I thought, "Fuck this, it looks like you don't want me." Terry asked me [to wait] for half an hour. I was walking [out], ready to go. The club president came in, looked me in the eye and said, "Do you want to sign for Barcelona?" I said yes and the deal was done.'

Once at Barcelona, Archibald adapted, learning the language and firing in the goals as Barcelona won only their second La Liga title in 25 years. The success rate of Brits in Barcelona varied and it did impact on the Spanish perception of English football. In the case of Mark Hughes, the former Manchester United forward who has since managed Blackburn, Manchester City and more recently Stoke City, the experience was, in his own words, 'a full-blown X-rated horror story'. Hughes had experienced debilitating problems with alcohol while at Manchester United, describing his behaviour as 'sheer lunacy'. In the six months before leaving United, Hughes was 'tortured and tormented'.

Things did not improve on arriving in Barcelona, where he was aghast to be placed in a hotel that was like 'something out of those holiday horror stories', with a 'so-called restaurant that would have been disowned by British Rail'. Hughes was exposed by the Catalan press after one night out when he failed to show for training the following morning. Venables described Hughes as a 'big disappointment'. In his autobiography *Born to Manage*, Venables said: 'He was only 22 and his age and a certain immaturity were responsible for his lacklustre performances as much as anything. His physical style caused problems. He feared nobody, including the Butcher of Bilbao, Goikoetxea, who had made his terrible mark on Diego Maradona. When he ran up against Mark and tried to intimidate him, he quickly learned that here was a player best left alone. Mark would rarely do other than defend himself but the match officials saw his name before an incident and kept pulling him up and showing him a yellow card. It got so distressing for him, I had to drop him.'

Venables returned to England in 1987 and he brought Nayim over a year later. Nayim had been at La Masia since the age of 15, having been scouted by Barcelona while growing up in Ceuta, and it was there that Venables had spotted his potential. At Barcelona, it is not unusual for the first-team manager to run sessions for the youth teams. 'The beauty of La Masia was the intermingling of the various age groups,' Venables said. 'We would all lunch together, and I would train and coach them when I could. It allowed me to keep in contact with the players, get to know them not just as footballers but as young men.'

Nayim had struggled to break into the first team at Barcelona and he headed to Tottenham on loan in November 1988. He had suffered from incapacitating injuries and had barely played for 18 months. His first appearance in English football was in front of only 200 spectators, as he scored a marvellous individual goal for Tottenham's reserves against Charlton. During his loan spell, he did enough to convince Tottenham of his merits and the following summer he agreed a permanent deal, becoming the first Spaniard to sign for an English club since 1947.

The deal was negotiated during a meeting between Venables, Spurs chairman Irving Scholar and Barcelona's director Joan Gaspart. The transfer was arranged as part of the package that would also bring Gary Lineker back to England from Barcelona. Venables called it an 'excellent double deal'. Lineker's four-year contract would be worth in excess of £250,000 a year. Nayim's was rather more modest. Barcelona thought highly enough of Nayim to include a buy-back option in the contract, a route they still take with many products of La Masia to this day.

For Nayim, it was a trip into the unknown. 'I remember when I joined, I had to wait a few months for my work permit to come through. It allowed me to build myself up physically in the reserves and then, once I was in the first team, I was primed and ready. I didn't have issues adapting. I lived in a hotel with my teammates. It was nuts. There was Erik Thorstvedt, Gudni Bergsson, Paul Gascoigne and Paul Stewart. We had a lot of fun.'

As with all Tottenham players from that era, Nayim has his own 'Gazza' stories. 'Lots of pranks,' he laughs. 'When I first came, I couldn't speak a word of English and he was taking the piss. It probably took me three months just to be able to go out and about in London by myself and catch the metro or a taxi. I learned the language quickly. I remember watching the BBC News. I'd read the tabloid newspapers at training.

At the start, it was just the pictures and headlines and then I worked from there. I remember cricket on the radio, *Test Match Special*. My best teachers were my teammates. I learned a lot in the dressing room. There were lots of jokes with Gazza and Paul Stewart. They'd nick my room key and move things around in my bedroom. I thought I was going mad! At the dinner table, they'd change my order with the waiter when I wasn't looking. I took it well, as intended, with a smile and a laugh. After a few months, I was part of the gang and taking part in the pranks.'

Nayim's voice softens as he reflects on Gascoigne. 'Gascoigne's quality was as good as I'd seen anywhere and I'd come from Barcelona. We are talking about hands-down the best footballer in the world at that time. There was nobody anywhere doing the things he could do with a football. When he was on it, he was unstoppable, a force of nature. He could shoot, tackle, beat a man, score goals. He was better than any Real Madrid or Barcelona player. It breaks my heart to see what has happened to him. He has the biggest heart of anyone I met in football. The people who surrounded him sometimes worried me. I was at a game against Spurs a few years ago and bumped into him. The truth is that I didn't recognise him in person anymore. He'd spotted me and came up to me. I saw he was doing a little bit better at that stage and he was trying to get himself right. I hope he finds peace.'

The change of football culture did take a bit of getting used to: 'You can't compare football in England now to those days. It was crazy when I joined. It's true that people in Spain feared for me a little, but I knew Terry and I saw a chance to play in a top British team. I'd say Tottenham, Nottingham Forest and Manchester United played what we'd call the right way. The rest were long ball, direct, brawny. In my first training sessions, Guy Butters was very physical with me. Opposition players thought they could intimidate me. Everyone was competitive, biting at my ankles. But my teammates protected me. We had a great team . . . Vinny Samways, Paul Allen, Gazza. It was easy to play in that team.'

Nayim's impact continued to grow. An excellent free kick crowned a 3–0 victory over Manchester United at Old Trafford. These were troublesome times for Alex Ferguson at Manchester United and Nayim's late strike sent thousands scurrying for the exits. One national newspaper match report read: 'Those that remained barracked their own team. These are testing times for Ferguson who after spending £12m on building a team must now squirm as they display a total lack of consistency.'

Nayim, by contrast, received only acclaim. He became a hunted man. On the first day of the 1990–91 season, Spurs came up against Manchester City, who had midfield terrier Peter Reid in the team. One match report of Tottenham's 3–1 victory describes how Reid 'snapped at everyone's ankles, until he came close to severing Nayim's from the rest of his leg'. Fortunately for Nayim, it was also the first day in English football history that it had become compulsory to wear shin pads.

In north London, they had taken to their talented Spaniard. In an interview before the FA Cup final in May 1991, Nayim received the nod of approval from the club's legendary manager Bill Nicholson: 'I like Nayim,' Nicholson said. 'He came on in the semi-final and showed nearly as many tricks as Gazza. He's a very clever player.'

Perhaps his best display in a Spurs shirt was a 2–0 victory over Graeme Souness' Liverpool in November 1992. One match report read: 'The goal that set them on their way was one that would have merited riotous celebration the length and breadth of the land had it come from the boot of Paul Gascoigne for England. The scorer of it was born in Morocco and there would have been much fez-tossing if it was repeated on Saturday night on African TV. The mosque-style bowing from the terraces underlined his contribution.'

His form by then was such that Spain manager Javier

Clemente flew to England to watch him in action against Aston Villa. A Spain manager travelling abroad to scout players was novel for the times. Clemente said: 'Everyone knows I'm a huge admirer of English football and I realise it's not easy for a foreigner to succeed there. From what I've heard he has added some of the English characteristics to his natural ball skills and that could be the sort of player I am looking for.'

Nayim did attract some controversy, earning a rebuke from new BBC commentator Trevor Brooking for his penalty-area amateur dramatics. Brooking had been a gentle voice in his early commentary days, leading Brian Clough, the bolshie Nottingham Forest manager, to say that Brooking 'floats like a butterfly and he stings like one'. In November 1992, however, Brooking fiercely condemned Nayim for feigning a foul to earn a penalty in a match against Oxford. 'The press came after me after that. The papers called me a cheat. I remember a controversy at Anfield, too. I tried to trick and deceive the referee and all I ended up doing was wasting a great chance. Terry Venables sat me down after that and told me to cut it out. He told me about the English mentality and the importance of integrity in England.'

To this day, Spanish players in England remain tarred by a suggestion that they are prepared to push the boundaries to gain an advantage. When I met Chelsea's £58m Spanish striker Alvaro Morata for an interview two months into his time in England, it was striking to hear his fear that he might be type-cast. 'I need to spend less time moaning at officials or falling over and focus on the game,' he insisted. 'In Spain and Italy, it's more normal to protest against the referees but here in England, they aren't interested. I think as well, the older I get, I see it is a bad look in front of the fans and in front of the little kids who are watching you. It's not very elegant.'

In 1993, Nayim left Spurs after 144 appearances. His greatest moment in Tottenham colours arrived in the 1991 FA Cup final. It remains the last time that Spurs lifted the trophy. In the final against Nottingham Forest, Gascoigne departed with an injury inside 17 minutes. Nayim replaced him and played a key role in the two goals, one scored by Paul Stewart and the winner, an own goal by Des Walker. 'I had two exceptional moments in my career,' Nayim says. 'That night against Arsenal was special. I was extra-motivated as an ex-Spurs boy. I loved London derbies, the passion, the build-up, the papers in the lead-up and the radio shows. And then the winning feeling! The team we beat in the Cup Winners' Cup was a proper team: Lee Dixon, Nigel Winterburn, Tony Adams, Paul Merson was an amazing player, Ian Wright up front. I wanted to win it for Spurs as well as Zaragoza. The only player I've ever spoken to from that Arsenal team was Merson, when I bumped into him at Sky. The first one was to win the FA Cup final at the mythical Wembley. Those were the days when everyone adored the FA Cup, when it was the pinnacle in English football, and the feeling that day was just amazing. I felt like I truly belonged in your game.'

CHAPTER 5

Wembley Dreams

It is mid-morning at the picturesque Talamanca bay, a calming oasis amid the hubbub of Ibiza's old town. By night, this Spanish island is an unfettered mecca for British revellers and partygoers, where the big dance-music names spin the decks, Premier League footballers pose for selfies and B-list celebrities pop the champagne corks at upmarket beach clubs. Perched on a deckchair beside a pristine swimming pool, Roberto Martinez smiles. It is a rueful smile. Everton brought his pilgrimage in English football to an end eight weeks ago and, already, he is becoming rather restless.

There is a certain kind of weariness to Martinez's appearance. Much of his hair has passed with time and his holiday stubble is now more salt than pepper. At his best, Martinez has the capacity to light up an entire room – infuriatingly handsome, immaculately turned out, splendid brown shoes. There are few more likeable characters to have touched the English game. I am pleasantly surprised to find a man who remains generous with his time and we end up spending several hours under the sun's glare.

Graham Barrow was the Wigan manager when a 23-year-old Martinez arrived into the fourth tier of English football in the summer of 1995. It was a surreal and, frankly, inexplicable step to take in an era when Spaniards did not grace English football. As the local Wigan newspaper put it, Martinez 'swapped paella for pies', as he left behind Real Zaragoza and signed for the Lancashire club alongside fellow Spaniards Isidro Diaz and Jesus Seba. The sense of intrigue was such that the trio posed with Mexican-style sombreros in promotional photographs.

Barrow would later become an assistant to Martinez at Wigan and Everton. 'Normally, with a British coach, a football conversation lasts half an hour,' Barrow says. 'With Roberto it's four or five hours. He's just obsessed, in the best possible way. It's odd, really, because as a player, I didn't see it coming from him. He was easy to coach but he listened to others rather than giving it back. When I managed him at Chester, I saw him returning with his own ideas more. Then I wondered whether his personality, amiable and charming, would work as a coach. I knew he had the intelligence and that he would be bold. But you know, British football has this thing that you need to be big and brash, ranting and raving. You have to be able to bollock people and really tell people. I wondered how he would handle that side of it, but he just did it in his own way and players responded.'

No other Spaniard has devoted as much of their career to English football as Martinez. As a player, he turned out in the lower reaches of the game, in the second, third and fourth tiers for clubs such as Wigan, Walsall, Chester and Swansea. His attachment to Swansea and Wigan was such that he managed both clubs with distinction, steering Swansea to a promotion before winning the FA Cup with Wigan. Now, he is waiting for his next job. There has been some subtle contact from Hull City, where Steve Bruce has surprisingly departed, but it is unlikely to materialise due to the club's volatile ownership situation.

'This would have been my tenth straight season as a coach,' he says. 'I started at Swansea in February 2007 in the lower leagues and then I had 265 consecutive Premier League matches at Wigan and Everton. It's really weird. I'm normally plotting and planning in June, but this summer I'm relaxing and enjoying my family. I've still not had a honeymoon. I got married in the summer of 2009 but I took the Wigan job and it was pre-season. We want to do South Africa properly. My wife Beth and I were together in 2010 in South Africa and the World Cup in Brazil and the Euro Championships in Poland and France – but that was work for me, too, whether it was punditry or scouting. The honeymoon's on the bucket list.'

For a man usually characterised by his relentless positivity, it is curious to find Martinez in reflective mood. He was hurt by the manner in which his three-year spell at Everton ended. On 30 April 2016, Everton defeated Bournemouth by a 2-1 scoreline. The victory on the field was in vain. The mood on the terraces had turned. An aeroplane flyover adorned the Merseyside skyline, carrying the depressing message: 'Time To Go Roberto'. On Gladwys Street, the road adjacent to the club's stadium, a hundred or so fans staged a sit-in, with fervent chants of 'Roberto Martinez, get out of our club'. In the *Liverpool Echo*, radio presenter and Everton supporter David Downie wrote: 'I think we could win our last four games 10-0 and it still wouldn't go far in regards to any sort of redemption for him, in what's been an appalling campaign. It's difficult not to feel exasperated and yearn for the end of May.'

It was a saddening and dispiriting fall from grace. The reasons for the opprobrium were clear. Critics argued that Everton had stuttered and regressed since a terrific first season in which Martinez's side finished fifth, a hair's breadth from Champions League qualification. Home form became a major concern and Everton ended the 2015-16 season with only 23 points from 19 games at Goodison Park, the same as relegated Norwich City and one point less than 17th-placed Sunderland. Middling teams such as Swansea, West Ham, Stoke and West Brom had taken maximum points from trips to Merseyside. Too many goals were shipped at home, with only Bournemouth and Aston Villa conceding more.

'The problem was at Goodison,' Martinez concedes. 'Too many goals, too lax, and it cost us. I maintain the level of football was fantastic at certain times in the season. But we had bad luck, too. For example, we played West Ham at home, we miss a penalty when we are 2-0 up and then we lose 3-2 with ten men and three goals conceded in 12 minutes. I think those moments scarred us. The fans were suffering at home, as we all were. The level of play in the first half of the season was fantastic. We scored more goals from open play than most sides during that period . . . I think more than Leicester, who became champions and even Arsenal. That's how I designed the team to play.'

The vitriol surprised Martinez and, after a nine-year coaching career and 21 years in England, he has perceived a change in attitude. 'Nowadays, we have social media, Twitter, and we live in a world where people can be aggressive and become very angry very quickly.' He shakes his head. He worries about himself but also his family.

Martinez was reared in Balaguer, a small town with a population of 15,000 sandwiched between the cities of Zaragoza and Barcelona. His father was a football manager for the local side and it was there that Martinez developed his eye for coaching and a dedication to his principles. He'd accompany his father to games and training sessions. On the car journey home, they would exchange ideas and plot for the matches ahead. He'd play with friends in the Plaza Mercadal, the main square, and he still remembers the sense of awe when he made his debut for Real Zaragoza against Atletico Madrid. 'As a child I had collected football stamps of star players in Spain and put them in my scrapbook. It was incredible to see those players come alive, in front of you in the flesh.'

As a coach, he learned from his father and he also inherited his competitive edge. The two often clashed over card games or Ludo at home or on family breaks. An excerpt from his autobiographical account of his promotion-winning season at Swansea is particularly striking. 'Sadly in later life I have reacted to results in the same way as my father,' Martinez wrote. 'As a player and a manager I have probably been impossible to live with if the result has gone against me. The people close to me suffer and I think you'd see that difficulty in every family where someone is involved in this sport. When you don't win, you feel miserable. I suppose you take for granted that at home you can be how you are and that means the people in the same house as you have to endure your misery.'

So we can ignore the charming facade and the optimism he finds in disappointment. Martinez hates losing. With time, however, he has grown more circumspect. 'I will always make sure my daughter has a strong network of friends and family,' he now says. 'She will grow up understanding that I am a public figure. In football, if you win you are the best in the world. And if you lose, you are the devil. I have one friend who tells me: When they see you on TV after winning a game, you are Paul Newman. When they see you after losing a game, you are Quasimodo!'

Martinez laughs. 'It's true, though,' he says. 'It's a world of extremes. English football has changed. I had been managing for seven straight years in the Premier League. During the last two years, there has been a radical change on a level of the attention you receive. On a domestic level, social media has an effect. It's a build-up of pressure and aggression and it's not good. To be a coach with a long-term project is more difficult. When you are constructing a plan, you're going to have set-backs. You have to try and survive because now there's such a build-up of pressure and public pressure adds to it. It's passion and people care and that's good, but we want things and we want them now. Every defeat and setback is pored over and you need a very solid approach to succeed. Look at Sir Alex Ferguson's first three years at United – nowadays he'd have been in trouble. It's a cultural change. If you have an owner who is ultra-protective of the coach, it can work, but owners need to be strong.'

Only two years earlier, Everton followers worshipped their new manager. Blue duvet covers were inscribed with '*Sólo Lo Mejor*' – 'Only the Best'. A stadium banner was unveiled that read: 'The School of Science Re-Opened, 6th June 2013', referencing the date that Martinez entered the club. Martinez excelled in his first season at Everton, 2013-14, as he built on David Moyes' long-term work. He walked into Goodison Park and transformed the club's mentality. He promised the chairman Bill Kenwright that the club would achieve Champions League football. The team evolved, playing more adventurously, going toe-to-toe with opponents at the top of the Premier League.

Supporters had grown to resent Moyes' habit of talking the club down, at times portraying a talented group of players as a rabble of scrappers. 'I'm going into a gunfight armed with a knife,' Moyes said before one Everton game against Manchester City in September 2011. This statement came despite Everton's record of seven victories from their previous eight matches against City and the team having won their four previous games.

Martinez enjoyed a brilliant debut campaign, as Everton pressed hard for the top four of the Premier League. They ended on 72 points, with a free-flowing way of playing that liberated young talents such as John Stones, Ross Barkley and Romelu Lukaku. Everton went to Old Trafford and defeated David Moyes' Manchester United. Then they went to Arsenal and enjoyed 63 per cent possession in the first half.

At the club's training ground, Martinez embraced and revelled in the club's history, inviting Howard Kendall, the manager who won two league titles with Everton in the 1980s, down for a cup of tea. He oversaw the installation of a series of canvases on the staircase of the club's Finch Farm training complex. Photographs of Everton's nine Football League-winning and five FA Cup-winning teams decorated the walls, and Martinez ordered one space to be left bare, in the hope that his Everton side would soon take pride of place among former heroes.

The local media eulogised Martinez's work. He arrived shortly before 8am and would sometimes not leave training until after 9pm. He initiated a points system to motivate players out on the training field. In shooting exercises or practice drills, the day's best player would be handed a point and the individual with the highest score at the end of the campaign would receive a prize. After scoring a free kick against Aston Villa, winger Kevin Mirallas ran to the bench to celebrate with his coach. Speaking afterwards, Mirallas said: 'I'd never celebrated with a manager at any point in my career. The reason I did that was because in the weeks leading up, we had long discussions about how I could contribute more and improve.'

The manager called Ross Barkley, the robustly built and dainty-footed midfielder, 'England's answer to Michael Ballack'. Barkley said: 'It's mad because the way the manager says I'm like Ballack, my Sunday league manager used to say that when I was 11. I knew I would get my chance under him. He had given young players their chance at Wigan. I knew I was the type of player to suit him because he is a tactical manager. I felt confident I could break through this season.'

Martinez was seen as a visionary when he declared a plan to convert left-back Leighton Baines into the next Philipp Lahm. The Bayern Munich defender Lahm had already enjoyed a marvellous career when Pep Guardiola arrived in Bavaria and sought to reinvent the German into a deep-lying midfield player. Guardiola described the captain of Germany as 'the most intelligent player' with whom he had worked, and Martinez saw similarities with Baines. So off Martinez went, with Baines in tow, to attend a Champions League quarter-final at Old Trafford between Manchester United and Bayern Munich. The aim of the night was for Baines to observe Lahm close-up.

Unfortunately for Martinez, it turned out to be a freakishly, fiendishly competitive season and a passport to the continental elite eluded Everton. Arsenal, who finished in fourth place, qualified with 79 points. Everton's 72-point haul would have been enough to secure a top-four finish in all but three of the Premier League seasons since the division converted from 22 to 20 teams at the end of the 1994-95 season. When Everton qualified for Champions League football in fourth place under Moyes in 2005, they did so with only 61 points. Manchester United's 1999 treble-winning team won the Premier League with only 79 points.

He grimaces. 'When Leicester won the league, Arsenal came second with 71 points and Tottenham had 70 points and finished third. As manager of Everton, you have two options. You hide from the history or face up to its standing as one of the iconic clubs of British football. They hadn't won a trophy since 1995. This weighs on your shoulders. The intensity the fans have is special. I never wanted the players or chairman to feel under pressure. I wanted to take the pressure off them. At the end, during my final four months of the last season, it was really tough. I felt at the centre of all the heat and pressure. It was a very young team that wanted to win titles. I was desperate to win a trophy and pushed for the cups. In the league, if you aren't near the European places and not in a relegation fight, it is difficult to push and motivate. We got to two semi-finals in the cup competitions.

'Once Everton get one trophy, the whole club will take off. When I arrived at Everton, we had the same budget as Aston Villa and Fulham. They both went down. We created a philosophy of giving chances to young players. We had John Stones, Ross Barkley, Romelu Lukaku, Gerard Deulofeu, Seamus Coleman – special players. This summer, it's sure that Stones and Lukaku could go for a fortune. This was the plan to put ourselves in a position to compete but we were doing it without investment. So we created a young team with big expectations.'

Martinez proves prescient with regard to Stones, who signed for Manchester City in a £50m deal. Lukaku went to Manchester United for £75m in another club record sale the following year, in the summer of 2017.

The death knell for Martinez's Everton career rang out during one gruesome week in April 2016, as Everton were pummelled 4-0 by Liverpool at Anfield before losing 2-1 to Manchester United at Wembley in the FA Cup semi-final. Everton were dire in the Merseyside derby on a night Liverpool had 37 attempts on goal, and they had to play most of the second half with ten men following a red card for Ramiro Funes Mori. Against Louis van Gaal's United, they were far more competitive and unfortunate to lose to a late Anthony Martial goal. Martinez nods his head. 'Yes, yes. Of course. Two huge games. We had bad luck with injuries, Stones had stomach cramps, Funes Mori was sent off at Liverpool. That week affected us terribly. After those games, the season was over. Finished. After that, the players were thinking mentally about the European Championships; the last games were very difficult.'

During that troublesome final campaign, a revisionist and jaundiced view of Martinez developed. He became chastised as the manager unable or unwilling to compromise his beliefs in order to move forwards. His previous achievements were recalibrated. Those who had celebrated his historic FA Cup win with Wigan now reconsidered his legacy, focusing only on consistently poor defensive records. Martinez's sunshine state of mind, seeing rainbows over the horizon when supporters could only sense storm clouds, began to rankle.

Writer Henry Miller, a New Yorker, once complained that 'the whole fucking world is going a hundred-per-cent-American' and Martinez did sometimes appear to be a descendant of those positivity gurus. He became known as the manager who took Wigan down, which overshadowed the remarkable story of the boy from Balaguer who had devoted his life as a player to the Football League and then scaled the heights of English football as a manager. Martinez knows the question around the corner, knows that I am about to ask whether he will become more pragmatic for the cause of self-preservation in future roles.

'No. You don't write off your principles,' he insists. 'No, no.

Football has cycles. We have been lucky that a type of creative football has been the key to success in recent years. Spain has taught this to the world but they've had their problems internationally, too, after three titles on the spin. So now we see a new debate over more defensive football, with more organisation and counterattacks. From my point of view, I accept all styles; it is a question of taste. My preference is to get hold of the ball, dominate the game, move defences around and score goals. To do that, you need a good technical level and good synchronisation.

'But there is this counter-revolution that is about defending well and getting people behind the ball. Some people are tired of training teams to construct play. You can only play defensive and counterattack against a team that wants to construct. Of course, you need to defend well and organise well. This is also an art and can be brutishly beautiful, like Atletico Madrid and Leicester at their best. Yet if we see two defensive teams, the spectacle of the sport diminishes. I don't think anybody wants to watch that. You need one of the teams to have ambition and want to break the defensive line. My aim is to make chances and entertain people. The defensive coach is the one building a house and then I want to be the person destroying the house.'

At heart, Martinez remains a romantic. It comes from his father. 'Dad managed Balaguer as if he were in charge of a top team such as Barcelona,' Martinez previously said. 'Whatever standard of team you manage, the principles are exactly the same.'

His childhood shaped his philosophy and his influences defined it. When he arrived at Wigan, he struck up a friendship with the Manchester United forward Jordi Cruyff, the son of the legendary Barcelona coach Johan. Jordi describes Martinez as 'the brother I never had'. The pair had the keys to one another's houses; Martinez was the best man at Cruyff's wedding and is also godfather to his son. 'I spoke to his dad Johan a few times. I was always nervous. I was so inspired by him. He became the godfather of modern football. He had an intuition. I believe not only in football but also in the transplantation of ideas and values. It's what I find fascinating. Not just winning but how you win.'

Martinez remains proud of his Everton legacy. 'I tried to stay faithful to my beliefs. I gave debuts to Brendan Galloway, Tom Davies, Callum Connolly, players for the future. Jonjoe Kenny, Mason Holgate and Dominic Calvert-Lewin have come on too since I left. The way of playing that we had in the second half against United in the FA Cup semi-final was a reference point. I felt we had clarity in being able to compete against the big boys. At our best, we would be rigid and stubborn defensively, and dangerous with the ball. We were developing this mentality with younger players, encouraging them to be fearless. Barkley never had continuity before I came. I gave real chances to Stones. Deulofeu had a big impact. Lukaku came on leaps and bounds. They were all young, needing patience, time to learn and chances to play. Everton hadn't really been bringing through young players. Wayne Rooney emerged but there wasn't a structural thing with Wayne. He was a once-in-a-generation talent. To regularly produce talents, you need a long-term plan. Behind the scenes, Joe Royle came back and he helped a huge amount. I think you will see more of this work coming to fruition in the years to come.'

A week after our meeting, a bolt from the blue. Martinez is appointed as the new head coach of the Belgium national team, grasping the opportunity to guide a group of supremely talented footballers to the World Cup finals in Russia in 2018. Martinez saw off competition from a long-list that included the Italian Cesare Prandelli, German Ralf Rangnick, Frenchman Rudi Garcia and the Dutch coach Louis van Gaal. Sources close to the Belgian FA explained privately how Martinez charmed the federation with a precise five-point video presentation, in which he dissected Belgium's humbling defeats by Italy and Wales at the 2016 European Championships.

I catch up with Martinez one year later, in the summer of 2017, for a newspaper interview, with his Belgium team edging towards World Cup qualification and growing in confidence. Back home in Balaguer, there are still pictures of Martinez as a toddler, wearing the Spanish national team kit in 1982 with the World Cup Tango ball. 'I still have my Panini stickers!' he grins. 'I was a nine-year-old excited during the Spain World Cup in 1982. Stickers get you hooked onto it. I was a huge Real Zaragoza fan and Carlos "Lobo" Diarte was my favourite player. He scored the first goal I saw live on television and I drove my parents mad until we found a Lobo sticker. To manage at a World Cup would be a dream.'

Freed from the high-voltage glare of the Premier League, he looks revitalised as he shows me around Belgium's Tubize training base. He is relishing the challenge of transforming Belgium's outstanding set of individuals, eliminated by Wales at Euro 2016, into a cohesive team capable of winning a World Cup. A roster including Tottenham defenders Toby Alderweireld and Jan Vertonghen, Chelsea playmaker Eden Hazard, Manchester City's creative fulcrum Kevin De Bruyne and Manchester United's striker Romelu Lukaku have embraced Martinez.

'There has been a lack of direction from previous generations. A German kid grows up knowing that a tournament means you have to get to the final. There is similarity with Spain. They didn't win anything for 50 years. The team was not ready. Now young players come through with the expectation to win tournaments. In France, it was the same. My assistant manager Thierry Henry brings experience of winning. He can see the difference between being a talented player in a group without know-how of winning titles. It's a lot of undeserved pressure on the players but the other side is this is a seriously talented group and we have to see where that takes us. When you don't commit to something, you can have regrets. We won't have a lack of commitment. I see players who care about their country and then whatever happens at the end, we can deal with that.

When I arrived, I didn't know what to expect. I'd been on the other side. I'd seen international football as something that got in the way of our seasons. I was pleasantly surprised to see how much the players care.'

He has settled in Waterloo, around half an hour from Brussels. His Scottish wife Beth, whom he met during his time at Motherwell, is learning French and Flemish with him, while their young daughter Luella has enrolled in a local school. He is regularly back in England watching Belgian talent in action. His assistant Richard Evans has visited every club with a Belgian international so that the player's individual fitness regime can be imitated with the national squad. All food in the canteen at the training complex is sourced in Belgium. His backroom staff prepare individual dossiers on every player under consideration for a call-up. Martinez watches at least one live match a day and travels every week to games in England, France, Spain, Italy, Germany and Belgium.

During our poolside discussion a year earlier, Martinez had expressed an attention to detail that bordered on the obsessive. On a Champions League night, he tends to watch seven games. He watches three games simultaneously, and then records another four. Meanwhile, his wife Beth enjoys *Emmerdale* and the other soap operas in another room.

'Generally, I'd watch a game between six and ten times,' he says, matter-of-factly. As much as coaches like to talk up their work ethic, this assiduousness is not the norm for a head coach in the Premier League. When we meet a month later and I ask Aitor Karanka, the former Middlesbrough manager, if he is similarly punctilious, he grimaces and replies, 'Twice, maybe three times.'

Martinez explains: 'I'm looking for things that I like and I don't like. Then I'm watching from different angles and seeing the movements players made. Often I'll track what we are doing with the ball and stop the video when we don't have it. There was one game that I watched ten times . . . no, 11 times.

I watched it from the perspective of every player on the field. It was a pre-season game, my first at Wigan. The jump from Championship to Premier League is huge. There are fewer margins for error. If you make a mistake in the Championship, you get away with it. In the Premier League, you're 1-0 down and, at a team like Wigan, it's hard to recover. I have no doubt that my different experiences, training in League Two, League One, the Championship and Premier League, helped my progression and learning. This is what allowed me to achieve my big dream at Wigan, the dream to win the FA Cup.'

To place Martinez's contribution to English football in its rightful context, we must return to the summer of 1995. The Wigan chairman Dave Whelan had opened JJB Sports in Spain and a company official based there, Paul Hodges, hit upon the idea of signing a few Spanish players to enhance the club's profile. At the time, Wigan languished in the fourth tier of the English league.

'Dave Whelan told us then that he had a dream, a vision to take little Wigan Athletic into a new stadium and into the Premier League. We were in the old stadium in Division Three. It was the beginning of an extraordinary story. We were kids, the three of us were in the academy and then, in that pre-season, Seba had made a big jump. He was 21 and in the first team. I think he made his debut against Atletico Madrid and Isidro the same against Bilbao. At that time, it was really a plunge into the unknown. Now there is so much info, you'd Google it. My parents were OK. I was already two hours from home when I played previously in Zaragoza. So two hours in the car became two hours by plane. My dad had been a footballer and he was over the moon. My mum said: "If you promise me you are going to learn English, then you can go." She was very strong on that because she knew that if football went wrong, at least I had gained a language.'

Martinez's family had always been strict on education and they remain close knit. His father had been fearful when he left home for Zaragoza at the age of 16, worried he would give into the temptations of alcohol and nicotine when exposed to the urban delights of the big city. Eventually, the family agreed a compromise. He could go, on the condition that he also enrolled in the University of Zaragoza, where he attained a degree in physiotherapy. When he signed his first contract and received his first wage at Zaragoza, he gave his father a fake Rolex watch and his mother a fake diamond ring. Later on, after he made rather more money at Wigan, he bought them the real things.

Seba's family were more difficult to please when it came to the big move away, as the player's grandmother warned her grandson that she would allow him to go – but only if he promised to bring Gibraltar back to Spain upon his return.

The trio moved into 317 Poolstock Lane, a semi-detached house in the heart of working-class Wigan. 'It was weird that shops closed at 5pm,' Martinez says. 'We couldn't even find a cup of coffee. I'm being serious. In 1995, in the north of England, it was tea, tea, tea. Maybe you'd find Americanos but a proper espresso – no chance. We were used to having a siesta after training and then we'd want to go out to the shops but everything was closed in the evening. We lived in the centre of Wigan, fans would knock at our house and we would chat. So things were hard but what a pleasure it was. The football was the seismic change. In that moment, you have to realise that there is no right or wrong. There were ways of understanding the game and you decide what you want to be.'

Seba, talking in a small café at Zaragoza train station, takes up the story: 'Fuck, it was hard. The first pre-season . . . hard, hard, hard. Brutal. It was all different. So much running. Running, running, running. In terms of organisation, the club had big potential. The training level, however, was miles behind. It was a big shock to the system. Every loose ball was a big tackle. Even in training, there was just this fierce intensity between team-mates that would never have been allowed in Spain. We had to run so much, sometimes 40 minutes non-stop. It was training you'd give to an athlete, not a footballer. There was nothing specific for football. We went a few times to watch the Wigan Warriors rugby league team and we spoke to fans. We took big stick from opposition fans. When you are in the lower divisions, insults were easier. Everyone's closer to the pitch. Opposition players and fans would call me "Fucking Spaniard". We got used to it. It didn't bother me. The way I suffered was more in the physicality. In Spain, the referees didn't let anything go and you were protected. In England, it was a free-for-all. Referees let players do anything.'

Off the field, the habits of English football surprised the three amigos. Martinez is a teetotaller whose only glass of champagne was on his wedding day. 'I grew up knowing you don't touch fizzy or sugary drinks. In a way, it was too much with me. I was maybe too restrained. In British football, in 1995, it was the opposite. Lads would go out and have 20 pints. You'd work hard and party hard. It made me curious. I was sat in the middle of guys downing pint after pint and then I'd be there looking after myself. Now everyone knows how to limit injuries but it made the squad happy in those days. It helped us compete. I've never touched it. We went out and they'd say, "It's a team night out." In Zaragoza, a team night out was maybe a nice meal at a normal time, some nice seafood, maybe a special steak. If you're daring, a nice glass of wine. In Wigan, it was straight down the pub. There was nothing to eat. It was pints for dinner. It made me laugh. It was fascinating – but odd.'

Seba continues: 'Players and staff didn't give any importance to nutrition. People were smoking and drinking. I couldn't believe it. I didn't take up smoking ... but I got to know the bottom of a pint glass! I think one of the reasons Mr Whelan bought us was to try and change the mentality of the dressing room and the level of professionalism. We had fun, though. At the start, we were staying in a hotel. It was part of our job to raise the club's profile. In the hotel on Friday and Saturday nights, there'd be a disco. The DJ made an announcement to say there's three Spanish lads here. He called us up, started playing the "Macarena" and we had to teach it to the whole room!'

Spanish football has long been ahead of the curve with regard to sports science, as highlighted by the recollections of Terry Venables from his period at Barcelona. The former coach reflected in his autobiography on the night Barcelona sealed a La Liga title by defeating Valladolid. 'In England the celebrations by the players would have been wild. But I was about to find out another difference in Spain. The captain Julio Alberto, who contributed brilliantly all season, wandered over to my table with a glass in hand. "Meester," he said. "I tricked you." Was he going to reveal some amazing incident or conspiracy that I was unaware of? No, Julio was referring to the fact he had not drunk red wine, but some Coca-Cola the night before the game, when it was a tradition for each player to have a glass of wine. The medical staff believed it was better for players to drink a glass of good wine than a soft drink full of sugar. Julio went on: "I tricked you, Meester. You think I was drinking wine, but I threw it away and drank cola."'

Venables was awe-struck by the discipline of Spanish footballers. 'They rarely drank, they didn't smoke, and they looked after themselves. Professional sportsmen are taught to look after themselves and not take chances with their fitness.' Spanish players could be trusted to stop after a drink or two, but it was a different story in England. Gaizka Mendieta, who arrived at Middlesbrough in the summer of 2003, was mystified to be told he would not be permitted to enjoy a glass of wine with his dinner the night before his first game. He told TalkSport radio: 'Someone on the manager's table said you're not having alcohol because one glass leads to another one and then another one, so it's better to not have one at all. I understand that, but I then asked why we were not having proper meals instead of fried eggs and ketchup, and pizzas and chocolate bars after the game. It was a long way from Spain.'

Not that the Spaniards were perfect. Jimmy Burns, in his book *Barça: A People's Passion*, recalls an episode during Rinus Michels' period at Barcelona in the 1970s when the legendary Dutch coach questioned the squad's professionalism. Barcelona lost a Spanish Cup tie against second-tier Sevilla and seven of the club's players headed for the hotel and a game of cards. 'They ordered two bottles of cava and seven glasses from room service,' Burns wrote. 'A few minutes later, there was a knock on the door. Opening it, the players came face to face with a stern-looking Michels holding the two bottles. In a rare display of emotion, the Dutch coach screamed at the startled gathering. "The trouble with Spanish footballers is that they are not professional!" and with that threw the bottles at the floor, splintering them into pieces, one of which lodged in the naked foot of a player.'

It was the sparkling wine equivalent of Alex Ferguson's flying boot, which was sent hurtling in the Manchester United dressing room before connecting with David Beckham's eyebrow. Heaven knows what Michels would have made of English football's lower echelons, where the three Wigan boys would have pre-match meals on match day at the local Asda café and relied on Ramon, a Spanish chef at an Italian restaurant called Milanos, for most of their evening dinners.

Martinez's journey from chip fat to champagne is characterised by his first FA Cup match in English football – a first-round tie on a sloping pitch at non-league Runcorn in November 1995. His management career began in February 2007, when he returned to Swansea, where he had spent three years as a player between 2003 and 2006. But his first experience in management came a decade earlier.

At the end of the 1993-94 season, Martinez was called into the military in Spain but received special dispensation to work within the community. It was there that he coached his first side, a group of under-nine children in their Sunday league. 'We had a code of conduct. As a young player, you rely on parents.

They had to have rules. I set them up a rota of taking the kids to games. Then I stopped them shouting. We sat down with the parents and set the boundaries. One of the parents wrote them all down. Parents can be very positive or very negative. We became one big family.'

His great friend Jordi Cruyff had concerns that Martinez would find it difficult to control a dressing room that included his former teammates. Martinez, however, was remarkably successful, achieving promotion with Swansea from the third tier of English football and ending the season ten points clear at the top of the division. He brought a Spanish identity to the club, and the playing philosophy has survived the regimes of subsequent coaches such as Brendan Rodgers, Michael Laudrup and Garry Monk. Yet a British edge remained. Graeme Jones, a former Wigan teammate, became assistant manager. The club's former coach Kevin Reeves became chief scout and networking was helped by the fact Reeves' wife worked for a budget airline. It allowed Reeves to fly abroad low-cost and aided the process of signing several Spaniards. Angel Rangel, a £15,000 right-back, was still playing in the Premier League with Swansea ten years later.

Martinez noticed a similarity between the Welsh national pride and the rich sense of heritage felt by Basques and Catalans, and signed forwards Andrea Orlandi and Gorka Pintado, along with midfielder Jordi Gomez. The aim was to blend passion and artistry, discipline and talent. The Spaniards did not have it easy. Garry Monk, a former defensive lieutenant of Martinez, who has become a fine manager in his own right, laughs as he recalls Rangel arriving at a beach in Swansea for pre-season training. Rangel had assumed that there would be some light ball-based sessions on the sand. Instead, Martinez had the team running up and down the hills on the beach at high intensity and Rangel ended the session with a vomiting fit.

'He got a shock that day,' Martinez grins. Michael Calvin revealed in his book *Living on the Volcano* that Martinez has previously punished any player 'who lost possession in a ball retention session by obliging him to drop to the ground and deliver a set of press-ups'. Martinez may be a romantic, but old-school methods have their uses, too.

In 2009, Martinez's circle in English football appeared complete when he returned to Wigan, the club he had joined as a player 14 years before. The objective every season was, in essence, to survive in the Premier League. In his four seasons, Wigan finished 16th, 16th, 15th and 18th. On two occasions, it went down to the wire to survive. Every season brought complications, as Wigan existed on a frugal budget and relied on bold and courageous coaching.

In his first season, there were some doubts among players. Seba had become one of Martinez's scouts and he recalls the extent of the angst. Chairman Dave Whelan, Martinez's biggest advocate, stepped in. 'Remember when he started at Wigan,' Seba explains. 'They were losing games and morale was low. One Friday, Dave Whelan went down to the canteen and addressed everyone. He said, "Roberto is my man, you boys get behind him, help him and work with him." Whelan went down to eat there every Friday, but that was important. It wasn't controversial but the players knew they'd be out before the manager would be. If only every club had that mentality these days!'

In Martinez's second season, the relegation battle went down to the final day, and Wigan survived by defeating Stoke away from home at the Britannia Stadium. The chairman and manager embraced emotionally on the pitch in front of the travelling fans. The next campaign seemed certain to be the end for Wigan's positive progress. After 29 games, Wigan were bottom of the table with 22 points. Then the most extraordinary thing happened, as Martinez's side won seven of their final nine games, beating Liverpool at Anfield, Arsenal at the Emirates Stadium, and striking a dagger blow to the title hopes of Alex Ferguson with a 1-0 victory over Manchester United at Wigan's DW Stadium.

Graham Barrow, who was in Martinez's backroom staff, explains that the upturn was no accident: 'We stuffed Newcastle 4–0 and deservedly beat United. We went to a 3–4–3. Sometimes, a manager might work on something for a week and then bring it in on Saturday. We worked on this for three months, two sessions a week, starting with very basics of the back three, the role of the wing backs, how the two in midfield should dovetail and then the front three. It was repetition, very basic but then gradually we improved it. When he unleashed it, it was phenomenal. The performances were unbelievable. He showed remarkable patience that season. Others would have panicked. It helped that he had a father–son relationship with Mr Whelan. He was bulletproof, really. It helped so much to have that support. He didn't have to panic and bring the back three earlier on. He is the perfect manager to give time because in time, he gets it right. That relationship allowed him time.'

One year later, in May 2013, even better was to follow: Wigan Athletic won the FA Cup for the first time in their history and defeated oil-rich Manchester City in doing so. During the previous summer, Liverpool head-hunted Martinez. In 2011, he had been approached by Aston Villa but turned the Midlands club down immediately. He wanted to honour his contract at Wigan. The Liverpool speculation was more tangible. Photographs emerged of the Spanish coach walking down a street in Florida with Liverpool's American owner, John W. Henry. Tit for tat followed. Martinez and Wigan claimed he turned down the role as Liverpool were keen to place a sporting director above him. Liverpool suggested Brendan Rodgers was the preferred candidate.

So it was that Martinez remained at Wigan, the club with the division's lowest wage bill, and he led them to FA Cup glory at Wembley. It was one of the great nostalgic mismatches, a result that defied logic and expectation. While Wigan's whole team was valued at £12.8m, every Manchester City player averaged a fee of £16.4m. It should have been a depressing stampede by the haves against the have-nots, but instead a new chapter was woven into the Wembley tapestry.

Martinez's smile widens once more: 'It was one of those things that deserve all the pain and sacrifice it took to get there. You know I left behind my family, went to a country without a language, adapted my life to something very different. Dave Whelan made it happen. He had his vision and he had his own incredible story. He had played at Wembley and broke his leg in the 1960 FA Cup final. He led the team out that day at Wembley after we got special permission from the Football Association. It was closure for him. I spent a huge amount of time with him and this was so special. He is a successful businessman, a big millionaire and all that − but in his football life, he was lacking something. He needed that day and for us to win the FA Cup for him, it was fantastic. However much money he had, the feeling of satisfaction he had that day will never be beaten. And for me, to come from Spain with nothing and play for six years at Wigan, searching for success, enduring many managerial changes, the new stadium and then finally to become the club's manager, coach in the Premier League … it's just … really special. I always felt I owed Wigan and it was the big dream fulfilled.'

On the eve of the game, speculation intensified about the future of Manchester City's under-fire manager Roberto Mancini. Wigan turned in the performance of a lifetime, as the players gave the impression they would run through plate-glass windows for their manager. Martinez signed off his Wigan programme notes with the Spanish words '*sin miedo*' (fearless) and this performance was the encapsulation of the motto. Adorning the walls at Wigan's training ground was a sign that read 'Courage, Possession and Arrogance'. On this day, Wigan embodied every catchphrase. They outplayed their elite opponents.

'When we were on the bus to the game,' Martinez says,

'I was sat there thinking, "We are ready." It wasn't a feeling about the other team. You'd have to be stupid to do that. It was Manchester City and Wigan, we were massive underdogs. At Wigan, it was as if every game was the opportunity to make history. We were breaking records and altering the narrative of a club. We had never won a game against the traditional top four before I came. We then beat Arsenal away, Man United at home, Chelsea when Carlo Ancelotti was there, Man City in the FA Cup, Liverpool at Anfield. Emotionally, we were good, the group was united, we knew our game plan. The beautiful thing was that we managed to put aside winning or losing during the preparation. To play well was the big thing. We'd played them three or four weeks earlier in the league and lost 1-0. However, we had three or four chances to score and we were the better team. We knew we could do ourselves justice. There was nothing to lose. We knew we were Wigan, playing at Wembley, with the chance to make history. This made the boys grow a few more inches.

'We'd played at Wembley in the semi-final so the team was accustomed to that. We stayed in the same hotel, took the same coach, went the same way to the hotel. We had the same dressing room as the semi-final against Millwall. At the end, the final whistle, it was like, "Fuck, we've won the cup with Wigan!", because we weren't thinking of winning, just playing really well. We knew what we could exploit. The big thing was our emotional control. There was nothing uncertain and we were in control. Our 22-year-old winger Callum McManaman was sensational; he tore Gael Clichy apart down the flank. He was a kid, really. He'd played against Bournemouth and Bradford in the League Cup and really struggled. He was so nervous before games, he wasn't sleeping or resting properly. Then we played Huddersfield in a cup game and there was a change. I had told him he wasn't going to play; he was annoyed with me. He said to me that he was rested and wanted to play. He played really well that day and from there, he was different.'

For Barrow, the man who first coached Martinez in 1995, it was beyond imagination. 'As we were getting closer, I thought, "Oh my God, this is actually happening." Roberto's strength is to win a one-off game. It's one of his outstanding talents. Paul Jewell and Steve Bruce did well at Wigan but Roberto was the one who could beat Chelsea, Liverpool, Man U and Arsenal. When you see his record, although it was always a relegation battle, we could always shock a big team. When we beat the big boys, we didn't just beat them, we merited it. We weren't on the back foot and with backs against the wall. It was through attacking football and finding weaknesses in the opposition. You would be on the coach back from away games and he'd be watching the whole game through twice. He'd already be outlining things. I've never seen anybody have that dedication and work ethic. He is the master of one-off games and that's what the cup is about. After the final, he just had the biggest smile on his face. We still had the relegation battle. We paid the price for winning the cup and lost the game at Arsenal.'

Martinez's cheery demeanour dims. Success was tinged with sadness. Wigan were relegated from the Premier League three days later, succumbing 4–1 to Arsenal. In doing so, they became the first club to win the FA Cup and be relegated – but few supporters would trade that trophy for a couple more years toiling in the top flight. Five clubs – Manchester City in 1926, Leicester in 1969, Brighton in 1983, Middlesbrough in 1997 and Portsmouth in 2010 – had previously reached the final, lost, and been relegated.

In the smart seats, Martinez's parents glowed with pride. 'I was at the semi-final and final at Wembley with Roberto's parents,' Seba smiles. 'They were so proud. We were in a box. His dad was going mad when they scored. Roberto had big confidence before the game but it was Manchester City! There was joy, happiness, incredulity. If you wrote it as a book, you'd think it impossible.'

Barrow concludes: 'You'd have laughed us out of town if

you'd suggested this 20 years ago. Roberto will be back. He'll
have his plan to win the World Cup with Belgium and then he
will come back, I'm sure.'

Martinez was not the first Spaniard to splatter his name all
over a Wembley final. Fourteen years earlier, in May 1999, a
Basque midfielder called Alejandro Calvo Garcia enjoyed his
own crowning moment. Calvo Garcia is another who destroys
perceptions of overseas footballers. I meet him and his wife
Leire for dinner in the town of Beasain, as the sun sets behind
the peaks of the Txindoki mountain in the distance. Their
friend, Jose, arrives midway through the meal and I am invited
to stay in the family's mountain ranch.

The geography of the region is spectacular and serene, with
rolling green hills and fresh pine-scented air in the mornings.
So it comes as something of a surprise to learn that Calvo Garcia
devoted eight years of his life to Scunthorpe United, the industrial and unappetising Lincolnshire town. Yet there is hinterland
to Calvo Garcia's character and all soon becomes apparent.
The couple were bosom buddies of Martinez and Jordi Cruyff
during the late 1990s in Manchester and remain in touch.

Calvo Garcia is remembered fondly in Scunthorpe, above
all for scoring the winning goal against Leyton Orient in the
third division play-off final at Wembley which earned promotion for the team. He likes them, too, writing a book with
British-based Basque journalist Iñigo Gurruchaga entitled
Scunthorpe hasta la muerte (*Scunthorpe Until I Die*). Calvo Garcia
was a bright youngster, working for the national construction
firm CAF, where he studied draughtsmanship and he was
offered a permanent contract. Instead, football remained the
dream. 'People were saying, "You are mental. What are you
thinking?" I just wanted to play football and I'd walk over hot
coals to get there.'

He signed for Beasain, where he played under Perico Alonso,
the father of former Liverpool midfielder Xabi Alonso. After
an underwhelming spell at Eibar, an opportunity arose in

England. Leire says: 'His agent said: "Alex, you have this option in England." He had to fly into Manchester. At first, he went by himself for the trials. When he called and asked me to join him, I didn't think twice. The people of Scunthorpe grew to love us and treated us well. I was having regular English lessons and went to work in the local surgery.'

For Alex, the adaptation was difficult. 'Back then, it was a freakish event. Where I am from, people live within walking distance of their parents all their life. I couldn't communicate. I was a mute. You are in laddish dressing rooms, which is like a micro-world in itself. They must have thought I was there for the taking. It wasn't a time where dressing rooms were welcoming towards foreigners. There were four or five who reached out. English football was very backwards and it was very protective of itself. But they warmed to me. When I first came, I landed in Manchester. Manchester to Scunthorpe is two and a half hours. It felt a lifetime. I couldn't say a word to the driver. I wanted to be friendly but I didn't know any English. That was a lot of motorway and some fear, too.'

Ahead of his first game, the local newspaper back-page headline read: 'From Spain to Scarborough': 'We won 2-0 at Scarborough but I didn't realise it was a reserve game. The phys-ical aspect of the game shocked me. It was like playing football on a different planet. There were players going out because they wanted to tackle, rather than play football. Basque play was more similar to the English style but, wow, it was hard still. I went to the gym, trained hard. I stayed behind for hours. Then came the first pre-season. We went to military camps!'

Alex and Leire felt a connection with the town. Their own working-class background shared parallels with their new home. Alex's father, Jose Miguel, had been a member of the *Comisiones Obreras* (Workers' Commissions) which were linked to the banned Communist Party in Franco's Spain. His revolu-tionary tendencies had earned him the nickname '*Zapata*', due to his moustachioed likeness to the Mexican guerrilla leader. In

1972, when Alex was only a baby, the family were touched by trauma. 'On 2 October,' Gurruchaga wrote, 'Alex's father was stopped by a Civil Guard road block along with two comrades. They were carrying leaflets to distribute in a nearby village. "What are those?" asked a guard, who had seen the leaflet on the dashboard. The men were pushed into the back of the police Jeep, beaten with the butts of submachine guns and driven to mountains.' The trio were taken to Civil Guard barracks. One of the three had his teeth smashed in. Alex's father was tied up and whipped with wire.

Gurruchaga continued: 'His collarbone was badly injured and his wrists had turned purple such was the intensity of tight handcuffs. He woke up in a bathtub, oblivious of how he got there.' The family home was searched, with Alex in his cot and older brother Mikel in bed. Alex's father was imprisoned, on a rotation system of Franco's most notorious incarceration centres: Martutene, Carabanchel, back to Martutene and then Jaen in Andalucia, southern Spain. The family's upkeep was aided by clandestine money from Eastern European Communist parties. Caritas, the Catholic Church charity, also helped Alex's mother, Mari Carmen.

Jose was released at the end of 1975, following Franco's death. Alex does not share the same political fervency but social justice matters to the family. *Schindler's List* is among his 'favourite' films and he has spoken out in Basque newspapers about inequality. He's irked by Britain's Brexit vote. His personal experience of working-class Britain had been of a community that welcomed a foreigner with open arms, and he worries about the tone of public debate with regard to immigration.

He explains: 'Scunthorpe was in the middle of nowhere but I had an industrial background with my family. When I went there, I saw many similarities. I saw a socially fraught society. I saw the poverty, the steelworks, and the challenges of modernisation. I identified with all this. There was the Iron Trust, a group supporting the club and also the workers. You have to be aware of your status and privilege as a footballer. I've seen people lose their heads and sense of reality. They think it will last for ever but it doesn't. So prepare yourself. People talk about superstars but I say, "What is a superstar?" A superstar to me is somebody who works extremely hard, who has the right ethics, who treats people the right way. People say, "Would you not change your career for Leo Messi's?" I wouldn't. I loved every minute.'

During the eight years, there were opportunities to move on from Scunthorpe. 'There was a moment when Crystal Palace and Walsall were in for me. I felt we had our life made in Scunthorpe. We had the money we needed. It wasn't like I'd be swapping Scunthorpe for Manchester United, was it? It might have been more money and a higher league but, I don't know, London would have been more expensive, too! I became very settled. I did an Open University course in technology there and I have a successful IT company now.

'I learned English in the dressing room and had lessons with a local man called John Costello. He taught me all about English football culture, not to dive, to be honest. He taught me the philosophy of English life, the mentality, British history. I loved listening to him. He spoke to me about the referees. The relationship between players and refs is different. In Spain, you are enemies with the referee. You can't say a word. You can't question anything. Within the first game, I was hearing, "Fuck off, ref" and the refs laughed it off in England. The refs, though, they knew how to manage games and personalities at that level. They'd wish you luck and have chats.

'I knew I was a foreigner and put up with the diving jibes and all that. They called me a cheater. But after a few years, I was another Englishman. I remember we were talking in the dressing room during a game and there was a French or Belgian guy on the other team who was tearing us to pieces. I was in the corner and muttered jokingly, "Fucking foreigners." Three years on, I'd become one of you!'

It was all a long way from his first winter in Scunthorpe, when starstruck locals asked if he'd ever seen snow before in his life. Upon announcing his departure in 2004, a testimonial was arranged. Gaizka Mendieta, Jordi Cruyff, Middlesbrough's Juninho Paulista and Roberto Martinez all turned out for the game. Now ensconced in the Basque Country once again, he has resisted the temptation to remain in professional football, coaching only his son's local team. 'There is a boy from Equatorial Guinea living in the town,' he said in *Scunthorpe hasta la muerte*. 'His parents died in prison and his aunt brought him here. I met him in the gym and we played 7-a-side together. One day he was sitting on the ground with his tablet outside the workshop and a truck ran over his legs. Doctors had to amputate one. But they were able to fit him with a prosthetic leg and he came to the office happy, showing how good it was. I asked him if he would speak to my team of 13-year-olds before our game about falling and getting back up again? He did. I left the dressing room. The kids told me later he was nervous at the start and at one point abandoned his notes and spoke to the kids freely. There were tears. The boys played great and every goal-scorer ran to Cristian to dedicate his goal to him. How can you compare that with watching the final of the Copa del Rey?'

CHAPTER 6

Teething Problems

Jose Antonio Reyes is laughing. The question put to him is quite simple: 'Who was the hardest defender you faced during your time in England?' At first, he attempts to dodge it. 'Well, coming up against Sol Campbell every day in training at Arsenal was a brutal induction. But you want an opposition player, don't you?' I suggest the Neville brothers, Gary and Phil, at Manchester United and Reyes laughs once again. 'Ah, *los hermanos* Neville!'

The episode that immediately springs to mind is the afternoon of 24 October 2004, when Arsenal travelled to Old Trafford aiming to extend their Invincible run to 50 matches. Sir Alex Ferguson's United stood in their way. It's a game so famous that it has its own Wikipedia page, which heralds 'The Battle of the Buffet' and recalls the infamous scenes in the Old Trafford tunnel where a mozzarella missile splattered over the United manager.

'Arsenal had stolen the title back from us in 2003-04,' Gary Neville wrote in his *Mail on Sunday* column in 2011. 'We couldn't bear another humiliation. The idea of Arsenal celebrating fifty Premier League matches unbeaten in our backyard was unthinkable. It's the only match when I've ever been accused of brutalising an opponent.' In the first half, United hit Reyes at every opportunity, disrupting his flow and trying to cow their opponents. *Los hermanos* Neville took turns on Reyes and referee Mike Riley was lenient in the extreme. The Spanish flyer nutmegged Gary Neville and the United defender responded by chopping his opponent down. Somehow, he avoided a caution. At the second go, Neville sliced him down with even more brutality. Yellow card. Then brother Phil cut him down to size a few moments later, joining Gary in the book. Reyes was substituted in the 70th minute and United won the game 2-0. Mission accomplished.

'I thought they were after me that day, for sure,' Reyes concedes. 'People see football differently, there are some who use those methods and try to be more physical. It's just one of those things in football.'

Neville's verdict on Reyes was ultimately damning. 'My job was to nullify the threat of Antonio Reyes. You are like a boxer trying to work out whether to jab and run or get in close. And while I could try to intercept, using my experience and positional abilities, I knew that above all I had to get tight, get physical. I had to make Reyes lose his confidence. If there were question marks about him – justified by what turned out to be a short spell in England – they were over his temperament. It was my job to expose that weakness. I'm not going to deny an element of intimidation but only because Reyes wasn't tough enough to take it. Cristiano Ronaldo would get that sort of treatment all the time, until defenders realised it didn't put him off, it just made him more determined. That sort of courage is part of being a great player. Reyes couldn't handle the rough and tumble, which is why Wenger ended up selling him back to Spain. He had the skills but he fell short of being a top player because he couldn't take a bit of stick.'

Reyes bristles: 'I wasn't scared of the physicality. It's true that the referees allowed more contact but do you think defenders in Spain hadn't tried these tricks with me? I got used to it. I was super-fast. Defenders just couldn't keep up with me and pace

terrifies them. Everything came very easily to me at that time.
But really, I wasn't scared of being kicked.' Reyes has statistics
to underline point. In the 2003–04 season at Sevilla, Reyes had
provoked 22 yellow cards by Christmas and he was the most-
fouled player in La Liga. He joined Arsenal in the January and
had previously said: 'Does it hurt? Damn right it does. Some
kicks hurt like hell and I am not made of rubber. This is football
and once the game is over it's all forgotten.' He tells another
story, about the time he was 17 years old at Sevilla and had
broken his toe. The manager Joaquin Caparros had to stop him
from playing in a plaster cast. It would appear, therefore, that
there was more to this case than meets the eye.

Reyes had arrived in English football to terrific acclaim. He
was only 20 years old but his talent had impressed sufficiently
to persuade Arsene Wenger to commit to a transfer that was
potentially worth £17m in the winter transfer window. One
year earlier, Wenger had his eye firmly fixed on a different
Iberian whiz-kid: Cristiano Ronaldo. The Arsenal manager
has since admitted that his failure to sign Ronaldo, who wound
up at Manchester United instead, is among his biggest regrets
in football management. Wenger saw Reyes as the next best
thing. Indeed, in Spain, he was deemed to be the greatest young
talent in world football. Reyes was the first example of England
prising away one of the jewels in the Spanish crown. *Marca*
described him as 'quite simply, a superstar: dribbling, magic,
vision and goals. The spectacular is guaranteed.'

After emerging as a 16-year-old in the Sevilla first team, his
impact on Spanish football had been devastating. His anarchic
turn of pace humiliated the finest of defences and his composure in front of goal defied his tender years. When Reyes scored
twice in a 4-1 demolition of Real Madrid, Zinedine Zidane
wondered whether 'the kid had a motorbike between his legs'.
Iñaki Saez, the Spain coach, described his dribbling as a 'controlled slalom at mind-boggling speed'. Some teammates went
a little too far. When a Reyes 40-yard sprint ended with the

net bulging, Sevilla's Francisco Gallardo bent down and took a brief nibble at the goalscorer's penis. 'I felt a bit of a pinch but I didn't realise what Gallardo had done until I saw the video,' Reyes said. 'I can understand it, though. It was a fantastic goal.' The Spanish Football Federation subsequently charged Gallardo, who was adjudged to have breached 'sporting dignity and decorum'.

Sevilla had discovered Reyes after he scored twice for his local side Utrera in an under-nines game. Reyes was reared in the murkiest depths of Andalucia and his background did not fit the stereotype of a region that is caricatured as a fiesta- and flamenco-filled paradise. The family lived in Arenal, one of the more forlorn *barrios*, and their modest home often suffered from a leaky roof. His proletarian upbringing drew comparisons to Wayne Rooney, as one of the last street footballers for whom sport would provide an escape.

Intriguingly, a lesser-known story is Rooney's own flirtation with Spain during this period. Barcelona watched the striker obsessively and sent the father of Bojan Krkic, who worked as a scout at the club, on a fact-finding mission when an England youth team played a tournament in Copenhagen. Krkic fell in love with the 16-year-old Rooney, sensing his power, dynamism and explosive potential. He did everything he could to track Rooney down. He attempted to catch him outside stadiums after games. He tried to see him at the England hotel but was unable to get through security. Eventually, he had clocked the time of England's flight out of Denmark and scampered to Copenhagen airport. As he rushed towards the gates, he spotted Rooney heading into a shop to buy a newspaper, and the two discussed the possibility of a move abroad. Rooney, as far as Krkic's father recalls, was reasonably open to the possibility.

'I love watching Wayne Rooney,' says Martinez Vilaseca, Barcelona's former director of the academy. 'I also scouted him for Barcelona when he was a young, strapping lad at Everton. He was 16 or 17 years old and I saw him play live at St James' Park, against Newcastle, the team of the great Sir Bobby Robson. He was a serious consideration at the time.' Barcelona are inclined to make ambitious bids at youth level, and also attempted to prise goalkeeper David De Gea away from Atletico Madrid when he was only 14 years old, but the family would not be persuaded to abandon their home in Madrid. Barcelona and Real Madrid both sought to sign Reyes, before Sevilla forced through the move to Arsenal.

As his progression accelerated rapidly through the age groups, the continent sat up and took notice, especially when Reyes became the top goalscorer at the European phase of Nike's Under-15 Premier Cup. When Reyes joined Sevilla as a teenager, the club worried about his reading and writing and a psychologist worked with him to prepare him for the trappings of fame and wealth. As a young boy in Utrera, he drew the crowds with his showboating. 'It's still what people talk about when I go back,' Reyes told the *Daily Mail* in 2004. 'I would play with my friends, sometimes my uncle Juan Antonio, and we would always be trying new tricks.'

Reyes was obsessed with Sevilla. He joined Biris, the club's hardcore ultras, and continued to pay his subscription fees to the supporters' group when he became a first-team player. He slept under a Sevilla duvet and, when the money started rolling in, he built a swimming pool in a new and more lavish family home. Sevilla's club crest was emblazoned across the bottom of the pool. This decision was much to the chagrin of his father Francisco, who was a lifetime supporter of Sevilla's bitter rivals, Real Betis.

In Andalucia, he may have been a patriot's pin-up but by the end of his ill-fated spell at Arsenal, he had become a *piñata*. In truth, the signs were there from an early stage. There were authentic concerns in Spain over his readiness to adapt. He cried upon leaving Spain and pleaded with his mother: 'Pray for me.' Lucas Haurie, a local journalist in Seville, commented: 'For Reyes, it's like going to the moon.' The *Guardian* reported another Spanish journalist as having quipped that Reyes would end up jumping in the River Thames if he went too long without his family in London. Sevilla's midfielder Pablo Alfaro commented: 'Jose Antonio is very *andaluz* and moving to Arsenal is a radical change.'

In Spain, the people of Andalucia receive a raw deal. There is a commonly held belief that they are a particularly insular community and rarely succeed outside of their comfort zone. It stems from an agrarian culture and prejudices against gypsies and travelling communities. It is a view that has been enhanced by the experiences of footballers such as Reyes and the Manchester City winger Jesus Navas, who suffered panic attacks in his younger years when he went away with the Spanish national squad. It rankles with the local population. 'Why is the Andalucian still a merciless target for insults from certain political groups?' asked the regional newspaper *La Opinión de Málaga*.

In 2008, Ana Mata, a politician from the mainstream *Partido Popular*, said that 'Andalucian kids are practically illiterate.' Joan Puigcercos, who served as the leader of *Esquerra Republicana de Catalunya* (the Republican Left of Catalonia) between 2008 and 2011, claimed that the Andalucians do not pay their taxes. The hostility is thought to derive from the gypsy heritage of Andalucia. As of 2010, 45 per cent of Spain's gypsies lived in Andalucia and there were 668 cases of discrimination noted in the country towards the community between 2005 and 2010. Perceptions in Spain, therefore, were always going to be complex to resolve for Reyes. 'It's a stereotype,' he says. 'It's true that less leave southern Spain. OK, it's not easy leaving Andalucia for England, but there are lots of players from all over Spain who have struggled in different countries. It's not an idiosyncrasy unique to people from Andalucia.'

Still, it is clear that his lifestyle altered traumatically. On his first day in England, London was held up by snow and he endured a three-hour traffic jam from the airport to Arsenal's training ground. In an interview with the *Guardian* in 2004, he admitted his difficulties. 'The first few months were awful. I wanted to go home, I was ill because of it. Many people couldn't understand why I left Seville and would tell me how difficult it was going to be to adapt. At first I thought they were right, that I couldn't cope. It has changed now, thank God. I feel protected by the club. Having the family around has helped enormously. If you are from the south, even when another club doubles or quadruples your wages, you think about moving a million times. Six or seven players at Arsenal speak Spanish and that has been very useful. But I cannot help but miss the rest of my family – my brother who just got married and especially my granddad. I would love to have him with me, but he has heart troubles and I am scared that the trip will kill him.'

His first game, a 2-1 victory over Manchester City, was a crash-course guide to English football. *The Times* match report read: 'A downpour, a pitch like a First World War trench, a punch-up and ninety pell-mell minutes must have left the Spaniard concluding that all the stereotypes of *Inglaterra* are true.' Wenger said: 'It was a good introduction because it was cold on the bench and physical on the pitch.' Just in case Reyes was in doubt, Wenger made his new signing warm up for 20 minutes in the rain.

Reyes' family moved over with him. The decor of their home in Cockfosters became lavishly Andalucian, and Reyes ate Spanish food and watched Spanish TV channels. The English language skills never did take off.

There were moments of joy. He scored twice in his third game to defeat Chelsea in the FA Cup, and there was a winner in a north London derby in April 2005. In his first full season, he began like an express train, scoring in Arsenal's first six games of the campaign. The Arsenal website summarises his career at the club as follows: 'Reyes had the potential to be a star at Arsenal but flickered briefly before fading. The defeat at Manchester United which ended that 49-game unbeaten run prompted a dip in Arsenal's form – and José Antonio was affected more than most.'

Reyes was subsequently sent off in the 2005 FA Cup final against United, although Arsenal won on penalties, and then he played only five minutes as a substitute of Arsenal's 2-1 Champions League final defeat by Barcelona at the Stade de France in 2006. 'I left for a multitude of reasons the summer after the Champions League final. The climate and everything contributed to a lesser extent but my role in the team was becoming reduced and I could see where it was heading. Real Madrid was an option for a season on loan, so I could return to Spain and it suited everyone. It's worth remembering I was only the 13th Spaniard into English football and I do think if I arrived now, with all the Spaniards in your game, Spanish coaches and the more progressive philosophy in English football, I would have been more successful. Back then, it was a more traumatic transition.

'I would do certain things differently myself, of course. The mid-thirties me would clearly act differently at certain times to the 20-year-old version of myself. That might have made my time happier. I wasn't the only one who found things a bit difficult. There was Marcelino, for example, at Newcastle . . .'

Outside a coffee shop in Palma de Mallorca, Marcelino Elena's toothy smile beams out. In the summer of 1999, at a time when Ricky Martin's 'Livin' La Vida Loca' patrolled the top of the music charts, Newcastle United made their first venture into the Spanish market. Ruud Gullit spent £5.8m on the Real Mallorca defender Marcelino, who had impressed as the Spanish side defeated Chelsea over two legs in the semi-final of the UEFA Cup Winners' Cup, before losing 2-1 against Lazio in the final at Villa Park in Birmingham. In four years at the club, he made only 20 appearances.

In the *Guardian* in 2002, Michael Martin, the editor of Newcastle fanzine *True Faith*, said: 'Marcelino is the worst signing in the history of Newcastle United bar none. He's the only Newcastle player who has ever been booed on to the pitch. There's a complete lack of respect for him as a man and as a footballer, and I've never experienced that at St James' Park. He's the worst example of a foreign footballer who has no stomach for the physical challenge of playing in England, and has no affinity with the club or its fans.'

Local newspaper journalist Alan Oliver was equally scathing: 'We had a row at the training ground last season. He asked me why I was writing not very nice things about him. I said he was never available to play. He said: "I'm a fucking good player." But not to me he isn't. The other players were laughing. When he plays for Newcastle, he reminds me of a rabbit scared by a car's headlights. He took part in the club's lap of honour at St James' Park last Saturday and I don't know where he got the bloody cheek to do that from, as he hasn't played this season.'

In 2005, Marcelino came fifth on a list of English football's worst imports, falling behind Massimo Taibi and Marco Boogers and just ahead of Corrado Grabbi and Sean Dundee. It is fair to say, therefore, that I did not go into this interview with the best impression of the former Spanish defender, who subsequently became a scout in his native country for Everton and then a football agent representing players such as Leicester's title-winning forward Leonardo Ulloa. So, is there a case for the defence? Certainly, Marcelino feels the need to set the record straight and, over an entertaining two hours, he does not hold back.

He begins: 'In Spain, it shocked my friends and family that I went to Newcastle. "Why do you need to take the risk?" they asked. Deportivo La Coruña and Valencia wanted me. Italian clubs were after me. I was a Spanish international and highly rated. I said very clearly to my agent, "Find me a club in England. I want to go to England." It was not just that a transfer came up; I actively wanted and pursued it. As a kid growing up, I'd watched English football every week on Saturdays. I identified with the spirit of the game and it became my life goal. I was over the moon when Newcastle came in. Leeds were also interested, around the time David O'Leary was there and the team included Alan Smith, Jonathan Woodgate and that brilliant young side at the turn of the millennium. Tottenham also scouted me. I chose Newcastle because I wanted to compete and win things. It was a competitive period for the team; they were in FA Cup finals and finishing high up in the Premier League. They seemed to be on the path towards glory and titles. I could have had a far higher quality of life in Coruña, Mallorca, Valencia or in the south of Italy but I was a professional and wanted to improve my game.'

Within a week of arriving on Tyneside, however, Marcelino sensed problems. 'Many things were different. The training sessions surprised me. There was a certain level of psychological commitment that I had been used to in Spain and everything seemed far more relaxed and improvised in England. It was as if the coaches didn't want to bother their players too much. Everyone seemed happy if players were not complaining and doing just enough to get by. In Spain, I was used to training in the morning and afternoon. In England, it could be half the number of sessions compared to Spain. That's a lot of hours I lost and it didn't help my body as I had a load of different injuries. It was just a total lack of rigour and intensity.'

Within three weeks of the season starting, Gullit resigned following a poor start to the campaign. The manager had clashed with captain and club icon Alan Shearer. New manager Bobby Robson arrived and changes were made. 'One of the cultural shocks in English football was the way that a manager would be sacked and then the previous manager's signings become the enemies of the next manager. This happens more in England than anywhere. Then you get players lining up saying how much they love and want to fight for the new manager. There's always three or four lining up to say, "This is the man for us." It makes me laugh. They are diplomatic statements by a player to secure their own position. They don't believe a word of it.

'I remember when I signed and a journalist asked me, "What do you think of Alan Shearer?" I said that he's a good player and he was a terrific striker of course. Then they asked me, "Is Shearer the best in the world?" Well, I thought Raul Gonzalez was the best striker in the world at that time. There was uproar. I wasn't allowed to think Raul was the best. So from there, I had to say Alan Shearer is the best in the world and I have a load to learn from him. Not true, of course. You say it to keep onside of the captain.

'Gullit signed me that summer, along with others like Duncan Ferguson, Franck Dumas and Didier Domi. Robson comes in and it's you, you, you, OUT, and Alan Shearer, Rob Lee, Steve Howey, the English ones come back in. I picked up the newspapers. Rob Lee says, "Bobby Robson is the best coach in England." Shearer is saying, "Rob Lee's my best mate and Robson's the best." I found it weird. On my contract, it didn't say Ruud Gullit United. It said Newcastle United.'

He paints a picture of a divided dressing room: 'After that, you aren't in a normal dressing room. There isn't a team. The principle of a team is a group of people with a shared aim. This wasn't the case. It was fractured first under Gullit and then under Robson. You knew the English boys didn't want to spend much time with you. It was difficult. It wasn't about being foreign; it was because I was seen as an ally of Gullit. There was mistrust, suspicion; I was treated differently.'

Marcelino does not want to speak ill of Robson, a former England manager and legendary figure in the national game for his work with Ipswich Town, Barcelona and Newcastle. 'Diplomatically it is unacceptable,' he states. 'Therefore, before I even begin, I am losing.'

In Robson's autobiography, *Farewell but Not Goodbye*, there are only a handful of mentions for Marcelino. The first concerned his own contract negotiations with the club upon becoming manager. 'They offered me £400,000 a year, at a time when Alan Shearer, I believed, was on around £3m. Later I found out what the players were on. Marcelino, who was signed by Ruud but barely played, was on £1 million a year. I was being offered less than half of what Marcelino was getting for sitting on a bench.' Eventually Robson did at least secure half of Marcelino's basic salary, with a £500,000-a-year deal plus hefty competition-based bonuses.

His second mention involved a training-ground incident that contributed to striker Carl Cort's long-standing injury problems. 'Finally, we had him sound and playing in a practice match when Marcelino, of all people, loomed from behind him and rocked him with a tackle. Carl was long-legged, slightly Bambi-esque, and in the impact of the challenge his knee went. The dark irony of this latest mishap was that Marcelino was having terrible injury problems of his own. So one recuperating player crocked another.'

Marcelino continues: 'It was more Mick Wadsworth anyway, his assistant. I'd signed in July and by September it was big trouble. In the first half of the first game of the season against Aston Villa, I picked up a thigh injury. Then I played through pain in a 3–3 draw against Wimbledon. I was recovering from injury when the new manager came in. In September 1999, I was a Spanish international, and there were a couple of games coming up. I had told the manager, Jose Antonio Camacho, that I couldn't go because I was injured. Wadsworth hauled me into the office to ask why I wasn't playing for Newcastle and then he insulted me. He called me a thief and said I wouldn't play or train. I said I'd even missed the national team because I was injured.

'The doctors didn't want to take responsibility. They would take a player's word for it whether they could play or not. So it was my responsibility according to the British culture. A few weeks later, they said, "Do you want to play on Saturday?" I said, "Of course I do but I can't." Again they said: "Do you want to play?" So I said: "I have been out for six weeks. If you want me to play, OK, but I'm not going to be able to do well. I

always want to play." We went to play Leeds and lost 3–2 and the
manager went out to the press conference and said Marcelino
was terrible and the two goals were his fault. That was after I
had risked my body for them.'

There was another episode in Italy, when Marcelino picked
up a muscle injury in training on the eve of a UEFA Cup game
against Roma at the end of November. He found some form and
continuity over Christmas but then came yet another injury. 'In
January in training, I had a collision with a teammate. It was a
big blow to my ankle. I didn't want to have another to-and-fro
where the staff would accuse me and say, "You don't want to
play." The physio told me not to play. I insisted I was playing
and training. Then I damaged the ligaments. It was a disaster
and I was out for the rest of the season. I went to Spain and I
was training for six or seven hours per day. It was an hour on the
bike, an hour running, an hour in the gym, in the pool, all that.
I got myself into brilliant shape. I arrived early for pre-season
and trained in the gym. The team were going to the USA on
pre-season. When the list came out, I was not on it. I had to
train with the reserves. The coach said there weren't enough
beds in the hotel and it was full. When you recover so well and
they still don't want you, it was hard. People turned on me.'

There begins a third-person diatribe on alternative facts and
fake news that would bring a smile to the face of the American
president Donald Trump. 'Journalists in England never know
what's going on. They know what they are told by the clubs.
They aren't there every day at the training ground. Everything
told to them is the "official truth". How can they know if
Marcelino is training today or if Marcelino is injured? We
weren't allowed to give interviews without the club's say-so.
Nobody was calling me to ask what was going on. In the press,
it was said that Marcelino is injured, he doesn't want to train,
Marcelino is out again. He won't be travelling to the United
States because he is recovering from injury. It was lies, lies, lies,
all the time.

'I did some interviews in Spain and then I had problems with the club and with the president. He said, "How could you say those things?" I said it was the truth. It made no sense. If you're the president and want to sell someone for £5m, you want to be telling the world that your boy is great and has been unlucky with injuries. You don't say he's unprofessional; that he doesn't want to train and that he can't cope with English football. Then you ask for £5m for that! It's nonsense. I was living there in this nonsense the whole time. There were teams in Spain and England that wanted me but Newcastle wouldn't let me go. Deportivo wanted me before I went there and still wanted me. Newcastle wanted a player in exchange and an extra £3m.'

Then came the moment that defined his Newcastle career. After the team returned from the United States, Marcelino was invited to train with the first team once more. Having followed a gruelling conditioning regime to recover from his injury, he was in prime shape to start the season. 'Do you know the story about my finger?' he asks. Only the 'official truth', I say, that Newcastle felt Marcelino was perhaps a little feeble in not being able to play with a finger injury.

He insists: 'I want people in Newcastle to know this. So here we go, the story of Marcelino's finger, told in the first person! Let's set the scene: 20 August 2000, Old Trafford, Manchester United v Newcastle United. Marcelino is starting. Marcelino had a good game. The coach came out in the press conference and said what a good game I had enjoyed. There was a corner kick and I was marking Ronny Johnsen. We were tussling for position, grabbing each other. Amid the grapple, my finger got caught and he went up and scored. On the field, my finger was pointing the wrong way. At the end of the first half, I said to the physio that I have a problem here. I played the second half, felt OK and then we had a game against Tottenham at St James' Park.

'On Monday, I go out to train and the physio said the tendon has come out of place. He said that if I left it, I would lose movement in the finger. I trained and Bobby Robson came storming down and told me I needed to go to the surgeon. I said, "I'm fine, I'm training, let's finish and I go afterwards." He's shouting: "Where's your fucking discipline? Go to the surgeon!" I said: "Gaffer, I'm training, then I go to the surgeon!" It goes on. "Go to the fucking surgeon!" I go to the surgeon at Nuffield hospital in Newcastle. He says if they don't attach the tendon I could lose my finger. I said I'm going to wait a couple of weeks because I've just started playing again and I don't want to miss this moment. "No, no, no," the surgeon said. He said it would be 12 weeks out and a very serious recovery. I thought he was joking. I said, "No chance, it can't be 12 weeks for a bloody finger." The surgeon said, "I want you to respect my job and it's a long three-month process of recovery." I said, "I'm not doing it." I went to the club and they said we had to operate.

'On the Tuesday morning, at the hospital, I had the operation under an anaesthetic. It looked really fucked the next day. I couldn't move my finger. *Horroroso*. On Wednesday morning, I left the hospital and then at the weekend it was the game against Tottenham. I went to the stadium and the telephone rang. It was the delegate from the Spanish federation. *'Hombre*, how are you?' I thought it was about a payment or something from a previous call-up. I explained the problem and they said the coach had watched the game against Manchester United and that I would be in the Spain squad. I was in the stand with my hand messed up and couldn't go!

'The next day in the papers, it was all this, "Marcelino doesn't want to play because he has a sore finger, blah, blah, blah." It was in the press, the radio, everywhere. I couldn't believe it. Is it sad, or what? This is the explanation that the Newcastle fans don't know. Nowadays, I'd have posted on Twitter or Facebook. Twitter would have saved my life! Nothing like this would have happened. Back then, there was the official truth of the club. I don't know who was driving it.

'It was an emotional rollercoaster. Everyone thought I didn't want to play for Newcastle. People in the street were hurling abuse at me. I couldn't understand what they said exactly in their Geordie accent. Nobody from the club protected me. Nobody said the truth. Five weeks later, Robson came out and said Marcelino has a genuine injury. That was the only time. I was hiding in the stadium on match days, I was scared to park my car and be seen. The newspapers were in the canteen every day. "Newcastle misfit", "Newcastle flop", all that. When the team lost, I was never playing. The team lost and it would be, "Marcelino doesn't want to play." Everything was my fault. They were calling me a thief and a layabout. I suffered a lot.

'It was a messed-up part of my life. For most of the last two years, I was with the reserves on a Champions League contract. My only hope was to continue being in shape with the dream of one day being free to continue my career. I was trying to find the motivation to train. The second year was most diffi-cult. It was when I felt my career was officially ruined. I knew I couldn't return to play and could see the team playing but offer nothing. I didn't form part of the first team in terms of eating or socialising. I was a reserve player. I lived near the training ground. From my window, I could see the first-team training sessions, which made it even harder.'

He left the club in the summer of 2003 and retired the follow-ing year at the age of 33 after playing a full season for second-tier Spanish side Poli Ejido. Newcastle's subsequent splurge on Spanish talent did not end much better, as they squandered £9.5m on Deportivo La Coruña striker Albert Luque, who signed in 2005 as a Spanish international, but his most memo-rable moment at Newcastle was a near-death experience. Luque was on the way to the airport to travel to Newcastle's UEFA Cup match against Eintracht Frankfurt in November 2006 when his Porsche developed a puncture. As he got out to make a telephone call, a lorry smashed into the car. 'I dived out of the way and jumped into a ditch. I was worried the wagon hadn't seen my car. If I had not dived, I probably would not have been here now. I feel lucky to be alive. If I had not seen the wagon or if I had been sitting in my car, I would not be here today.'

Marcelino grimaces: 'It's funny, I spoke to Luque when he joined. I said, "Don't do this, do that, etc." When bad things started happening, I could see a similar path. I was worried for him but he actually seemed OK and to be enjoying it. I had to clock in every day before midday, even when nobody was in. It was so I didn't go on a trip anywhere. If the team had a couple of days off, I still had to clock into the training complex. It was a punishment, I presume. With Luque, there'd be times he'd fly back to Mallorca for a few days and he seemed very happy. Luque played only a few more games than me . . . so that perhaps says it all!'

CHAPTER 7

Breaking Free

Brian Clough used to like it here in the 1970s. It was here that his Derby County team discovered that they had secured the English league title in 1972. Later on at Nottingham Forest, Clough and his assistant Peter Taylor became so fond that they came to refer to this place as their 'branch office'. *Here* is Cala Millor, the Mallorcan resort where the attractions start and end with *sol y playa* (sun and beach). In his autobiography, Clough gushed: 'Nobody ever wanted to miss out on a trip there – whether in the close season, or in mid-season when we just fancied a break from the old routine. We've enjoyed some of the finest times of our lives in Cala Millor. In fact, I still follow the practice of keeping a few peseta notes in my bedside drawer. I take a look at them from time to time to remind myself that it won't be long before I'm out there again.'

Clough attributed his greatest success, Nottingham Forest's 1-0 victory over Hamburg in 1980, in part to the Mallorcan hideaway. Forest's triumph in Real Madrid's Santiago Bernabeu stadium ensured a second consecutive European Cup trophy, and Clough's side remain the last English team to achieve such a feat. After a 60-game season, some relaxation was on the menu.

Pep Guardiola would shudder at Clough's approach to

preparation. 'We were in brilliant nick,' Clough said. 'We spent the week prior to the final in Cala Millor – doing absolutely bugger-all. I told the players there would be no training, no formalities. It was a case of get your shorts on and into your flip-flops and down to the beach. And at night have your few drinks – but if you've got a bad head in the morning, don't come complaining to me. We didn't bother with deadlines, or whatever they call them, either. The players came and went as they pleased. And if they weren't in till two in the morning they slept till eleven. The last thing they wanted was a physical hard slog or being bored out of their skulls, practising free-kicks. They didn't even want to see a football at that stage. But I knew that when they next set eyes on one, out on the grass of the Bernabeu Stadium, they would welcome it like a long-lost friend.'

Nearly 40 years on, I discover Cala Millor to be less invigorating. It is three days before Christmas and, out of season, Cala Millor bears all the scars of a ghost town. A desolate melancholy grips the deserted stretches of sandy, wind-blasted beach. Many of the local restaurants have the shutters down. One convenience store is open around the corner from the hotel, rather optimistically flogging Lilos. Visitors are invariably retirees, a German couple here, a Russian septuagenarian there, a few bridge-playing British widows in the ballroom of the hotel in the evening.

In the poolside bar, a footballer glances around at the surroundings. He is not a player you would know by sight. Only the swottiest of football anoraks would know him by name. Many of the players and coaches interviewed in this book admitted they could not recall him at all. Yet Lionel Messi should know his name. Once upon a time, he was Messi's captain. Now, he is 32, retired and a hotel receptionist. *He* is Arnau Riera.

His story is a sad one. It is not a misery memoir or the tale of a lost genius but, rather, the narrative of potential unfulfilled, of the uncertainty of sport, and a cautionary tale for those Spaniards who take the plunge and move to England. Riera grew up in the Balearic Islands, playing for Real Mallorca's youth side before being scouted by Barcelona. He was not one of those, like Andres Iniesta, spotted at an early age and reared at La Masia. Instead, he was recruited at the age of 19 in the year 2000.

Riera explains: 'My contract ended with Mallorca. Then an opportunity came to have some trials at La Masia. I had a Catalan agent and we knew that Barcelona had tracked me for a few years in the *juvenil* age group. I scored against Barcelona twice at youth level. I fitted their profile. I was a good passer, a quick thinker and always looking to break the lines. I suppose I was in the Guardiola or Busquets *pivote* mould. I went for trials. I spent a week there and signed a deal. It was worth around €700 per month and I lived in one of the dorms overlooking the stadium. I started with Barcelona C. Very quickly, the coach Quique Costas wanted me in Barcelona B. There was Iniesta, Thiago Motta, Victor Valdes, Oleguer Presas, Fernando Navarro – a bloody good team. I played every game and we were champions.'

Riera became the B team captain. In a 2004 poll in *Mundo Deportivo*, he was tipped to become the next player to break into the first team. Then, a little Argentine came along. 'At Barcelona, you are accustomed to kids arriving with big talent. We'd heard the stories but Messi was only 16. I remember a very fast, agile player but he was very introverted. When he picked the ball up, though, he blew our minds. Normally when a kid comes in from the younger age group, they shrink when they have to take more responsibility. For him, it was natural. It was like he was immune to pressure. He just played for fun, like a toddler doing a jigsaw, totally focused. I was always more anxious. My biggest handicap was I thought too much. I spent too long thinking about what could go well and what could go wrong. We had sports psychologists to improve performance, both individually and as a group. I depended on them. Messi worked with them, too.'

Riera signed a contract extension and he was by now earning £2,000 a week. He saw his teammates disappear one by one, over the horizon into the first team. Then Riera's opportunity came along when Barcelona manager Frank Rijkaard invited him to join the team on pre-season in the summer of 2004. 'We were in the mountains. I remember I had gone there without feeling totally ready or prepared. Barça B had a high level but the first team was in the stratosphere. There was Ludovic Giuly, Samuel Eto'o and Ronaldinho. They signed Deco that summer from Porto. We are talking about superstars. I really struggled with the rhythm of it all. It was a whole different speed of thought, speed of movement, reaction time, everything. The atmosphere was hard, too. You have to earn their respect and that's hard. It's all that masculinity stuff. The dressing room is driven by testosterone and you have to respond. If you don't respond then it's very difficult.'

He pauses, taking a sip of his coffee. 'If I'm honest, I felt isolated. It's just . . . I saw them as great players and wanted them to think the same about me. I knew they didn't really. It was quite a cold feeling. I wanted to belong but I didn't belong. I wanted to prove myself but I couldn't. You'd say a few pleasantries with them all but my relationships didn't warm up.'

I wonder if more could have been done to help the integration, whether it is a healthy environment for young people? 'In general, there is individualism. It's weird. You ask me what I miss most about football and it is being in a dressing room. Yet it was also the hardest thing in football. I had five years in total at Barça. I had a few squad selections with the first team. I never really believed I could make it. I saw how high the level was. I don't know if I maybe lacked enough ambition. I came from a little village and had smaller expectations. I arrived at a club with extraordinary social dimensions. It was like I had vertigo, dizzied by the heights I needed to scale. You arrive in the squad, get to the stadium and it was daunting.

'The amazing thing about these guys who make it is their consistency, in training and matches. That's what separates the best from the rest. They don't accept two or three little errors. They are punished. I suppose football puts you in situations and you have to cope. During the time I was at Barcelona, there were midfielders like Xavi, Phillip Cocu, Luis Enrique, Andres Iniesta, Thiago Motta, they were all there.'

To use the racing parlance beloved of Sir Alex Ferguson, Riera did not 'train on' and become a Barcelona first-team player, but there is no shame in that. English football's recent history is littered with examples of players who had to leave their Barça education behind and embark on adventures in the Premier League. Mikel Arteta is one of those footballers.

Arteta grew up in San Sebastian, the picturesque Basque town that was chosen to be Europe's Capital of Culture for 2016. The Haussmann-style avenues are lined with *pintxos* bars. 'It's a unique place,' Arteta grins. 'There is something particular about the Basque people. We have our language, we have a national story that is passed down through the generations, and this always leaves a very powerful feeling within you. In school, everything is imbued into you. It's an ideology; our grandparents only speak Basque to one another. We have a strong, slightly introverted character. I think it is loyal and honest at the same time.' His recommendations for *pintxos* include *txakoli* (the local dry white wine), *guindillas* (pickled chillies) and *bacalao* (salted cod).

I meet Arteta in a small room at Manchester City's training campus, where he is now a coach in the backroom staff of Pep Guardiola. At the age of 14, he took the decision to leave his hometown behind for Barça. 'Twenty years ago, this wasn't normal but my parents knew that my dream from a really young age was to sign for Barcelona. I remember a passion stirred me as I watched them as a kid. I don't know how to explain it – but it excited me, it made me smile, it made me want to be like them. It was that team with Michael Laudrup, Pep Guardiola,

Romario, Ronald Koeman, Hristo Stoichkov and then later the Brazilian Ronaldo ... the list goes on.

'I wanted to form part of this amazing tapestry. I saw Barcelona as the most beautiful expression of football. I've always felt that you should be happy doing what you do and the style Barcelona play is the one most capable of putting a smile on your face. My parents knew they didn't have a say in it. There would be no "wait and see" or "maybe you should stay?" No, no, no. I had been training a bit with Athletic Bilbao and my parents tried to argue the case but I was 14 and had it very clear.

'Leaving my family was very, very difficult. I arrived into a strong age group, though, and we formed a really close relationship. Pepe Reina was on the same bunk beds as me, him on top, me below. There were times we all needed each other emotionally. You miss your parents, your family.'

Reina recalls similar anxiety upon joining La Masia. 'I remember the date: 28 August 1995. I was 12 years old, ten days short of my 13th birthday. I just remember being nervous, like really trembling. I was moving out of my home. My dad made a point of emphasising to me that it was about more than becoming a footballer. He kept saying it was about becoming a good person, studying hard, all that stuff. I arrived there alone and it was scary. You think, "Am I good enough?" "Will they like me?" I started receiving these long letters from my parents and they were making me upset because I was hankering for home. In the end, I had to plead with them to stop sending them because I was going to become homesick. I said to my parents, "We can talk on the phone but really, that's it."'

Arteta continues: 'In our dorms, there was Reina, Valdes, Iniesta and Carles Puyol. I remember there was this guy called Haruna Babangida. Wow, at the age of 15 he was the best player in the world. I cannot put into words how talented he was. He ended up in Greece, Cyprus and Russia. He should have been a star. There was Nano, a winger who went on to play for Barcelona and Atletico Madrid. Jofre, a midfielder who has had a good career in Spain, and Mario Rosas as well, who was very close to Xavi.' Arteta shakes his head as he recalls Babangida's untapped potential.

It must be a strange adolescence at La Masia, where every friend is a rival, where teenage impulse is inhibited. 'We had very strict rules,' Arteta says. 'But when we were able to, we did certain things. When you're 15 years old, you have certain needs! You are discovering yourself, the hormones are going crazy and it's a process. It's an academic test as well, because our days were split between school and training. It's painful when it's very clear that a kid won't come good for reasons beyond his talent. All you can do is guide, warn and advise but if they don't want to listen and can't change . . . then that's their problem. If you're in an environment and if you have everything you need, all the tools to succeed and know it's your dream and you throw it all away, then it's clear you don't want to make sacrifices.'

At La Masia, coaches are looking for the intangibles that go beyond pure talent. Martinez Vilaseca was the director of the academy at a time when a glorious generation entered their teenage years. He is responsible for discovering Carles Puyol, Cesc Fabregas and Bojan Krkic, guiding players through the age groups.

He says: 'It is about the person, his attitude, how he trains, the intelligence in the game. Cesc was a midfielder who passed precisely, who could battle, and he scored goals from midfield. At the age of ten or 11, you could see those same qualities that we see today, that positional intelligence, that eye for a pass. Xavi was the same. There is something else, though, other than the quality. It is about their personality, their determination, their desire to succeed. I watched Mario Balotelli play for Liverpool against Manchester United and he was trying to change the game. He did two or three really good things but he did stupid things as well, irresponsible things. Throughout a career, composure and behaviour is important. For me, it is the most important thing. You have to develop human beings and set them up not just to be a footballer but also to succeed in real life. Not everybody is going to make it at Barcelona and we have to teach them the right way to act.'

Arteta was one of those who did not make it at Barcelona, joining Paris Saint-Germain at the age of 19. He had spent some time with the first team under Louis van Gaal, sharing those same insecurities as Riera as he entered a dressing room with Luis Figo and Rivaldo. 'I've always had this niggling doubt inside of me, about what would have happened if I didn't decide to leave Barcelona. Thiago Motta, for example, stayed for a while but there were times he wasn't playing at all and he didn't become a starter. I had an opportunity to play regularly at PSG. I was very self-critical and perhaps had self-doubt too. Pep was still there, doing his thing at a high level. Xavi was Xavi and even he couldn't get a game at that time! So I felt it would take me maybe three years to break through. I couldn't afford to stop for two years and stunt my development. Luis Fernandez, the manager at PSG, told me that he would play me. My dream was to play at Barcelona but above all it was to be a professional footballer.'

In recent years, we have seen a similar fate befall La Masia graduates Pepe Reina at Liverpool, Oriol Romeu at Chelsea and Southampton, Bojan Krkic and Marc Muniesa at Stoke City, and Gerard Deulofeu at Everton. Even Fabregas, the prodigiously gifted midfielder, had to return to England with Chelsea as he was unable to force himself into the starting picture at Barcelona. Riera's experience, however, was rather more jarring. In the summer of 2006, the time came to leave Barcelona behind. He was by then 25 years old. England appealed. Rafa Benitez had arrived at Liverpool and won the Champions League. Spanish players were travelling more freely.

He takes up the story: 'A British agency called SEM got involved and an agent called Craig Honeyman took me on. They suggested a move to England and I said it would interest me a lot. I wanted a change of culture. I wanted to learn a language. I was treading water at Barça. There had been offers previously that I turned down to stay with the B-team coach Quique Costas. Craig called me and said Hearts were interested in a trial. I caught a plane to London. Then Sunderland came in out of the blue. I said I don't know much about them but let's see, OK. I went to the Academy of Light, three or four days' training, and stayed at the Marriott Hotel by the sea.

'We played a game against an Under-21 side and then Craig was negotiating the three-year deal for me. I was very happy. We had the first few pre-season games and I remember after one, my friend Andy Mitten [a journalist in England] was walking back with me from the stadium to the hotel. We stopped by a pub for a drink and got talking with Sunderland fans. He introduced me to supporters and one guy on the table happened to be letting a flat. It was a nice apartment near the sea in Sunderland. Lots lived in Durham but I wanted to be close to the fans, to feel the club.

'Sunderland were in the Championship and in total chaos then. This was nuts, though. Niall Quinn had become the chairman but was also the manager. That didn't last long. I'd never seen that before ... Imagine Jose Mourinho as president and manager! The results went badly. The training sessions were poor. I spoke with my dad and I told him we were losing because we were training like an amateur team. It wasn't good enough. The methodology was poor, it was badly organised and we trained without the right tactical and physical preparation. There was nobody to physically prepare us. It was just games in training without objectives. I don't want to sound arrogant but imagine that compared to Barcelona. We needed to do defensive shape and work on the transition. Given the size of the club and ambition and the capacity of the stadium, it was poor to see. Sunderland have a bigger stadium than Valencia, probably the fifth biggest team in Spain. They are always in a relegation battle or in the Championship. The area deserves better.'

Four games into the season, Roy Keane arrived as manager.

It was the former Manchester United midfielder's first job in management. 'Roy had clear ideas. There were six signings straight away and nearly as many out. I was sent on loan to Southend for a month. Keane didn't want me and he was typically honest. He called me into his office. I had been sent off in a cup game in my second match. It was a stupid action. I was too desperate to impress and overcompensated. Straight red. It was a four-match ban that coincided with Keane's arrival. He had never heard of me, I presume. The president had signed me. Keane didn't give an explanation. All he told me was I wouldn't be part of his plans.'

The mechanics of change in sport can have a dehumanising impact, as Riera discovered. 'It was a massive shock. I'd signed a three-year contract and moved country. I had grown up watching Roy Keane and was so looking forward to learning from him. I was training, always on my own. The only time Keane spoke to me was when he needed a couple of extra players for a training session to make up the numbers.'

The one-month loan to Southend was a failure and he then headed north of the border to Falkirk. 'Dwight Yorke came to see me at the end of that season. He'd been impressed when he'd seen me train. He said to me, "I have a friend in Falkirk, think about going there." So I went up there and had two great years. I scored a brilliant goal against Rangers at Ibrox. There was a fun tradition where we'd play crossbar challenge and then you'd jump into the mud at the wettest time of year. I started working with the Carrongrange School in Falkirk. It was a school for children with additional support needs, where I went to volunteer for one day every week. I am studying for a qualification in social education and would like to see that through.'

After Falkirk, he joined Atletico Baleares in Mallorca. That same summer, in 2009, his former teammates Valdes, Iniesta and Messi had lifted the Champions League trophy after defeating Manchester United in the final in Rome. 'I wanted to return to Spain but I came back and suffered a terrible, horrible injury – a cruciate ligament injury. Everything became more difficult. I knew that was the end at the highest level. They operated on it and during the recuperation period, I went to Sunderland and used their facilities. Niall Quinn let me use it all for free and I stayed with Julio Arca.

'When I recovered, I then damaged the other knee because I overcompensated. The knee ligament injuries are real bastards. Six months, at least, the muscles need strengthening. It destroys your confidence. Things you took for granted before, you think twice about after. Can you whack a shot from 25 yards? Can you slide-tackle? In England, you can't have that at the back of your mind. You have to be all guns blazing, at 100 per cent to succeed.

'At the age of 31, I retired. For a while, there was this bleak vacuum. Little by little, I had other muscle problems. It was a natural decision to stop. It killed me but I felt I had to. It was so hard. I loved football as a kid. It's my life and will always define me. As a child, I read the magazines and collected stickers, talked tactics with school-friends, grew up worshipping my idols. My frustration is that I never reached the level I could have done. I didn't approach it, in truth. Now I am ending my studies in social education. It is fascinating. I can work in the reception of the hotel, thanks to my English. I need to work.'

Arteta blows out his cheeks when he is reminded of Riera's trajectory. He also arrived into the north of the British Isles when he was forced into a move to Glasgow Rangers in the summer of 2002. Fifteen years later, he is still working in the UK, spending only one year back in Spain with Real Sociedad during the 2004–05 season. He subsequently enjoyed six years at Everton under David Moyes and five years at Arsenal under Arsene Wenger, where he became the club's captain and twice lifted the FA Cup.

On Merseyside, he lived almost next door to his club rival and close friend, the Liverpool goalkeeper Pepe Reina. 'The truth is, I wanted to stay in Paris, I was really happy and we had a really talented side. It was a crazy dressing room – Ronaldinho, Mauricio Pochettino, Nicolas Anelka, Jay-Jay Okocha, Gabriel Heinze. There was big freedom and trust there. If you wanted to go out at night, you went out. If you wanted to go and drink, you drank. There was little rigour or control. The problem was that Barça had made some poor signings; they needed money and were asking PSG for big bucks to sign me. Rangers came with the cash and Barcelona said, "You're going there."

'Rangers were a huge club in the Champions League. Ronald de Boer, Claudio Caniggia, Fernando Ricksen – we had a great team. They were offering money to set me up for life and I took that decision. It was a good bridge for me before the Premier League. My parents and sister came over with me and it was a surreal, beautiful experience. None of us spoke a word of English. Now we all speak with a Glasgow accent! Mine is mixed with Scouse. We won the treble at Rangers for the first time in I-don't-know-how-many years. We went to a language school. My sister started working for the BBC and she stayed there for a few years. We went as a family to this open language centre and made friends from all over. We had Moroccans, Lebanese, Greeks coming over to our house for dinner, a total mish-mash. We just threw ourselves into it completely.

'The football is clearly a different way of thinking. If you go somewhere, you have to be realistic and know you can't demand everyone conforms to you. You have to adapt, change, convince yourself of the new way. I could have been negative. The climate's crap, it's windy, it's cold, it's rainy; it's long balls in small stadiums, but I saw it as an apprenticeship. The first thing, always, is to understand what the manager wants from you, then get to know the players alongside you in the best possible way. If you do those two things, you don't go far wrong as a footballer.'

As a player, Arteta has competed in the most ferocious of derbies, as a Rangers player against Celtic, a Real Sociedad player against Athletic Bilbao, an Everton player against Liverpool and an Arsenal player against Tottenham. So which was the most febrile? 'Glasgow!' he grins, without a second's hesitation. 'If you're talking about atmosphere, Rangers v Celtic blows everyone out of the water. *Joder* [fuck], I've not seen anything like it. It's aggressive, passionate and historic. In the dressing room, it's tense. There's a lot of shouting and getting up for it. It's electric. I remember the first time I played in it . . .'

He purses his lips together to make a buzzing sound and his index finger whizzes around at speed. 'It's as if you're in a washing machine at a thousand miles per hour. I am a player who tries to dictate play but in that game, you can't. Don't even bother. It doesn't stop. One touch, bam! Next touch, boof! Tackle, shot, corner, we go again! It's nuts.'

Carlos Cuellar, who would later play for Aston Villa, Sunderland and Norwich, also signed for Rangers in 2007. 'The Old Firm game, it's just . . . the best. The week leading up was like nothing I've ever seen. There's passion, history, authentic rivalry. The dressing room is on fire before the game. Everyone's in the zone. The Scots go round the foreign players, leaving us in no doubt what it means. It means deciding people's mood for the next few weeks, it means settling family feuds. I was sent off in one! It feels like a badge of honour! It's blood and thunder, anything goes, players will walk over hot coals for the jersey on those days.'

At Arsenal, Arteta returned to the elite, playing under a manager who appeared to share his beliefs about the game. One journalist wrote in *The Times* that Arteta 'could scarcely be a closer manifestation of Arsene Wenger's ideals if he took to wearing one of his manager's oversized puffer jackets'. As Wenger's powers wane and fans scream blue murder at their manager, he is accused of falling behind the times. So we should remember that he brought visions of artistic perfection long before Guardiola arrived on our shores.

Arteta's new role as a coach has brought deeper reflection on Wenger's contribution and longevity. 'The way things are going, nobody will repeat what he's achieved at Arsenal. I don't see anyone with that profile to put up with 20 years or more. Nobody will do that. It's impossible. Arsene has a very straightforward idea of what he wants. He knows the profile of the player he wants and what he wants them to do. He gives players licence and freedom to make their own decisions on the pitch. He puts big trust into players because he wants the player to express himself and take decisions for himself.

'He is incredibly loyal: loyal to his players and loyal to his style of play and staff. It's rare to find that in football. I know he's been criticised for being too loyal to certain players in recent years, but I'd rather someone be too loyal than not loyal at all. To be too much is not a bad thing. Of course, you cannot hide from big decisions, but he has made many of those too in his career.'

He becomes agitated in his seat, anxiously rubbing his hands together and then running his hand over his stubble in a manner spookily similar to his mentor Guardiola. 'Everyone has an opinion now. It's too much analysis. Now we have millions of football managers. Everyone fancies themselves. People talk about politics and think they can be prime minister. Then they have the answers to the economy. But however many think they know about politics or economics, it's small fry compared to how many think they have the answers to football management. In the stadium, there are 70,000 coaches!'

Arteta is defensive over Wenger but it is clear his enduring influence remains Barça, his first and only true love in football. It is why he followed Guardiola to City. He sees in Guardiola the execution of how the game should be: speed, skill, fluency and adventure. He, like Guardiola, was most comfortable playing at the base of the midfield. Some in football believe that this offers an authentic advantage as a coach. We needn't look too far for current examples, as Antonio Conte, Luis Enrique, Pep Guardiola all filled that position in their playing days. Promising coaches such as Roberto Martinez, Slavisa Jokanovic and Oscar Garcia provide further evidence.

Certainly, it is the view of Jordi Cruyff, who worked as a sporting director at Israeli club Maccabi Tel Aviv in recent years. 'I played with Pep at Barcelona and you could tell he had the intelligence to be a great coach. He was not a fast player, or a strong player. It meant his technique was excellent on the ball. I don't mean juggling with the ball and tricks – that's not technique – but technique in decision-making and his first touch, and with his two-touch football. It gave him a sixth sense because he didn't have the speed, the explosiveness, or the stamina – he didn't know how to jump. Everything was based on intelligence, movement and anticipation. Everything was considered and thought-out.'

Arteta brings the vision to life. 'It's much more simple for a player if you can process the image of where your teammate will be before receiving the ball. If I am in the kitchen and I know the glasses are always in this cupboard, I get my glass of water more quickly. If my wife starts moving the glasses from one cupboard to another every day, you go stir-crazy and it takes you longer to get your glass of water. It's the same with football. If you have a clear methodology and are always looking around, it improves your performance. If we know our wide man will be hugging the touchline, first touch, ping and it's there. Paul Scholes was excellent at that.'

Arteta's excursion into English football was so successful that he very nearly became an England player. In 2010, Arteta had given up hope of breaking into the national picture in Spain and England manager Fabio Capello made contact. Under European law, he was able to become a British citizen after five years living in the country. It was a move backed by England captain Steven Gerrard, who said: 'I'd certainly love nothing better than to see Mikel Arteta available for England. You want to play with the best players, and if it makes the England squad better, of course I'd like to see it.'

Some did not take the news too well, suggesting that playing for England should be reserved for those born and educated in the country. Behind the scenes, FA officials were uncomfortable with the idea, which was certainly rich considering they had employed a man in Capello who was barely able to converse in English. Germany, Portugal and Spain have long since considered residency permits when enticing players.

There were historic precedents. Alfredo Di Stefano, the legendary Real Madrid forward, played for three nations. After first turning out for the country of his birth, Argentina, he then represented Colombia after signing for Millonarios and then played for Spain when he joined Real Madrid. Ferenc Puskas and Laszlo Kubala both played for Spain after defecting from their home country, Hungary, during political revolutions. More recently, Winston Reid, the West Ham United defender, represented Denmark at Under-21 level before becoming a senior player for New Zealand. Reid's family left the Kiwi nation behind for Scandinavia when he was ten years old.

Arteta is a sophisticated man, with dark beady eyes and a sharp intellect. He speaks seven languages. He grew up around Spanish, Basque and Catalan, picked up French at PSG, then English at Rangers before learning Portuguese when he made friends with Nuno Valente at Everton. A dabble in Italian completes the set. 'It's very much true that I now feel part-English. I will always feel Basque, too, but I am very grateful. I was up for it when Capello made contact. On a bureaucratic level, it was complicated and it was difficult. It was a serious consideration. I felt English and I was up for it but ultimately it wasn't possible due to FIFA regulations. I'm very proud of English football, though. The game has evolved massively. When I first came, it was really a million miles behind what was expected from a top athlete in Spain. When I came, it was one-way traffic. It really was long ball and big challenges.'

At the turn of the millennium, this was the perception of British football: clumsy and overbearing, arrogant and insular, our way

or the highway. If those in Iberia considered themselves pur-
ists, the backwards English were apostates. Yet a view evolved
that cast the Premier League as a gentle grazing ground for
famous names from the Spanish game. Players such as Fernando
Hierro, Michel Salgado, Gaizka Mendieta and Ivan Campo
made lucrative transfers to England at varyingly late stages of
their careers. Some renowned imports from La Liga, such as
Noureddine Naybet and Patrick Kluivert, also found cushy and
well-remunerated existences in England.

After spending 14 years at Real Madrid, lifting the European
Cup on three occasions, it was hard to take Fernando Hierro at
face value when he declared it to be a 'fairytale' to sign for Sam
Allardyce's Bolton Wanderers in 2004. Yet as he talks inside his
office at the Real Oviedo training ground, where he is now the
head coach, he appears sincere. Hierro was a majestic figure in
Spanish football, a goalscoring central defender who amassed
29 goals in 89 games for his country. He grins as he recalls his
days as the *jefe* (boss) of the Real Madrid dressing room. Steve
McManaman once admitted that 'absolutely nothing happened
without Hierro's say-so.'

Yet when he arrived in the north-west of England in his
mid-thirties, anxiety took over. 'I was always wondering what it
would be like for me, as an icon of the Spanish game, to try my
luck in England. It was a difficult decision. We'd always had this
conception of very direct, perhaps even unsophisticated football.
When I saw Spaniards start to go over, I remember saying to
Real Madrid teammates: "What the hell are they doing?" These
guys weren't very powerful physically and I feared they were
taking a huge risk.

'Truth be told, I was completely terrified when I went at 36.
I was scared of what it would be like to adapt. I had a fantastic
reputation but a reputation is a fragile thing. It takes a long
time to form and a very short time to unravel. I loved watching
English football on the TV; I'd been to the stadiums and revelled in the atmosphere. After 14 years at Real, I spent a year in

Qatar and I'd all but packed it in. I was going to retire. Then, out of nowhere, this approach came in from Bolton and Sam Allardyce. It was like instinct. I didn't think twice.'

His previous experience in England had been unhappy: he missed a crucial penalty in the shoot-out against England at Wembley during Euro 96. 'I was excited, but nervous. Would I make myself look daft? Could I cope with the physicality? Lots of players had come to England and flopped. The problem with English football is you can be a physical centre back but there might be an even stronger centre forward. I remember during the first half of my first game, I stopped and thought, "Fuck, it's fast." Every challenge hurt. It was a unique, almost bestial physicality. Every challenge was a collision, as though it was the opponent's last one in a cup final.

'In Spain, if a ball goes long, your team win it or they don't win it. Bolton obsessed over the second ball, the third ball and keeping pressure on. I noticed that the fans applauded you when you won that second ball. I was used to the admiration of the fans but it was normally for a trick or a great pass. In England, the fans enjoy a tussle, a scrap, a big tackle. I realised quickly that you have to earn the right to play in the Premier League. An English footballer has this instilled into their character. They've been told to win those second balls since they were a child. For Spaniards, Frenchmen, Germans, Africans, South Americans, it is a bit different. The atmosphere carries you into it; it's like a tidal wave.

'I had opportunities to go to England before Bolton, at my peak. I won't say which club because I don't want to make it sound like I was arrogant and rejected a big club. I had an amazing career with Real Madrid and Spain but if I could have had a second career, I would have spent it in England. I loved everything about it.

'At Bolton, we competed with the big boys; we went beyond the fans' wildest dreams by qualifying for the UEFA Cup. It was a little family club. You knew everyone, from the tea lady

to the stewards. I'd seen the other signings that Sam had made –
Jay-Jay Okocha and Youri Djorkaeff. He took people with big
names and enhanced their reputations. He drew new ability
out of players. I arrived a couple of weeks into pre-season and
I was worried I'd struggle physically. There was far more gym
work, far more running. It amazed me to be in the gym the
day before a game.

'We had a great dressing room. I'd come from playing with
Zinedine Zidane and Luis Figo but it wasn't hard to adapt. Your
job as a player is to follow exactly the orders of your coach. It's
what you're paid to do. You can't waltz into the Premier League
and expect everyone to change to suit you. Who do you think
you are if you do that? At Bolton, we felt we could trouble
anyone. I could sense in the tunnel that teams hated the idea of
playing us, particularly at the Reebok Stadium. We had Bruno
N'Gotty and Ivan Campo. Okocha provided brilliant set-pieces.
We saw every set-piece as a chance to score. It's not just about
having big people. It's where you run, who you block. It wasn't
rocket science. Sam had one or two players right on the goalkeeper. Radhi Jaidi, Kevin Davies, Nolan, me, lots of players!
Then there was Gary Speed, who had a *cabezazo* (a thunderous
header) on him. I've never met anyone who could head the ball
like Gary and I was devastated to learn of his passing. We had
great strength.'

Hierro had spoken to McManaman and Campo before signing on the dotted line. Campo, a frizzy-haired, slightly podgy
player, had joined Bolton in the summer of 2002. He arrived
with a fine reputation, having formed part of the Real Mallorca
squad that reached the UEFA Cup Winners' Cup final in 1999
and then picking up two Champions League winner's medals
with Real Madrid. He played the full 90 minutes against
Valencia in the 2000 Champions League final and four games at
the France 98 World Cup. He stood between Hierro and Zidane
in the Madrid team photo in the 2001–02 season.

As Hierro implies, however, reputations are brittle and can

be dismantled with consummate ease. Campo had the misfortune to come up against a teenage Wayne Rooney, who had burst onto the scene at Everton. A rampaging Rooney took a sledgehammer to Campo's standing in the space of 90 minutes at Goodison Park. In the Sky Sports studios, Rodney Marsh, the former Manchester City forward, offered a brutal conclusion: 'The bloke's a clown.' One national newspaper mused that his 'unruly mop of hair and taste for hippy chic gave him the appearance of someone returning from a mission of self-discovery in the Andes'.

In the *Guardian* sometime later, Simon Hattenstone summed up the stereotype that surrounded Campo: 'The Spaniard does not just look like a pub footballer, he looks like a pub footballer who has sunk 14 pints with William Hague on a Friday night, gone down the rankest curry house for chicken vindaloo and chips, missed the last bus home, slept on a park bench, not washed and turned up at the Reebok, 2.55pm on the Saturday, to play for Bolton Wanderers.'

Campo arrived at Bolton at a low moment in his life, with self-doubt clawing away at his mind. His form at Real Madrid became so poor that white handkerchiefs and merciless jeers greeted him, while the Madrid press went into vindictive mode. Quite simply, he was no longer a Happy Campo. In 2001, he had been struck down by a crippling bout of anxiety. He spent several months out of the picture and his rehabilitation supervisor Juan Carlos Hernandez admitted the player faced a struggle to 'return to normality'. Campo's sleeping pattern was disrupted; he suffered panic attacks, and was beset by constant headaches. He spoke out, openly and courageously, long before it became more commonplace for young males to discuss mental health issues publicly.

Campo told *El Mundo*: 'I was upset because I was the black sheep of Madrid. Everything I did was wrong, everything I tried was wrong. The criticism felt personal and professional. I was consumed by a real fear. I don't know why. I think we are always keeping certain things inside. Anxiety is when these things keep reproducing and it reaches a point you can't live with it, it all builds up and explodes. It was a fear that something terrible was going to happen to me. I thought I was going to die.'

Campo sensed a 'campaign' building against him in the Spanish media and he harked back to an evening in the spring of 2000 when he played at Old Trafford on a night Real Madrid led Manchester United 3-0 inside an hour in the quarter-final of the Champions League. 'One thing that struck us that night, and we talked about it for a long time afterwards in the dressing room, is that even though we were 3-0 up there was one time when United got the ball and everyone stood up and cheered them on. That would never happen in Spain. If you were 3-0 down people would be more likely to throw stuff at you. It was out of this world.'

Campo wanted to be loved and, in Allardyce, he found affection. In his autobiography, Allardyce said: 'I was warned Campo was too much to handle and was on tablets to calm himself down but I was confident I could sort him out. If I could liken him to anyone today, it would be David Luiz. He looked like him and played like him, not always reliable as a centre back but accomplished on the ball in midfield, and you had to accept he would make the odd mistake in exchange for the benefits he gave you in launching attacks. Campo wigs flew off the shelves in the club shop.'

Not that Allardyce spared Campo his notorious tongue-lashings. In May 2003, the club faced a crucial match against Southampton as they battled relegation and, with the team under-performing, the coach took aim at Djorkaeff, Okocha and Campo at half-time. He scathed: 'You've won the World Cup [Djorkaeff], and you've played at two World Cups [Okocha] and you've been to a World Cup and won the Champions League [Campo]? What the fuck's the matter with you all?'

Campo enjoyed living in the north-west of England, often

stopping by Harper's restaurant in central Manchester, which was a popular haunt for footballers. On the walls of the restaurant, there were signed pictures from Diego Maradona, Luis Figo and Ferenc Puskas. Ivan Campo has his own piece of wall reserved, too. He would remain at Bolton for six years, but he was cautious when Hierro arrived. Allardyce recalls: 'It was, oh hell, here we go, he comes in and I'm out. He wasn't exactly putting out the welcome mat. Fernando was unbelievable. There wasn't a better passer in the Premier League, and I include Paul Scholes who was the master. His accuracy was laser-like and the others only had to make their run and Fernando could find them. He was intercepting 15 balls per game. Nobody in the league was doing that. He'd win 20 headers every match; no midfielder was doing that either.'

Allardyce admired Hierro's quality and commitment, valuing his composure as a shield in front of the back four. In each of his teams since, he has always sought to find a similar player. Steven N'Zonzi performed the role at Blackburn, Jan Kirchhoff did the job at Sunderland, and when he was made England manager, Allardyce drew comparisons between Eric Dier and his old Bolton flames Campo and Hierro. 'What a player, eh?' Allardyce said. 'Like a Campo or a Hierro. He's got that vibe. It's very important, that position. When out of possession he keeps pressure off the back four with interceptions and his reading of the game seems to be very good.'

The week I meet with Hierro coincides with Allardyce's appointment as England manager, a reign that would prove to be short-lived, as Allardyce fell victim to a newspaper sting by the *Daily Telegraph* and lost his dream job. Hierro has previously been an assistant to Carlo Ancelotti at Real Madrid and, before that, the technical director of *Real Federación Española de Fútbol* (Spanish FA), where he appointed his former Madrid manager Vicente del Bosque as head coach of the national team and outlined a nationwide blueprint for age-group teams. He was there as Spain transformed from pretenders to contenders and eventually *conquistadores* on the global stage. His belief that Allardyce's appointment represented progress, therefore, should not be taken lightly.

'He knows what it takes to succeed at English clubs. He has done well everywhere. He has huge experience. He knows the players and what they need. I always wondered how he'd cope if he tried a different league. Would his methods work? He's a Premier League master. He did extraordinary work with me. He was extremely advanced, miles ahead of his team and, remember, I'd just come from Real Madrid. He'd have clear statistics and data within an hour of the game and he'd be passing it on. We had a sports psychologist even then, who did fantastic individual work with me. The only thing he might find hard is organisation and set-pieces. We did it over many months every single day. With England, he'd have only a few days every two or three months. That's not easy.'

In a column in *The Times* in 2016, Kevin Davies, the bulldozing Bolton forward, explained why the big names enjoyed working with Allardyce. 'We had a big room where he'd use a touchscreen, all the technology, to go through games. We'd be given CDs with clips of players we were coming up against [it's all done on phones and iPads now]. Leicester City's use of cryotherapy was heralded last season; we were doing that 12, 13 years ago. Fish oils, beetroot juice. Every two or three months, you would go and see him for an evaluation; watch videos, get data on your performances, be given targets. It was daunting at first, but I'd walk out feeling 10 feet tall. We were given the "Bolton Bible", a little booklet going through all the rules and regulations, the standards required. He made sure the players went into the community and did their appearances – he'd stamp down on anyone who missed one.'

As Campo and Hierro flourished at Bolton, the Spanish success stories became more common. In the north-east of England, a Basque talent arrived at the Riverside in the summer of 2003. Only two years earlier, Gaizka Mendieta had played in a second consecutive Champions League final for Valencia. A player of devastating skill, the Valencia president Pedro Cortes declared that he'd 'rather go hungry than sell Mendieta'. UEFA named him as the continent's midfielder of the year and he'd scored 48 La Liga and Champions League goals in four seasons, including a memorable volley into the top corner in the 1999 Copa del Rey final.

Real Madrid pursued him vigorously. When Juventus' Zinedine Zidane became available, however, Real's interest reduced and, following Juan Sebastian Veron's departure from Lazio to Manchester United, the Italian club moved for Mendieta in a £28.9m deal. It was a catastrophic failure. *Gazzetta dello Sport* labelled Mendieta 'a terminally ill patient'. Another Italian paper suggested he had a face like a sphinx. He returned to Spain inside a year, on loan at Barcelona, but was unable to recapture his previous form.

Middlesbrough, who had a track record for luring the continent's distinguished names, decided to be bold. In the 1990s, they had recruited a stellar cast of flamboyant names such as the Brazilian Juninho, the Croatian Alen Boksic and Italian forward Fabrizio Ravanelli. Manager Steve McClaren boarded a plane with chief executive Keith Lamb, and McClaren described what followed as 'the most important half an hour of my managerial career'. This was of course before he stood pitch-side at a rain-soaked Wembley with only an umbrella for shelter as his world caved in as manager of England.

Mendieta, whose Christian name Gaizka translates from Basque as 'saviour', was rapidly convinced and produced some memorable displays in Boro colours. He had taken advice from Lazio teammate Jaap Stam, who had been coached by McClaren at Manchester United when he was an assistant to Alex Ferguson. Now entering his forties, a new hobby occupies Mendieta's time and he is more likely to be seen in Liverpool's Cavern Club, a former haunt of the Beatles, than Merseyside's two football stadiums.

'DJ-ing has always been my passion,' he told the *Daily Mail*. 'My friend in Valencia, who owned a record shop, used to DJ. If I played on Saturday I would then sneak into the club, but it was always off the record, I would wear a hat and go in disguise. I would then DJ and no one would know it was me. I loved it. It was an escape. It is the possibility of making people happy, seeing them having fun and going mad at your choice of song. I don't have a setlist of what I'm going to play. We take a box of vinyls and we only arrange the first few songs and then see how the mood is and what people want. When you are on the pitch you have a split-second to decide a pass; it is the same as a DJ picking the next song. It is the same feeling of tension as playing football and I do get nervous before I DJ. I play everything from Aretha Franklin to Kings of Leon to Lou Reed. Wherever I am in the world I always find the record shops.'

For all the progress, however, doubts still surrounded Spanish players by 2005. Writing in *The Times*, Bill Edgar concluded: 'Spanish footballers, like their English and Italian counterparts, are less inclined to move abroad than those from other countries, partly because their leagues are wealthy enough to prevent much economic migration. Spaniards may be further discouraged from coming here by the dismal record of players who have made the switch.'

Disolodging stereoytpes takes time. Too many had failed. Albert Ferrer and Campo were steady and endearing rather than spectacular. Bolton's punts on Javi Moreno and Salva Ballesta each lasted less than six months. Enrique de Lucas arrived at Chelsea as a goalscoring midfielder and proceeded to score no goals in 25 appearances. Manchester United took Spanish goalkeeper Ricardo, whose only consistent party trick was his aptitude for rushing out of the goalmouth and conceding penalty kicks. Raul Bravo was a calamitous presence in a Leeds United side that was on the treadmill towards Premier League oblivion. Javier de Pedro had been an integral part of a Real Sociedad side that very nearly won the La Liga title, finishing only two points behind Real Madrid. He arrived at Blackburn in the summer of 2004 but made only two appearances.

But times were changing. As the first decade of the new millennium progressed, Premier League managers began to scout more closely in Spain. Arsenal had full-time employees monitoring La Liga talent. Wenger had signed the excellent defender Lauren from Real Mallorca in 2000 and still regards it as one of his greatest steals. From retirement homes to nurseries, English clubs spotted gaps in the market, poaching young Spanish teenagers such as Cesc Fabregas at Arsenal and Gerard Pique at Manchester United. Arsenal, too, made a play for Pique.

In the boardrooms, directors were also taking note. In the 2003–04 season, there were still only three foreign managers in the Premier League – Wenger at Arsenal, Claudio Ranieri at Chelsea and Gerard Houllier at Liverpool. Yet English football was becoming more open. The FA had appointed Sven-Goran Eriksson as their first foreign manager of the national team, and the bigger clubs with the bigger budgets increasingly cast their gaze overseas. A Spanish manager was only a matter of time.

CHAPTER 8

Misunderstood

Liverpool's 2005 Champions League triumph remains the most inexplicable and extraordinary in history. When Liverpool were 3-0 down against AC Milan at half-time, bookmakers offered odds of 360/1 against a victory for Rafa Benitez's side. In *The Times*, Simon Barnes wrote: 'A person who made such a bet would be certain to have a serious interest in crop circles, Elvis's second coming, flying pigs, a flat earth, extra-terrestrial landings and the innate goodness of humankind.' Barnes called it a 'night of perfect insanity'. For Benitez, it is the evening that will always be cast in stone. French daily newspaper *L'Equipe* roared: 'Liverpool Eternal'. In the Spanish sports pages, former Real Madrid coach Jorge Valdano said he 'longed for a seismograph that could measure human passion. In the six minutes where Liverpool scored three goals to equalise, the seismograph would have reached its upper limit.'

Yet matches involving Benitez are rarely so enthralling. As a child, Benitez grew up playing basketball and handball, while he also attended judo classes. Football, ultimately, was his chosen pursuit. As a young player, Benitez entered into Real Madrid's academy and represented their C team in the Spanish third division. He played as a holding midfielder and Franz Beckenbauer was his idol, but an embryonic playing career was cut short after Benitez struggled to recover from a knee injury suffered at the World Student Games in Mexico. He progressed through the ranks at Real Madrid's academy before being promoted to B team head coach and then assistant to the first team under Vicente del Bosque.

Yet Benitez had a second love and that was chess. Indeed, it was the sport of Bobby Fischer that really stimulated Benitez. During his time in military service in Madrid, he outmanoeuvred all those who dared to take him on across the chessboard. In his days working at Madrid's academy, he would often play chess against first-team boss Radomir Antic. Xavi Valero, his former goalkeeping coach at Liverpool, tells me Benitez sees coaching as akin to being a military general. In essence, Benitez views his players as his pawns and it is his job to strategise and outthink, outflank and outgun his rivals.

Benitez said in 2012: 'Have no doubt at all that chess has stimulated my football brain. In football, we have to think ahead and analyse what is coming next. We need a plan A, a plan B and even a plan C. We need to calmly evaluate moments before putting them into practice.'

Benitez is, therefore, a far cry from the more fluid Spanish style of more recent times. In a column for the *Independent* during his time in charge of Napoli, Benitez said: 'Everyone seems to be talking about statistics in football and managers' philosophies about offensive football. Well, I'm sorry, but the philosophers were Plato and Socrates. The essential part of winning games for a coach is the work done on the field, helping players deal with the systems thrown at them.' They may both be loath to admit it, but Benitez sees the game in a manner similar to his sparring partner Jose Mourinho. After Manchester United won the Europa League final against Ajax in 2017 with only 31 per cent of the ball, Mourinho said: 'There are many poets in football but poets don't win many titles.'

Benitez finds his stimulus in control rather than expression. His greatest influence was the Italian mastermind Arrigo

Sacchi, but the analytical mind of Felipe Gayoso, a lesser-known coach in the Real Madrid academy, also shaped his thinking. Fernando Torres, the striker he signed for Liverpool and later coached at Chelsea, explained the scientific approach of a man who has studied medicine and physical preparation at degree level: 'Rafa calculates everything, the distances, long passes, everything is drawn up on his computer. If he tells you that you must stay a certain number of metres from the penalty spot, you must obey and follow the instructions. He is showing you how to find the extra space that is the difference between a goal and a missed opportunity.'

In a newspaper column, Jamie Carragher said that Benitez made his team virtual 'robots' in training sessions. 'If you asked me to say the one word I heard most during training and games,' Carragher said, 'it would be him shouting "compact". We knew exactly what he wanted us to do and when to do it. This came about through repetition on the training ground, the drills being done over and over again until he was satisfied. It demanded a high level of concentration and there was no laughing or joking.'

The rigid and pragmatic football on the pitch has rarely charmed the British public. Benitez, as a character, appears to be a riddle of contradictions. He offers a sense of robotic detachment in many of his dealings. Steven Gerrard wrote in his autobiography that Benitez is the one former manager he no longer feels comfortable to call over the telephone. Take the text message Benitez sent to his Liverpool goalkeeper Pepe Reina, one of his most outgoing players, after Spain won the European Championship in 2008. It simply read: 'Congratulations, RB.' Take his first meeting with Craig Bellamy before he signed for the club, in which he sat the fiery Welshman down and pro-ceeded to ask him to state the benefits and downsides of the 4-2-3-1 formation.

Benitez focused on detail rather than emotion. Luis Garcia, the attacking midfielder, admitted in one interview that he had never heard Benitez shout. He is one of those managers who often respond to a goal by reaching for the notepad rather than wrapping his arms around the nearest person to him. Thus emerges a caricature of Benitez as dispassionate and cold. Yet in Benitez's character lies a fundamental paradox, for he is also prone to moments of sentimental outpouring. Upon being named Real Madrid manager, he had to hold back the tears in his first press conference. He decided to remain at Newcastle United after relegation because the supporters pleaded throughout the final match of the season, a 5-1 victory over Tottenham, for Benitez to stay. '*Rafa, no te vayas*' ('Rafa, don't go) read the placard held up in the Gallowgate end of St James' Park.

Benitez is respected around the world, perhaps far more than he is in Great Britain. When the Argentine sports magazine *El Gráfico* celebrated its 90th anniversary, he was one of only five coaches to make their list of 90 men who had shaped the game. As a neutral observer who had often found Benitez's demeanour to be rather standoffish – in truth, I have never really *got* Benitez – I wanted to gauge the feelings of those who worked alongside him and those who played under him. I wanted to bring some understanding to a man whose advocates believe to be misunderstood.

Certainly, it is true that few coaches share his compulsive addiction to the sport. In 2015, his wife Montse gave an interview to *La Región*. 'On our first date,' she began, 'we went to a Madrid pizzeria. I had no idea about football. So he picked up a pen and started drawing diagrams to teach me the 4-4-2 formation. He loves cinema but take the football away and well . . .' The pause summed up his dedication. Montse added: 'Rafa was out of work for a year and went to help out a local school team on the Wirral. It was very funny. He stood on the sidelines, gesticulating furiously and waving those arms as if it were the Premier League.'

In his time in England, Benitez has also won an FA Cup and

a Europa League with Liverpool, and a Championship title with Newcastle, but that night in Istanbul remains his most significant contribution to English football; the night that will never be usurped. Yet Benitez's true impact can be seen in his endurance and longevity, in the way he keeps coming back for more, first at Chelsea and then at Newcastle United. Benitez's connection with English football runs so deep that he tolerated the pain and pleasure of the Championship, all within 12 months after becoming manager at his beloved Real Madrid.

At Liverpool and Newcastle, he is admired and beloved by a large section of supporters even though many across the country have often felt detached. 'If you want an idea about how his fans feel about him,' goalkeeping coach Valero says, 'just look at our last game at Real Madrid, which was at Valencia and we lost 3–2. As bad as it was for Real, he was blown away by the support and reception he received from Valencia fans that night. They respected his work and what he did for Valencia. There is warmth for Rafa wherever he goes back. He is loved. I would say Valencia and Liverpool are the big connections but even in two years at Napoli, he grew to love their passionate city and fanbase.'

Benitez's imprint on English football can be uncovered in many places, but a feud with Sir Alex Ferguson is always a good sign that a mark has been made on our national game. Ferguson reserved one of his more brutal literary kickings for Benitez in the autobiography that followed his retirement. The former Liverpool manager, Ferguson mused, had been left to appear a 'silly man' after one particularly high-octane bout of psychological warfare with the Manchester United manager. Ferguson concluded: 'The advance publicity was that Benitez was a control freak, which turned out to be correct . . . Jose Mourinho was far more astute in his handling of players. And he has personality. If you saw the two together on the touchline, you knew you could pick the winner.'

Against that hostile background, it can appear something of an illusion when we are reminded that Benitez's first significant exposure to the intricacies of English football in fact came courtesy of Ferguson. Pako Ayestaran, who worked as Benitez's assistant at Liverpool, tells me: 'It's funny, but one of our first tastes of the Premier League was actually with Sir Alex Ferguson. We were between jobs, so we went to visit Manchester United. Ferguson let Rafa and me watch his first-team training sessions with Roy Keane, Ryan Giggs, everyone in that great treble team. At that time, it wasn't as normal to let foreign coaches come over to observe. It was very kind.'

Ayestaran is referring to the period that followed Benitez's departure from Extremadura, when the pair embarked on a European tour in which they also observed the work of Fabio Capello, Marcello Lippi and Claudio Ranieri. At Manchester United's old training ground, The Cliff, Benitez was afforded privileged access to Ferguson's methods and also those of Steve McClaren, who was the Scot's assistant manager at the time.

Even after taking over at Liverpool, Benitez continued to enjoy the respect of Ferguson. Did you know, for example, that in the autumn of 2004, shortly after Benitez became Liverpool manager, the two men in fact sat next to one another on a flight heading to a UEFA conference in Switzerland? These days a photograph from the flight would no doubt have been leaked on social media and we might have been talking about something approaching a 'bromance' between the Manchester United and Liverpool managers. When Benitez won the Champions League in the most extraordinary circumstances in Istanbul, he returned to Liverpool's training ground to find a signed letter of congratulation from Ferguson.

For a while, the relationship continued to blossom. In May 2006, UEFA invited Ferguson and Benitez, along with the two managers' wives, to the Champions League final in Paris between Barcelona and Arsenal. Following the game, Ferguson and his wife Cathy were walking the Parisian streets when they stumbled upon some of Arsenal's more raucous followers. Benitez intervened, calmed down the Arsenal supporters and guided the Fergusons away from the situation.

To reflect on that moment now is rather sobering, as we consider the disintegration of the friendship born out of mutual respect. To mention Benitez's name in the presence of Ferguson, particularly during the Spaniard's time at Chelsea, could be akin to unloading petrol into a diesel engine. For his part, by the end of Ferguson's period in management, Benitez was giving the distinct impression that if he saw the United manager drowning, he would chuck him both ends of the rope. The English football establishment generally sided with Ferguson and this may not have helped the public perception of the Spaniard.

The fuse was lit during the 2008–09 season, when Benitez's Liverpool threatened Ferguson's United in the title race for the very first time. As tensions rose during the month of January, Benitez delivered a press conference in which he unveiled a sheet of paper and started to list 'facts', railing against Ferguson's treatment of referees, Ferguson's complaints about the fixture list and Ferguson's generous treatment by the Football Association. It was a remarkable monologue and the relationship never recovered. Some say that Benitez's Liverpool tenure did not recover. United won the title and, 15 months later, the Spaniard left Anfield.

Liverpool's dressing room did not appreciate their manager's intervention. In his autobiography, the former Liverpool captain Steven Gerrard said: 'Rafa went off on a ramble about how Manchester United and "Mr Ferguson" had not been properly punished for various misdemeanours. Rafa was sounding muddled and bitter and paranoid. He was humiliating himself. It was a disaster. I couldn't understand Rafa's thinking in wanting to take on Ferguson, a master of mind games, when we were sitting so calmly on top of the table early into a new year. When I met up with England, all the Manchester United players told me Fergie was just laughing at Rafa, saying: "I've got him. I've got him."'

By March 2013, Ferguson's final season in management, the pair would not even shake hands. Benitez had also fallen foul of Ferguson's cohort of supportive contemporaries, including Sam Allardyce. Benitez and Allardyce had an uneasy relationship from their first contest in August 2004, when Bolton beat Liverpool 1–0 and the Spaniard refused to shake his rival's hand after Sami Hyypia had his nose broken by Kevin Davies in a challenge for a high ball.

Benitez was angered when Ferguson did not seek him out to offer a welcoming hand before Manchester United's FA Cup quarter-final tie against Chelsea at Old Trafford in March 2013. Ferguson went even further, neglecting to mention Benitez in his programme notes for the game, something he would customarily do for any opposing manager. Rather, Ferguson only highlighted what he considered to be the harsh dismissal of Chelsea's previous manager Roberto Di Matteo.

When Benitez complained about Ferguson's snub, the United manager said: 'I never even saw him at Old Trafford, so I don't know why he went and made such an issue of it [the handshake]. At the end of the game, we always shake hands and always have a meeting in my office with both sets of staff. It is a fantastic thing to do. You don't get it abroad, but it is the right thing to do. He came in once when he was at Liverpool, but I don't think he's come in again. He never even came in when we went to Anfield.'

It was all daft and petty but very few managers riled Ferguson to quite the same extent. Kevin Keegan, perhaps, for a while at Newcastle United. Arsene Wenger, for a period, at Arsenal. In many ways, it is a compliment to Benitez, a manager who has offered so much to English football and who became so popular on Merseyside and, more recently, on Tyneside. As Benitez told the *Sunday Times*, 'It's exactly what Arsene Wenger was saying one day [about Ferguson]. When we were rivals, we were no longer friends. When we were 20 points behind Manchester United, he liked me.'

*

For Benitez and his wife Montse, the Wirral Peninsula has become home. Benitez has been known to drive around in a Union Jack Mini convertible and he enjoys the vantage point of his home, overlooking the River Dee. It is a far cry from urban Madrid, where Benitez spent his formative years. Growing up in Spain's capital, Benitez followed Real Madrid, just like his father, although his mother was an avid Atletico Madrid supporter.

It is curious to reflect now that Benitez was not a straightforward choice for Liverpool back in 2004. He may have won two La Liga titles and a UEFA Cup with Valencia but, in England, momentum was building behind the impressive Irishman Martin O'Neill following his success with Leicester and Celtic. The Liverpool board also considered Steve McClaren, Alan Curbishley and Gordon Strachan as replacements for the outgoing Gerard Houllier. Fresh from winning the Champions League with Porto, Mourinho was the object of desire for most European clubs. *The Times* suggested Mourinho had indicated he would prefer the Liverpool job to Chelsea, but while the Merseyside club offered a £30,000 weekly wage, Roman Abramovich blew rivals out of the water with an £80,000-per-week proposal.

At Liverpool, Ayestaran became Benitez's assistant, having previously worked with him at four Spanish clubs. To this day, he keeps a property in Merseyside and we meet in a bar near to his Kirby home. 'We loved it in England from day one,' the coach said. 'I was in Lime Street station and people were coming up to me, saying, "Thank you, thank you for coming." I'm thinking, "Fucking hell! I was in Valencia for years with Rafa, where I was only stopped in the street to be criticised and then I come here and they are saying thank you before I have even started." After my time at Liverpool, Carlo Ancelotti allowed me to go to Milan and observe his methods. I spent a week there and he was so intrigued by England and I was encouraging him to go there one day. Of course, he later came to Chelsea.'

When Xavi Valero joined Benitez to replace outgoing goalkeeping coach Jose Ochotorena in 2007, he was similarly charmed by the English culture. He had enjoyed a previous taste of English football during a one-month loan spell at Wrexham in January 2005. In a Madrid café, he explains: 'Andy Dibble, the ex-Man City player, was injured and they needed an emergency goalkeeper. We had the winter break in Spain and I hadn't been playing. I played four games and I loved the experience. The Premier League is tough but maybe the top flight is easier to adapt to than lower down. To go into League One or League Two, where anything goes, that was a real shock. It's incredibly physical and the conditions are worse on muddy pitches. They allow contact in the area while any light contact is a foul in Spain. I'm a big guy but there were bigger strikers!

'At Liverpool, I was also head of the goalkeeping development. I remember one game in the Johnstone's Paint Trophy. We had a reserve goalkeeper, Dean Bouzanis, on loan at Accrington. I went to Leeds to watch him on a Thursday night. I could not believe what Elland Road was like that night. It was an amazing atmosphere, beyond all logic for a pretty minor game like that. I went back with Chelsea when we beat them 5-1. It was a huge rivalry between the fans. I could imagine from those games how that stadium could have been in the 1970s. As a player and coach, that's why you want to be in England.'

Ayestaran adds: 'I've always kept my house here in West Kirby and my kids and wife love it here. In Spain or Mexico, where I also worked, it takes a long time to get the affection you receive immediately here. It's the feeling of belonging to a club, to a community, and a responsibility to the people in your city. I think Rafa sees similarities between Newcastle and Liverpool, in the town and the fans. It's no surprise to me that he is popular there. I've seen his mentality, work ethic, attention to detail, and that brings results.

'I think the big thing for Rafa is that he feels loved and wanted. He couldn't walk away. It's a club that has Champions League potential. They are one of the traditional big clubs with an extraordinary fanbase and an authentic culture. It should be a magnificent club to manage and it needs to become that again.'

Arsene Wenger went a long way to modernising attitudes and methods at Arsenal in the 1990s, but when Benitez arrived at Liverpool, he introduced his own progressive formulas. Ayestaran says: 'I believe we arrived at a juncture when there was far more emphasis over the control of the physiology of the footballer. In England, there wasn't really this mentality. We began to implement a stricter diet, monitoring of training and far more physical tests. Rafa started building a database of players. He has what can only be described as an obsession – in a good way – over control and being right across things. The idea of worldwide scouting was quite new but he had this database of over 10,000 players, which was novel and pioneering for the time.

'He had different ways of training and took into account factors that influence recovery and recuperation. He carried charts of exactly how many minutes a player played in a season. There were some more old-school methods too. We dug our man-made hills, dubbed "Pako hills", which were three mounds with different gradients, at the club's training ground for stamina and resistance training.'

Benitez has a record for clamping down on dietary issues. At Extremadura, he discouraged his players from chewing gum in public because he felt it was bad for the club's image. At Valencia, he provoked a dispute by asking the chef to stop serving fatty foods such as the ice-cream dessert that one of his predecessors Claudio Ranieri allowed his players to indulge in. The decision to do away with paella, olives and second helpings at lunch even yielded showdown talks between the players and the club doctor.

At Liverpool, players were surprised by his attention to detail. He was strong on some issues and more lax on others. For example, Benitez outlawed baked beans at the training ground but also brought an end to Gerard Houllier's ban on mobile phones being used there. Yet when he noticed early on that his players ate their lunch rapidly before heading off, he held a team meeting in which he told his squad that in his experience at Valencia, men such as Pablo Aimar and Roberto Ayala would spend an hour talking together and bolstering squad unity over the dining table. Even the most loyal of Benitez lieutenants would not escape his attention.

Pepe Reina, the goalkeeper Benitez signed for Liverpool and Napoli, is one of those who speak glowingly about the coach. Reina was a popular and charismatic figure around the Liverpool training ground and he is entertaining company when we meet during his summer holidays in Ibiza. He has a swanky apartment by the beach and we meet for lunch at a local bar. He's drinking water today but recalls an episode that followed a game in 2007. Liverpool lost at Besiktas in the Champions League and, on returning to the hotel for the team's post-match meal, Reina ordered a beer. Soon enough, the barman came over to explain that Benitez had blocked the order. Reina challenged his manager, who stood firm. Reina stormed to his bedroom and felt disappointed his coach did not trust him to have one drink.

Craig Bellamy once said that Benitez trusted his players less than any other manger he encountered. On the day of games, he would wait until the hour before kick-off to reveal his team. Bellamy said: 'Rafa said it was because he didn't want to give the opposition an advantage. What he meant was that he didn't want anyone to leak the team early and he didn't trust players to keep it secret.'

At the training ground, everything was regimented. Ayestaran recalls: 'They were a bit surprised by the level of monitoring and control. We were taking decisions for them over many facets of

their daily life that had previously been left alone. We wanted
to know every detail of their diet, training commitment and
their sleeping patterns.' Spanish defender Josemi, Benitez's first
Liverpool signing, adds: 'The mentality changed. The English
view was very different in terms of discipline, dedication and
training. I was surprised how much butter is used in England,
for example. Rafa brought in more physiotherapy. Many things
were behind the times and certainly behind the level you expect
for top clubs with 30 million-pound players.'

In 2017, when Benitez was experiencing tensions with
Newcastle's unpopular owner Mike Ashley, Jamie Carragher
described Benitez in the *Daily Mail* as 'the most political figure
I've come across in football'. Many who have worked with
Benitez would see his point. Ayestaran was alongside Benitez on
the bench on the night Liverpool lifted the Champions League
trophy in 2005, the day the club won the FA Cup against West
Ham in 2006, and when they lost the Champions League final
against AC Milan in 2007. Yet in the summer of 2007, Ayestaran
suddenly left. The pair did not speak for at least six years but
they are now back in touch, with the families living within a
quarter of an hour's walk from one another.

Benitez felt his assistant had talked to other clubs behind his
back. In a cutting remark, Benitez said that 'power and auton-
omy' changed Ayestaran, yet the assistant always insisted Benitez
was made aware of any interest. Ayestaran explains: 'I had no
hidden agenda. After I left Liverpool, one of the things I said
was that I would not go to direct rivals. When Jose Mourinho
was sacked, Avram Grant called me and asked me to join his
technical team at Chelsea. It was a great opportunity but I felt
it would be wrong. We had some great moments together and
went through a huge amount together. He lives around the
corner and we are fine now.'

The two men have not worked together since. Ayestaran
formed part of the backroom teams of Quique Sanchez Flores
at Benfica and Unai Emery at Sevilla, and he became a manager

in his own right with Israeli club Maccabi Tel Aviv, Mexican team Santos Laguna, before spells in charge at Valencia and Las Palmas. Others have experienced Benitez's darker moods. At Real Madrid as B-team coach, he fell out with the first-team manager Jorge Valdano when the Argentine made demands as to who should be picked in his side. At Valencia, his rivalry with the board was a weekly item on the news agenda. He memorably accused the board of buying him a 'lamp' when he had 'asked for sofa'. Sporting director Jesus Garcia Pitarch had signed attacking midfielder Fabian Canobbio when Benitez wanted a winger.

At Liverpool, former chairman Rick Parry has recalled how Benitez responded to the club signing Fernando Torres by asking why they also failed to sign Florent Malouda. During his time there, he would often end a season by making public pleas for new signings, and Carragher recalls Benitez suggesting he could jump ship to Juventus, Bayern Munich or even the England job if he so desired. At Inter Milan, Benitez railed against the veteran age range of the treble-winning squad he inherited from Jose Mourinho and criticised the lack of transfers.

Yet while board members are irked by Benitez's demands, supporters rapidly grow to like him. At Liverpool, his commitment to the victims of the Hillsborough disaster endured long beyond his time in charge of the club. Shortly after leaving in 2010, he donated £96,000 to support the families who lost their loved ones on 15 April 1989. When he returned to Anfield for a commemorative event the following year, he and his wife wept when they were thanked publicly for their support.

While manager of Newcastle, he laid a wreath at the Hillsborough memorial before a game against Sheffield Wednesday. His immediate promotion-winning return from the Championship triggered local journalists Martin Hardy and Mark Douglas to write, respectively, books entitled *Rafa's Way* and *Rafalution*. He charmed administration staff by buying each member a Christmas present to say thank you for their work.

Yet it is striking that many of his former players pass up the opportunity to eulogise his personality. Carragher and Gerrard respect him and recognise he improved their performances, but there is rarely a warmth when it comes to their personal relationship with Benitez.

I decided to meet Spanish fullback Josemi, a £2m signing from Malaga and the first addition of the Benitez era, to better understand the manager's early intentions. Some Spaniards, such as Pepe Reina, Xabi Alonso, Luis Garcia and Fernando Torres, were spectacular successes. They became known as 'El Benitels' in the Spanish media. Yet Josemi, Antonio Nuñez, Fernando Morientes, Antonio Barragan, Mark Gonzalez, Dani Pacheco, Francisco Duran and Dani Ayala failed to make the grade.

At his home in Torremolinos, Josemi, an unused substitute on the night, has a montage dedicated to Liverpool's win over Milan in the Champions League final. 'In the previous years under Houllier, they'd bought quite a few French guys in. We knew a few would be moved on and Rafa had the idea to bring a few Spanish guys in. However, he was very insistent we wouldn't be arriving as an enclave and isolating ourselves. He'd been concerned by French cliques before he came.

'At the training centre, we had to mix with everyone but I had Spanish TV in my house so we were often all around mine. Xabi Alonso and Luis Garcia were outstanding talents but they were very young rather than superstars. Carragher and Gerrard tried to help us from the very first day. They were the reference points. They made it clear what the club stood for. The French ones were a bit different, a bit odd, and a bit more individual. The Spanish are more open, friendly with everyone rather than insular. The French guys had a different mentality.'

Josemi was steady for a while at Liverpool but Steve Finnan ousted him and the Spaniard returned home, joining Villarreal, midway through his second season. 'I had offers from Atletico Madrid, Sevilla and Valencia before going to Liverpool. Rafa had wanted me while he was at Valencia. Malaga told me about

Liverpool's interest and there was a lot of excitement about Rafa at the time. I didn't know English, my family had never left Spain and we'd never given the impression of wanting to leave.

'How do I define Rafa? Hmm. He's . . . peculiar. He has his mentality and that's it. It has worked very well for him. The only weakness I see with Rafa is his relationship and personal contact with players. I've always said that Rafa's flaw is his inability to be a footballer's friend. He has very little contact. Players like a manager to ask how they are and what they are up to. He is more on the margins. Modern footballers are different. We like managers to be close to us. We can have problems, whether family or personal, and it can affect everything. We need to have that personal relationship.'

Josemi was affected by a series of injuries and he insisted on a return to Spain for the recuperation period. 'The gaffer didn't want me to go back to Spain. Many things happened. I was out with a knee injury for five months; my wife was pregnant with my daughter. It was right for my family. The club wasn't great with my recuperation. I think they could have done more. Medical care was catching up at that time. I remember Xabi Alonso had some treatment in San Sebastian and Djibril Cisse went to France. I went back to Malaga where I trusted the medical team to get it right. I went to Barcelona every week for further sessions. Villarreal made an offer and I wanted to go for the family. I needed a change of atmosphere. Benitez barely made contact during those five months. It was like he was never bothered.'

Yet for Pepe Reina, the story could not be more different. Benitez first tried to sign him for Tenerife, when Reina was a 17-year-old at Barcelona. He then bombarded him with calls to sign for Liverpool while Reina played for Villarreal. The pair won the FA Cup together in 2006. It was a topsy-turvy afternoon for Reina, in which he was at fault for West Ham's second goal when he spilled a shot into the path of Dean Ashton, and he was then deceived when Paul Konchesky's cross sailed into the top corner of his goal.

'I know you're meant to say, "I never stopped believing,"' Reina says. 'But the truth is that it was a really bad game for us. We started awfully, 2–0 down; it was a warm afternoon and difficult to recover. It became a tough afternoon. I was very anxious throughout the whole game for some reason, but Gerrard scored two and made one. I then made one of the best saves of my career to tip Nigel Reo-Coker's header onto the post.

'Then, it went to penalty kicks and all my nerves suddenly fell away. I made three saves. It is funny, though, because we had information for the penalties. Rafa gave me a sheet. It had instructions about Teddy Sheringham but he scored. But then for Bobby Zamora, Paul Konchesky and Anton Ferdinand, there was no detail at all about them on the sheet and I saved all three of those. Sometimes life just works like that and my relationship with the fans really took off from there.

'I loved Anfield. I liked looking to the stands and seeing the legends Ian Rush and Kenny Dalglish looking down. It was actually great when Dalglish became manager after Roy Hodgson left because the whole place just lifted. The fans dreamed again. It was clearly a romantic, nostalgic decision; he maybe wasn't a manager completely up with the times. But we got to a cup final in 2012 and at least we competed well. Nobody at Liverpool would ever say a word against Kenny. He was always underlining the responsibility we had to the supporters; that was the minimum he expected. It was more an emotional reign than tactical, if I was to compare him to Rafa.'

Reina grew close to Benitez, who would often challenge his players by pointing out areas to work on rather than offering praise. Recordings of mistakes and imperfections were always at the ready, and although players sought validation, Benitez often brought about improvements through cold analysis. In the 2008–09 season, Liverpool finished second on 86 points and just four behind the champions Manchester United. On Merseyside, it is seen as one of those that got away, as Liverpool continue to seek their first top-flight title since 1990.

Xavi Valero nods: 'It was a very balanced squad and the team was filled with confidence. There was youth, experience and a core of players and leaders at their peaks. We had Reina, Carragher, Hyypia, Alonso, Mascherano, Gerrard, Kuyt and Torres. They were world-class players. We had energy, youth and character. We created huge occasions at Anfield. We beat Real Madrid 4-0 on the Tuesday and then went to Old Trafford and won 4-1 at United. On those nights, the atmosphere was just ridiculous. I've seen major European teams, like Real Madrid, Arsenal and Inter Milan suffer in that environment. I would observe them before the game on the pitch. They would look around the stadium, hear "You'll Never Walk Alone" and be affected. I wouldn't say intimidating. The word is *stimulating*, but that has a different effect on individuals and groups.'

Reina concurs: 'For sure, the biggest regret of my career is that this team did not win the title. I was desperate to win a title with Liverpool; the fans were craving it after so many years. We had a chance that year. Manchester United were an amazing team, though, with Cristiano Ronaldo, Carlos Tevez and Wayne Rooney.'

Many reflect that Benitez's 'facts' monologue against Ferguson tipped the scales United's way. Liverpool won only two of the next seven league games that followed his speech. 'Ah, the facts . . .' Reina winces. 'Look, it was a decision he took. Everyone was trying to seek an advantage, but nobody was expecting it. It was his way of defending us but he went on the attack. The United rivalry always felt huge. OK, Everton is a local derby but you can't compare it with United or Liverpool in the modern era. Ultimately, posterity does not cast it well as we didn't win the title. It was Rafa's decision, but people do forget we ended the season with ten wins in 11 games.'

During the summer that followed, Alonso departed for Real Madrid. A year earlier, Benitez bizarrely wanted to sell Alonso to fund a move for Gareth Barry. When he did move on, it left a gaping chasm. In his book *Ring of Fire*, Simon Hughes interviewed Alonso and the author concluded that Benitez 'instilled a sense of resentment that made Alonso's departure inevitable'. Regardless of the politics, Alonso was a giant loss.

Reina says: 'Xabi is one of the best players of the modern era. He could play with anyone; he worked in partnerships with all sorts of players: Dietmar Hamann, Mo Sissoko, Stevie Gerrard, Javier Mascherano. They all liked playing with him. He was incredibly competitive. When he went, we dipped. He left Liverpool to better himself at Real Madrid. It was the same thing with Torres and Mascherano. Sometimes people do not understand that, as footballers, our career has a small shelf life. We want the best for our lives and for our families.'

From near champions in 2009 to seventh place and his acrimonious exit from Liverpool the next summer. Hostility and politicking with the club's American owners, Tom Hicks and George Gillett, took its toll and with four years left on a five-year contract, Benitez departed in the summer of 2010. Liverpool suffered for a lack of transfer-market ambition and, one by one, their stars slipped away. At the start of May, Benitez had pointed the finger at the owners. He said the club was short 'in terms of money and power, so you can analyse carefully and then you have answers'. He followed the line up with a classic Benitezism: 'The fans are very clever; they know what is going on.' This is Benitez's trademark media approach – provoke the blazers and cosy up to the fans.

Yet when it came to taking over at Chelsea in November 2012, he needed to find a new approach. Chelsea and Liverpool endured a dramatic rivalry during the Benitez and Mourinho years, so the decision to sack the popular Champions League-winning manager Roberto Di Matteo and replace him with the Spaniard went down like a bucket of cold sick at Stamford Bridge. Those fierce Champions League encounters took their toll and Benitez was about as welcome at Chelsea as Tom Henning Ovrebo, the Norwegian referee whose catalogue of errors saw Chelsea eliminated from the Champions League semi-final in 2009.

His first home match, against Manchester City, was a 0-0 draw but the atmosphere was startling in its toxicity. From all sides of the ground, the insults came hurling down. Shouts of 'Fuck off, Benitez, you're not wanted here!' rained down from the Shed End. The stadium announcer made the mistake of actually mentioning the new manager's name and boos followed. In the *Guardian*, Daniel Taylor wrote: 'The mutiny was loud and sustained and, for Rafael Benítez, callous in its intentions. He shrugged his shoulders afterwards, insisted it did not trouble him and tried to convince us of his selective hearing. But it had been shocking to witness the vitriol that was waiting for him.'

Chelsea's decision-makers did not aid Benitez's position. His title 'interim manager', which he resented, made him appear a temporary solution. It suggested he was expendable, it meant the supporters had little reason to nurture a relationship of depth with the manager and the players knew he could be off with a moment's notice. They knew he was makeshift, a stopgap, a light substitute; a bit like lighting a candle when the electricity fails.

The situation was exacerbated on the first day of his tenure, when an alleged quote from 2007 emerged on social media. 'Chelsea is a big club with fantastic players. Every manager wants to coach a big team. But I would never take that job, in respect for my former team at Liverpool.' It immediately spread, causing widespread outrage among Chelsea's fanbase and damaging Benitez's credibility and integrity. And yet, here's the thing. It was not true. He could not have said Liverpool were his former team, owing to the fact that he was still managing the club in 2007. In the days before the Russians waged cyber warfare on Hillary Clinton, this was fake news before the fake news era began. The quote, it transpired, was made up and shared on Twitter by a 15-year-old from the Czech Republic. Benitez denied saying it but the sentiment lingered.

Benitez was Chelsea's eighth manager in eight years – one reason why Pep Guardiola has always resisted Roman Abramovich's advances – but Benitez was the most immediately vulnerable. After the draw against City, his opponent Roberto Mancini said the only way for Benitez to succeed would be to 'win, win, win, win'. So without the club or the fans entirely on board, that is exactly what Benitez did. He beat Manchester United twice, won the Europa League to secure Champions League football and claimed 26 points from the final 33 available in the Premier League.

Coach Valero linked up with Benitez once more at Stamford Bridge. He recalls that first day as being one of his most 'difficult' afternoons in football. 'Yes, it was hard,' Valero says. 'The main lesson from our time at Chelsea was that even in difficult circumstances, we could still do really well. We won the Europa League; we played the FA Cup semi-final at Wembley and lost to Manchester City. Rafa is one of the best coaches of the past 15 years. He has had the trust of many clubs. Chelsea knew it would be difficult but they trusted him to take them to the final destination.

'We knew all the speculation and how it might be with the fans. We knew the big rivalry after the Champions League nights. He was seen as a Liverpool man going into their territory and their dugout. But Rafa saw lots of energy that we needed to redirect in the right direction. The players were mostly very good with us and, for all the noise about Rafa, a club always remains about the club. The fans did not stop turning up. They came to Japan in the Club World Cup, to Leeds in December for a Capital One Cup game. They were always there. And, trust me, fans are more expressive in Italy and Spain, even compared to what happened at Chelsea.'

It was reported that Benitez encountered problems with senior players such as John Terry, but in the club's strong and popular Spanish contingent, he discovered important allies. 'It is obvious that the environment was not easy at the start for

Rafa,' says the defender Cesar Azpilicueta. 'A section of the fans were unhappy with the decision to give Rafa the job. From my point of view, I just got on with my job of playing and it was an important time because we were all united by the pressure and desire to change results. It was a good season in the end. He needed to deflect from the noise and get us working. He took the emotion out of it really well. It is his way of training. He prepares in huge detail for every opponent. He got results and that was the proof of his work.'

Juan Mata was named the club's player of the season for the second time in a row, scoring 19 goals and creating 35 in a remarkable campaign. Mata says: 'On a personal level, I actually really enjoyed playing with Rafa. I had one of the best seasons of my career. It was obvious that the atmosphere around the club at the time was not ideal but, on the training ground, players increasingly bought into the work he was doing. We won the Europa League. He overcame a lot and showed his character.

'He is a coach who prepares methodically. It's rare to meet somebody who thinks about football as compulsively as Rafa. I think it is his whole life. He is a real strategist, everything is controlled, and he has an obsession, in a positive way. Every coach has his own way of working. Van Gaal, Mourinho, Rafa … they all prepare the smaller details and reduce the margins by which luck can decide things and Rafa is right up there.'

Southampton midfielder Oriol Romeu, who came through at Barcelona before signing for Chelsea at the age of 19, has played under Luis Enrique, Pep Guardiola, Andre Villas-Boas, Roberto Di Matteo, Jose Mourinho and Ronald Koeman. He reserves unique praise for Benitez. 'I know he has been criticised but he worked unbelievably hard for us on the tactical side of the game. His organisation and attention to detail was staggering. I broke back into the team, started three games in a row for Chelsea but then I injured my cruciate ligament at Sunderland. In the little time I was actively working with him,

I learned an awful lot. I still have some notes I took from his training sessions. I loved his video analysis sessions, where I'd make a list of [the opposition's] strong and weaker points and try to capitalise, and I will take his qualities into my own coaching career one day.'

At Chelsea, Benitez was reunited with Torres, the striker he signed for Liverpool in 2007 from Atletico Madrid, who scored 65 league goals in 102 appearances. His Chelsea tally, meanwhile, was only 20 goals in 110 appearances. The chronicles of a doomed £50m move have now been well told. At Liverpool, he was utterly explosive. He could poach goals in the penalty area or unleash glorious strikes from 30 yards out, as he did with one marvellous goal against Blackburn in 2009. He could score headers. He could go toe-to-toe with the league's most fierce defenders. Most people point to the day he terrorised Nemanja Vidic in a race of pace and power at Old Trafford, but there was another goal against United that was perhaps even more impressive. It came at Anfield later in the same year, where Torres outran and outmuscled Rio Ferdinand before hammering the ball past Edwin van der Sar.

Yet at Chelsea, Torres toiled. It took 14 games to score his first Chelsea goal. In 2011–12, his first full season, Torres scored only six league goals. In his first 61 Chelsea games in all competitions, there were eight goals, nine yellow cards and one red card. Staff at Chelsea's training ground remember an individual becoming increasingly quiet and isolated. He would rarely be persuaded to stop by the media mixed zone after games. It remains hard to pinpoint the diagnosis of the malaise. Some suspect a Michael Owen-style burnout. Torres made his Atletico Madrid debut by the age of 16 and was captain by 21. Groin and hamstring injuries took a toll at Liverpool. Hamstring problems damage a footballer's pace and certainly their confidence while sprinting. He also underwent two significant knee operations before signing for Chelsea. Some argue Torres' physiology had changed. But was there more to it?

Pepe Reina was his neighbour while they both lived in Liverpool. Reina frowns and shakes his head. 'I don't know, I just don't know,' the goalkeeper says. 'It's really difficult to understand. Thank God, I only saw the fantastic Torres. He trained extraordinarily well; he was unbelievable as a front-man. And then he went to London and . . . oof . . . it's hard to explain. It was a really bad spell for him. Maybe . . . in Chelsea, he was just another player; for us he was the superstar. Chelsea always gave me the impression of being a colder club, less of a family environment and maybe this affected Fernando. The transfer fee may have had an impact too. The figures can weigh heavily on your shoulders. Fernando was always a player who exposed space in behind and perhaps they didn't always play to his strengths in that respect.'

Under the weight of responsibility some players grow a few inches and others retreat further. I recall a conversation with Alvaro Morata shortly into his time with Chelsea, in which he explained the impact of a goalscoring dry spell on his frame of mind. 'It's really hard as a striker. It's cut and dried. Your job is to put the ball in the back of the net. OK, we like to say how a striker creates space and influences matches in other ways but let's not pretend: at the end of the season, the best striker everyone talks about is the top scorer. I had a spell of around a hundred days, where I couldn't score at Juventus. You start driving yourself mad. It goes through your head constantly: "I need a goal", "I need a goal". The more you think, the harder it gets.

'Goals flow when you play with a smile and don't think too much. I can overanalyse. I can think a lot, maybe too much, about chances I've missed. Sometimes I've scored in a game we have won, but I will go back home and watch again the chance I missed or say to my wife, "I should have scored here or there."

'At Juve, during that spell, I changed my car, my haircut, my boots, everything to try and end the duck. The dressing room helped me through. They were direct, face-to-face. Gianluigi Buffon would give it to you straight. No secrets or hiding, it was like a family. When you have a problem at Juve, you don't moan and you don't cry; you confront it, work through it together and improve yourself.'

Torres, sadly, did not improve as a footballer at Chelsea. Yet after stuttering under Carlo Ancelotti, Andre Villas-Boas and Roberto Di Matteo, Torres did rekindle something approaching his previous form upon being reunited with Benitez. He scored 15 goals between December and the end of the season, including the winner in the Europa League final against Benfica. Valero recalls the relationship between Mata and Torres being essential, with the playmaker operating in behind the forward and providing a direct supply line Torres had not enjoyed since his time with Steven Gerrard at Liverpool.

Azpilicueta agrees: 'We played in a different way with Rafa with regard to Torres. We changed a few things that helped Fernando and played to his strengths. We knew as well that Torres had been a star with Rafa before and I'm sure that gave him more confidence. He scored a big goal in the final. He got close to his old self for a bit. But look at the trophies he won at Chelsea: the Champions League and Europa League – that's what should be remembered.'

Benitez exited Chelsea at the end of his one season and back came Mourinho. Yet Benitez had by now showcased new qualities, primarily the ability to succeed when faced with obstacles in every direction. He could not cosy up to the fans but still he managed to bring performances from the players. For the supporters, success brought *détente* but the Europa League final still saw signs that read 'We want Jose'. And Jose they received.

After arriving, the Portuguese coach gradually moved on Benitez's favourites. The first victim was Juan Mata. It mattered little to Mourinho that Mata was popular with supporters and the club's best player for two consecutive years. Mata did make ten Premier League starts by New Year's Day but Mourinho often substituted him. At a Football Writers' Association dinner in Mourinho's honour, Frank Lampard explained how

Mourinho not only improved Eden Hazard's flair but also convinced the Belgian to adapt to his defensive demands and hunt down marauding right-backs.

In Mata, however, Mourinho did not appear to see the same qualities. Mata became unhappy, so unhappy he held a meeting with owner Roman Abramovich, who agreed he could leave the club if the situation continued. In January 2014, Mata left for United. Azpilicueta recalls: 'Juan had been our best player for two straight seasons. We had a lot of success and we won trophies. The fans adored him and everyone around the club loved him. He wasn't playing as much as he would have liked and he had a fantastic chance to join Manchester United. I felt really sad when he left the club but, above all, I think everyone around the club wanted him to be happy.'

To discuss the situation with Mata was complex. By the time we carried out our interview for this book in early 2017, a twist of fate had seen Mourinho now become his manager at Manchester United. 'I was always calm in the summer he arrived at United,' Mata insists. 'Of course I briefly wondered. Jose made it abundantly clear to me that he wanted to work with me at United and wanted to count on me. From my point of view, that was all I needed to hear. As far as I was concerned, it was the end of the matter.

'The first season went well, I am very proud and it reflects well on us as people. Many people talk a lot and create stories. I can't control all that but for all the rumours when Jose arrived, the reality was clear for me from the first week. I try to avoid all the noise. You'd drive yourself mad. Someone calls you and says, "Have you seen this story or that story?" I knew the reality and I just focused on working hard for the manager.' Mata became an influential figure in Mourinho's team and before the Europa League final victory over Ajax in May 2017, the manager insisted he needed 'Mata's brain' within the team.

For Torres, there would be no second coming with Mourinho. Torres scored a total of 11 goals in the Portuguese coach's first season back with Chelsea, but he and fellow strikers Samuel Eto'o and Demba Ba each scored under ten league goals. A memory stands out from a match between Crystal Palace and Chelsea towards the end of the 2013–14 season. Chelsea lost 1–0 in a bitter blow to their title aspirations and the club eventually finished third in the Premier League. Asked to diagnose his team's frailty, Mourinho teased: 'I will not say it in front of the television cameras but I will write it down on a piece of paper.' The notepad scrawl was direct and to the point: 'BALLS'.

Mourinho knew the *cojones* he needed. Three weeks later, Chelsea played Atletico Madrid in the Champions League semi-final. Diego Costa, the Atletico striker, had already scored 34 goals in 39 appearances – more than the combined tally of the Chelsea starting XI on the night. In the summer of 2013, Costa received interest from Liverpool, but Mourinho persuaded him to wait a year and link up with him at Chelsea the next summer when the funds would be available.

At Chelsea, Mourinho was constructing another winning machine. Azpilicueta, with his dogged defending, strong leadership skills and quality on the ball, embodied Mourinho's new team. The coach said: 'Azpi is the kind of player I like a lot. A team with 11 Azpilicuetas probably could win the Champions League because football is not just about the pure talent. Football is also about character and personality and Azpilicueta has all those traces of a winning personality.'

Azpilicueta arrived at Chelsea in a bargain £6.5m deal in 2012. He started as a right-back but ended up at left-back under Mourinho before excelling in a back three under Antonio Conte. 'When Jose arrived, I had huge expectations. Above all, I knew he would improve me as a footballer. I wanted to learn from him and win titles. We did these things – it's what he does. I always felt he placed huge trust in me. I felt it was sad that it ended in the way it did. It was not positive for anyone.

'I don't mind being versatile. People agonise and think, "I am right-footed so how can I play on the left?" As a player, it is our job to make it work. I found that a lot of teams now play with inverted wingers, so they are always shifting onto their stronger left side and that gave me an advantage as I could tackle with my stronger foot. Of course, it's harder to attack, though, because you lose that half-second to shift onto your stronger side. I now feel equally comfortable on either side. If I change from one position to the other, I adapt. You adapt and survive.

'I practised with my left foot after training sessions. I focused hugely on the position of my body, passing drills and extra video analysis. I had to visualise the situations to give myself the best chance. It was clear that during Jose's first season we improved but by the second season we were really prepared to challenge and win the title. In the Champions League, we reached the semi-finals in that first year. We weren't treading water. But Jose was imposing his ideas and then, in the summer of 2014, he made four very clear signings that enhanced our level and we made a big jump. Filipe Luis, Cesc Fabregas and Costa had a very high level, while Didier Drogba also came back. They signed at the beginning of the pre-season and everyone was prepared. We knew exactly how the season was going to go and that we had a great chance to win the title.'

Costa has his character flaws but he was a competitor of courage and talent in equal measure. Perceptions of him are skewed, not unjustifiably, by the dramatic summer of 2017, when a devastating row with Antonio Conte brought an acrimonious end to his time at Chelsea. By the final denouement, some at Chelsea may have sympathised with the end point of Costa's time with Albacete, where he became known by some teammates simply as 'that fucking Brazilian'.

When the *Daily Mail* sent me to knock on his door in his hometown Lagarto, with Costa on strike during the opening weekend of the Premier League season in 2017, I discovered a character who could not be more different from the snapping and snarling striker who terrorised defences. He was warm and welcoming, funny and insightful. Mourinho once described

Lagarto as 'beyond the sunset'. Most people I later encountered on a trip to Sao Paulo and Belo Horizonte had never heard of the small town. Yet this is where Costa was nurtured and this is where his heart lies. It is where he would walk over half an hour every day to play football with his local team or offer a cycle ride to a deaf and dumb friend who lived on his street.

It is also where he chose to spend several months on strike from Chelsea, happily going without pay and ignoring emails and letters demanding his return. He was single-minded in his determination to return to Atletico Madrid and he eventually did so in September 2017. The details of his spat with Conte – the abrupt text message from the manager that declared his time with Chelsea was at an end – are now well documented. 'It was clear,' Costa said. 'It was saying that he didn't count on me and wishing me the best for the future. Full stop.'

He accused Chelsea of treating him 'like a criminal' and refused to rule out legal action. He said he will always keep Conte's text message on his phone and claimed the Chelsea manager 'lacked charisma' in comparison to his former manager Mourinho. Costa also accused Conte of blocking his contract negotiations at Chelsea. This, of course, was one side of the story. Chelsea subsequently filtered details that Costa had, in fact, asked to leave the club before Conte's first season in charge. He was eventually persuaded to stay but in January, with contract talks stalling, interest came from the Chinese Super League. Chelsea even held a meeting in January, including Conte and the players, in which the club explained that Costa wanted to leave. In the end, he stayed, fired 20 goals on the way to the Premier League title and scored in the 2-1 FA Cup final defeat by Arsenal. From Wembley, he headed to Lagarto.

Yet in three seasons at the club, Costa spearheaded two title charges and, at his best, he would decimate Premier League defences. He was one of those players opposition fans claimed to loathe but secretly wished he were one of their own. Costa

The devastated streets of Guernica after the bombing of 26 April 1937 that left hundreds dead, and caused thousands to flee for their lives. *(Alamy)*

Basque refugees arrive in Southampton on 25 May, packed onto the *Habana* – with Emilio Aldecoa and Antonio Gallego among the children onboard. *(Getty Images)*

Nayim's long-distance shot for Real Zaragoza caught out David Seaman during the 1995 Cup Winners' Cup final. When he joined Spurs in 1988, he became the first Spaniard to make a real impact in the English league. *(PA)*

Roberto Martinez and Isidro Diaz celebrate winning the Third Division title in 1997. When they moved to the town in 1995, it was a rare leap for Spanish footballers to com to England – but that would soon change. *(PA)*

Los hermanos Neville close in to stop Jose Antonio Reyes on 24 October 2004, when he Invincibles were finally beaten and the young Spaniard came in for some tough reatment. *(Getty Images)*

Reyes had a brief moment in the sunlight, then Marcellino at Newcastle and Falkirk an signing Arnau Riera – the man who once captained Lionel Messi – were two for hom Britain's stadiums did not bring fresh glory. *(Getty Images)*

Lost in translation: Pepe Mel found it difficult to get his message across as manager of West Brom. *(PA)*

By contrast, Quique Sanchez Flores came from a privileged football background, but even that wasn't enough to keep him at Watford. *(Getty Images)*

Aitor Karanka's meticulous preparation helped him earn a draw at the Emirates, but a lack of goals at Middlesbrough saw him ousted. *(Getty Images)*

Rafa Benitez, seen here with Liverpool goalkeeper Pepe Reina, has been the most successful Spanish manager in England to date. *(Getty Images)*

…nchester City manager Pep Guardiola celebrates with assistant Manuel Estiarte after …omfortable 3–0 win over Arsenal in the Carabao Cup final in February 2017. He …uldn't have to wait much longer for more silverware. *(Getty Images)*

Standing on the back row, third from left, David De Gea is already a champion – but not yet a goalkeeper.

Juan Mata took his first steps towards glory as a young boy in Asturias.

Mata and De Gea are joined by fellow Spaniard Ander Herrera as the three Manchester United stars celebrate victory in the 2017 Europa League final.

(Getty Images)

is an antagonist and provocateur. He is mischievous and snide
on the field. He would stamp on opponents such as Liverpool
midfielder Emre Can. He would mercilessly wind up Arsenal
defender Gabriel Paulista. Norman Hunter, the legendary Leeds
centre back, admitted Costa is the one modern striker he would
love to go back in time and face.

But Costa is also a magnificent leader of the line and a pro-
lific scorer of goals. Alvaro Morata, the Spanish striker who
followed Costa, could hardly have been a more contrasting
individual. Costa has a hardened, battle-wearied physique with
the face of somebody many years beyond his true age. Morata
is a boyish, immaculately presented, dashingly handsome
madrileño, nurtured in middle-class suburbia and married to an
Italian glamour model. He is, of course, a superb forward in
his own right and he admirably embraced the task of replacing Costa. Morata had learned the trade the hard way himself,
training against Pepe and Sergio Ramos at Real Madrid and
dealing with Giorgio Chiellini, Leonardo Bonucci and Andrea
Barzagli slashing at his ankles in his time with Juventus. 'Kick,
kick, kick!' he grins.

At Chelsea, Costa was always going to leave a huge hole. He
was superb in Mourinho's title-winning season yet he was one
of many who faded away in a desperate third campaign that saw
the manager sacked by December. I expected Costa to be critical of Mourinho but instead he said: 'People really liked Jose.
We won a lot with him and everyone was happy. You win but
you have to win, win and win again. He has called me during
pre-season, direct to my phone. He called me to see how I am
as a person. He wished me good luck. There was really never a
problem between us.'

Former Chelsea colleagues also reflect that the pair had a
good relationship. Mourinho would rev up Costa's engine in
training and before games, ordering him to tear around the
field, provoke his opponents and win matches. When the tenor
of media coverage turned against Costa for his indiscretions, it

was Chelsea's communications department that felt the brunt of the striker's frustration rather than Mourinho, who cared little. Instead, Mourinho sensed a chance to further unify his squad with the 'us against the world' mentality. Above all, he was simply happy Costa was winning games for his team.

Mourinho's final season fell apart and Costa was dropped to the bench for some games. 'I can't explain it,' Azpilicueta says. 'It was the same coach and the same squad. It's complicated. From the start, things went wrong. Things unravelled very quickly. OK, in some games, it seemed luck was against us. But the dynamic became very negative and that played out in the results. I could not see a solution to the problem. I saw a manager and staff doing their absolute maximum to change the tide and get results but it just wasn't working. We couldn't get out of the rut.

'It's hard to pinpoint a moment when we knew it was gone. From the start, we drew our first home game against Swansea. Then we lost to Crystal Palace at home. It was a sequence of negative things, one after the other. We were hitting the post, having shots cleared off the line. We weren't accustomed to being in that situation. The truth is, we weren't even used to losing two games in a row so it was a new challenge psychologically. Football is ever more competitive in England. When you win, you know it is going to get harder the next season. Teams find it hard to defend the title. You have to adapt yourself but it is not easy.'

Chelsea and Costa recovered their mojo under Conte and it seems a shame that the relationship between manager and striker was so short-lived. The small Brazilian town provides an insight into Costa's single-minded personality. He is a man whose fuse can be ignited at the slightest provocation. In a small-sided match at school, he responded to a nutmeg by punching the player in the face. He has risked the wrath of employers before. Under Quique Flores at Atletico, he was late and overweight for pre-season. 'Blame my mum, she's far too good in the kitchen,' was his excuse for his rounder shape. In Conte, Costa met his match.

Costa is, those who know him insist, a man of principle. Yet he is also a man who grew up in Brazil, dabbled briefly with the country of his birth and then changed his nationality to play for Spain. His father, known as Zeinha, is the man who named his son after Diego Maradona, while Costa's elder brother is Jair, after Jairzinho, the Brazilian 1970 World Cup icon. Zeinha told the Bleacher Report: 'That's because Luiz Felipe Scolari just gave him ten minutes, so of course he was pissed off. Those few minutes, that wasn't enough to show his ability, so I don't blame him. You appreciate who appreciates you, and Spain gave him everything. The Brazil media here don't appreciate him; they never gave him any value.'

Yet there are more attractive traits to Costa's personality. He speaks with a level of candour that eludes most modern footballers. He has invested in local land in Lagarto and is providing a safe environment for young children to enjoy sport with his *Balón de Oro* social project. At Chelsea, despite it all, many players and support staff still smile broadly at the mention of Costa. He exasperated and enthused his contemporaries in equal measure. At the club's Cobham training ground, he took up a pastime that involved stealing the keys to the club's medical buggies on a daily basis and then dumping the vehicle in a ditch. He thought it was hilarious, as he did when he tried, together with accomplice Nemanja Matic, to enclose Eden Hazard in a cardboard box. On one occasion, he ransacked the physio's hotel room along with teammates Willian and Ramires.

There is a charming naivety about Costa. As an 18-year-old arriving in wintry Spain to sign for Atletico Madrid, he wore flowery beach shorts and flip-flops. The Spanish journalist Fran Guillen wrote a fascinating biography of the striker and some of the stories are Costa classics. At Albacete, the police turned up at Costa's home after his female neighbour complained about a loud social gathering as teammates got together for a barbecue.

On another occasion, the same neighbour complained to his club about a porn movie being on too loud. 'What's the matter? Don't you like making love?' Costa asked her. There is no shortage of entertaining anecdotes.

Yet Costa also retains a strong sense of self and sticks by his principles. He tells me a story about his time at Albacete. The club was embroiled in financial problems and the players received their pay cheque during a week when many support staff at the club went without their salary. Costa refused to train until everyone received his or her money. When he believes he or a friend has been wronged, he feels an obligation to stand firm. In the case of Conte, he felt mistreated and had to stand his ground. But he remains fond of Chelsea. When I joined him in his living room during Chelsea's 3-2 defeat to Burnley, he was up and down like a jack-in-the-box as his side pursued an equaliser. This is a man who retains man-of-the-match awards from games against Everton and Crystal Palace in his parents' home despite being almost 8,000km away from London.

'Here, come and look at this. Meet Ben!' Who's Ben? I ask. 'Big Ben, of course!' he says, fiddling with a little ornament of London's famous landmark. Costa, like Benitez, may be hugely misunderstood.

CHAPTER 9

Artists and Pragmatists

On a biting cold January evening in the Midlands, a vehicle is parked up on a side road adjacent to Aston Villa's Villa Park stadium. Sleet lines the pavements and streetlights flicker occasionally. Inside the car, a balding middle-aged man is jabbing in exasperated fashion at a satellite navigation system. The robotic voice giving out instructions repeats the order: 'Please make a U-turn.'

We've all been there. So, unfortunately, has Pepe Mel. 'On my first day at West Brom, they gave me a car,' he begins. 'It was a freezing night and pitch-black. We finished training and I left the training ground at 6pm. You head out of the training ground and travel through the Black Country. Anyway, I got lost. Very lost. The satnav they gave me was in English and this bloke from the machine is giving me instructions and I can't understand any of it! I was unable to redirect the machine, as I couldn't even read anything on it. I had to call up West Brom's media officer, who came and found me. So there I was, parked up on the side of the road for over an hour, and it was even worse because I'd managed to park up on a road that was only a hundred metres from Villa Park, the home of our big rivals!'

For Mel, it was the first of several false starts after being appointed as manager of West Brom at the beginning of January

2014. His tenure at the club lasted only five months and, in truth, English football barely scratched the surface of one of the more zany characters of Spanish sport. He is an entertaining raconteur, both in person and in his prose. Intoxicated by the novels of Dan Brown, Mel's debut work *El Mentiroso* (*The Liar*) was published to both critical and commercial acclaim in 2011. *El Camino al más allá* (*The Road to the Beyond*) followed before Mel ventured into the realm of children's literature more recently. 'Escapism,' he smiles.

In the brittle and insecure world of football management, where social media amplifies every tactical misjudgement and 24-hour news channels offer up odds on the next managerial sacking, a distraction is required. Some managers prefer the temptations of Silicon Valley, luxury gadgets and zooming sports cars. For Mel, writing is the soothing balm that diverts attention from the raging fires. I suggest it may even be a coping mechanism. 'Certainly, writing is a way of escaping the pressures of football. I am not in work right now and therefore my writing is terrible. Yet when I'm coaching and stressed, that's when the adrenaline flows and the words fall onto the page beautifully. It may not be a surprise to learn I wrote a lot at West Brom!'

El Mentiroso is a riveting read, as protagonist Cail Lograft uncovers rare archaeological finds from ancient Egypt before embarking on a worldwide adventure, pursued by Middle Eastern mafias and implicating the Catholic Church. 'I am drawn by archaeology, mystery and fantasy,' he grins. 'That first one brings those three things together. The third book, which I've recently published, is a children's book. It's harder, a different way of thinking. Do we really understand the audience? How do I make it accessible for children? I felt the best way was to return to my own childhood, and it's actually semi-autobiographical, capturing the thoughts, feelings and experiences of a young boy breaking into football.'

He sees similarities between management and writing, in

the series of instincts and the endless tweaks and adjustments. 'Deciding tactics or deciding the words on the page. You are always asking: Is it better like this? Or like that?'

At West Brom, there was no shortage of self-assessment for Mel. He had been a left-field and courageous choice to replace the underperforming Steve Clarke. The club were 14th in the Premier League and only four points above the relegation zone when Mel arrived. Sporting and technical director Richard Garlick said upon his appointment: 'Pepe was a strong contender from the outset due to his impressive achievements and has emerged as our number one candidate. He is a forward-thinking coach whose teams are renowned for playing an attractive and positive style of football.'

Mel's mandate was clear: to revolutionise the club's identity and instil a progressive and sophisticated style of football into the team. The success of the Spanish international team had encouraged clubs to follow the curve of the latest trend. For a club whose previous managers had been Clarke and Roy Hodgson, and whose subsequent coaches have been Alan Irvine, Tony Pulis and Alan Pardew, it seemed rather out of character. Yet West Brom boasts traditions of flamboyance and attacking flair. Bryan Robson, the former England and Manchester United midfielder, managed the club for two years, while the Argentine wizard Osvaldo Ardiles had coached the Midlands side during the 1992–93 season. West Brom followers hark back to Vic Buckingham's free-flowing side of the 1950s and the pioneering, buccaneering 1980s team starring Laurie Cunningham and Cyrille Regis. Mel suspects these traditions guided the club's thinking when they appointed him.

Mel had earned a glowing reputation at Real Betis in Spain. A former Betis striker and a graduate of the Real Madrid academy, he had returned to lead the club to promotion into La Liga and then rode the crest of a wave as the club confounded the realities of crippling debt to finish seventh in 2012–13 and qualify for the Europa League. When he was sacked in December 2013, with the club rooted to the bottom of the table and the team's form dreadful, supporters still came to his defence. The Betis ultras threw stones at the windows of the building where Mel was dismissed. The affection was mutual. Mel once told reporters that he would rather his daughter 'came home and told me she was pregnant' than see Real Betis relegated.

'I had a very successful time at Real Betis. Then things went less well and the sack came. Curiously, my first contact with West Brom was over Skype. We had a video conference with Garlick, the director, and then organised a meeting in London. West Brom wanted to change their style of play. It was – or is – a very typical English club. They asked me to change their whole way of thinking. Two weeks later, we met in London and decided to take the adventure on together. The first Skype meeting was odd, because I didn't speak any English. Garlick had Dave McDonough next to him. He speaks Spanish really well and he was also an assistant to Rafa Benitez at Liverpool and Valencia. It was exciting for me, a new adventure but with the handicap that I could barely speak English.'

Some characters in this book exaggerate their English language deficiencies. Mel does not. Bizarrely, the club did not recruit Mel's backroom staff and the situation worsened when McDonough exited the club shortly after the Spaniard arrived. 'I don't know why he left. But after that, nobody at the club spoke Spanish except for David Gomez, who came in as a fitness coach. I didn't speak English. Naturally, it affected my confidence. Everyone at the training ground seemed lovely and wore a smile but it was almost impossible to have a conversation that lasted even a minute.'

Out on the training ground, the language barrier bred a culture of insecurity and mistrust. Mel inherited Keith Downing and Dean Kiely as his assistants and, as the team's form dipped, he was not entirely sure whether everyone was on board. 'My biggest mistake was obviously my inability to make myself understood to the players. It was naive, looking back. We've perhaps seen a similar case with Gary Neville's difficulties at Valencia. I had to spend all day trying to explain things to the assistant Keith Downing. He was on the field transmitting my orders. That's how we did it.

'The most important thing on a technical staff is that every component thinks the same way as the head coach. For me, it was difficult because I remember for example I was desperate to get the boys to play out from the back with confidence. Not everyone agreed. Some were saying, "If Ben Foster has a big kick and can get it straight up to Victor Anichebe, why do we need to waste time playing out?" It was the way West Brom played. Fine, I respect that, but they'd brought me in under an instruction to change things. If you want to play like that, get Tony Pulis in! To be fair, they did in the end. The lesson for me is that signing a Spanish coach without a Spanish coaching staff is not the brightest idea if you want to change the mentality or way of playing.'

Mel did try to correct his deficiencies. 'I had one English teacher paid for by West Brom and one paid for by myself. I started with football vocab: throw-in, corner, man-on, set-piece words. I always like to have meetings with senior players and I wanted to do that with lads like Gareth McAuley and James Morrison. I wanted to motivate the team but it was impossible. I always needed someone holding my hand. There was a week where Stephane Sessegnon needed me with something and I needed my female Spanish teacher there to translate because I couldn't say what I was thinking. The important thing for me was that when we finished the season, West Brom stayed up. I remember especially a game at Swansea where I changed the system; we played with five at the back and that week was important to keep us up.'

Mel, however, was scarred by the experience. He wanted to impose his romantic view of football but, instead, he encountered obstruction at every turn. Idealism gave way to pragmatism after players raised concerns. Once the West Brom players decided that Mel was leading them off the edge of a cliff, he was doomed. After failing to win his first eight Premier League games, the controversial midfielder Joey Barton took to Twitter. Barton wrote: 'Remember, for every Mauricio Pochettino, there's a Pepe Mel.' By the spring of 2014, the impressive Pochettino had guided a youthful Southampton team into eighth place in the Premier League, before joining Tottenham, where his reputation continues to be enhanced as one of the continent's most promising managers.

Yet Barton perhaps failed to realise the extent of Pochettino's own dependency on Mel. 'Pochettino is Argentine but he's one of my pupils,' Mel says. 'I trained him in the tactics module at the Spanish FA, along with others such as Aitor Karanka and Fernando Hierro. Pochettino has very clear ideas and transmits these very clearly. When he arrived at Southampton, he was in trouble because he couldn't speak English. I remember he told me how worried he was. However, he had my friend and his assistant Jesus Perez with him, who speaks fantastically and thinks the same way. I do think that this was the only difference between the experience of Pochettino at Southampton and myself at West Brom.'

Ultimately, a malevolent cocktail of his own linguistic shortcomings and dressing-room scepticism saw him off. 'It was very difficult with the players. They clearly had doubts. We played Aston Villa at Villa Park and we were playing 4-3-3 and trying to keep the ball and press fast and early. We went 2-0 up but the moment it all changed was the injury to Nicolas Anelka, and then he was suspended for the "quenelle" salute he had shown in a game before I arrived. We lost the game 4-3 against Villa and the footballers stopped believing in the project. They weren't used to what I was asking them to do and this was the game that damaged it all. They couldn't see it and we decided to give in to the players' wishes.

'It was sad because I like my teams to play with freedom and a smile on their face. My teams should be happy. It was difficult to make this happen at West Brom because the players have to believe for this to happen. It was very hard to sacrifice my beliefs. You need to be able to talk to players, to smell and feel the football, and my messages were second-hand. Even then, I don't know if my message was transmitted how I wanted in a positive way.

'In truth, I knew from the moment I arrived it wasn't working. Internally, West Brom didn't really want to change things. I didn't fit into the vision of football the players had. That is not to say England does not possess technically gifted footballers. I believe sincerely that English football has produced magnificent footballers and, in recent years, I have spoken with Real Madrid, Barcelona, Valencia, anyone who will listen in Spain and underlined the potential of Saido Berahino. I had him as he was coming through and he really could have been anything he wanted to be. Every week he doesn't improve, it's a blow to English football. He played every game under me. He is a special kid, but his family situation was hard; his friendship circle wasn't great.'

For all parties, hindsight suggests mistakes were made. West Brom's intentions were progressive and Mel's ambition was commendable. Mel led the club on a leap from insularity but the change was too sharp, too radical and too unnerving to succeed. It is unjust to paint Mel's vision as light and the West Brom of Tony Pulis as darkness. The former teetered on the brink of Premier League oblivion, while the latter secured a top-half finish in the 2016–17 season. In 2013–14, West Brom stayed up with a couple of games to spare but Mel's future was clear.

'Before the final two games against Stoke and Sunderland, we had a meeting with Richard Garlick and chairman Jeremy Peace, and we decided it was best to part. We never had discussions about summer transfer targets. It was a very clear situation. I would like English football to know the real Pepe Mel. I am always trying to improve. I had offers from Dubai that I turned down because I wanted to prepare better for an opportunity in England. Last summer, Nottingham Forest were interested and also Aston Villa looked very closely before recruiting Steve Bruce. Bruce was very much first choice. When Quique Sanchez Flores was at Watford, he let me come in for ten days and observe everything. It gave me the smell for English football again. I love my job. It's a passion for me and I want to show I have made improvements.'

'Quique, would you like to pick that name up off the floor?' Quique Sanchez Flores smiles mischievously, coming alive as he reels off a list of his greatest influences. 'Where do I start?' he grins. 'My father, Isidro, who played for Real Madrid is the first. Then my godfather, Alfredo Di Stefano, he was like my second father and one of my dad's best friends. I had a fantastic relationship with the Portuguese legend Eusebio.'

A cynic might conclude that Flores is a merciless name-dropper but he has, in fact, simply enjoyed a quite remarkable existence. He is magnificent and charming company, full of anecdotes, inspired by artistic influences and intoxicated by a thirst for knowledge. His family life is sport and theatre, and, out on the field, his two passions converge. His father played in the Real Madrid teams of Di Stefano and Ferenc Puskas, his mother Carmen and his aunt Lola were celebrated stars of the stage and cinema in Spain. In the small town of Jerez de la Frontera, Lola has her own statue in one of the squares, posing gracefully as a flamenco dancer. His uncle Antonio Gonzalez is a renowned guitarist on the Catalan rumba scene. Cousin Rosario is a feted singer and actor, starring in a Pedro Almodovar film.

I first met Flores at his home in the Madrid suburb of Alcorcon. It was a Sunday morning, during the 2014–15 season, and he opened the door wearing his slippers; just out of the shower, he ran his hand through that jet-black hair of his. For box-set connoisseurs, the likeness to Hugh Laurie in *House* is unnerving. At the time, he was out of work, having brought an end to a spell managing in the Middle East. I had visited him to discuss the remarkable development of David De Gea, the Manchester United goalkeeper who had emerged in the Atletico Madrid first team under Flores' guidance.

Yet it became a wide-ranging discussion. Flores had been learning English, readying himself for an opportunity in the Premier League. He studied English football forensically, watching games back to back in his living room and asking Jose Mourinho for tips to break into the Premier League. During a lunch in the Middle East following a coaching seminar, the Portuguese urged the Spaniard to come to England and make his name in what he believes to be the world's most compelling league. When he was Real Madrid manager, he pulled a similar trick on Mauricio Pochettino. Mourinho invited Pochettino, who at the time was the head coach at Espanyol, to attend Madrid's Champions League victory over Ajax in 2012. Mourinho took Pochettino into the team's dressing room after the game and it was there that he told the Argentine that he must try his luck in England.

Flores, for his part, had been a contender for the West Brom job as the Midlands club pursued a continental coach before settling upon Pepe Mel. His opportunity came, in unexpected fashion, at Watford. The Hertfordshire side had been promoted under the management of Slavisa Jokanovic, but the two parties were unable to agree a new deal. Jokanovic claims that Watford offered him a salary that was worth half of what the lowest-paid Premier League manager was earning at the time. A move for Flores was put into place. Scepticism greeted the appointment.

Watford went through four managers by the October of the previous season, as Beppe Sannino fell foul of the owners, Oscar Garcia fell ill, Billy McKinlay lasted only eight days, and then Jokanovic arrived and led the club into the Premier League. In the *Sunday Times*, the columnist Rod Liddle wrote: 'The question is: will Sanchez Flores still be manager by the time you read this? You have to doubt it. Well, I mean, you don't have to, because by now you'll know. But it wouldn't surprise me terribly much if he was the first Premier League manager to bite the dust, and did so before the final Test gets under way, or maybe even before Root and Broad et al have recovered from their hangovers.'

Yet Flores had arrived primed and ready to make an impact. He retained Dean Austin, the former Tottenham Hotspur defender, as part of the coaching staff, who provided continuity and a local voice. 'It was Quique's decision to keep me on,' Austin says. 'The owner gave me a good reference to Quique and he rang around some people. He knew some people I'd worked with before. I spoke to him when he came in to check he wanted me. I had been there with Slavisa and I remain life-long friends with both him and Quique.

'It was actually quite interesting watching as an ex-player and as a coach to observe Quique during the first three days. We didn't go out on grass for two days. There was testing but there was no big meeting. He was working away in the office, having a walk around, introducing himself. We were all sat there thinking, "Is he going to have a meeting? What's happening?" Then, on the Wednesday afternoon, everyone congregated in the gym, medical staff, players, everyone. This guy started speaking and all the players sat there and, as he was talking, you could see the players' ears prick up. It was one of those where they said, "He is the real deal." He outlined his organisation, what he expected: to play with a smile, to have respect for each other and fans, all the little details that players want. We had someone proper.'

In truth, it should not have come as a surprise. Flores had a fine playing career of his own, including a decade at Valencia and some time at Real Madrid, where he lifted the La Liga title in a team featuring Raul, Fernando Hierro, Fernando Redondo and Michael Laudrup.

Moreover, he has been able to lean on some of the sport's

most iconic individuals for guidance. 'I spoke with Di Stefano very often. When I was very young, I was quite daunted by him but we became good friends. He was my coach at Valencia and he was honorary president at Real Madrid. When he was my coach, I put big pressure on myself. I thought people would say that I'm only playing because Di Stefano is my godfather. He was demanding with me and my own levels of self-determination were higher. I played out of my skin and scored nine goals from defence that season he coached me. Alfredo was saying, "What is going on? Now you are scoring goals?"

'I loved spending time with Eusebio. When I was managing Benfica, he travelled with us to every game. We would have a snack before the game and I would bombard him with questions, probably too many. He is an amazing person, such a wealth of knowledge about the game. I asked him, "Eusebio, who is the best player for you of all time?" He replied: "I don't have any doubts. Alfredo Di Stefano." My father says the same. Maybe they are right. I was too young to see him play live; I can only read reports and study old videos. My father, who was his teammate for five years, always told me that Alfredo had a speed of thought that separated him from the rest. He could defend, attack, lead, create and score. A complete player.'

As a coach, Flores has managed some of the continent's most gifted talents, including Juan Mata and David Silva at Valencia and David De Gea and Sergio Aguero at Atletico Madrid. He took Valencia to a Champions League quarter-final and won the Europa League and Super Cup with Atleti. His character was nurtured in childhood. He grew up in the 1960s, in a family of thespians. 'Aunt Lola – "Lola of Spain", they called her – had these Christmas parties. As the youngest, I had to dance and sing in front of everyone. It was typical Spanish flamenco dancing – all very embarrassing for me. I was only eight years old, and for four years on the trot it was the same. When I was older, I could say, "OK, please let's stop this now!"

'If anything, I think this made me more timid and shy as a

child, very much so. Over the last few years, I have seen the shows like *Strictly Come Dancing* but I could never go on that. I have responsibilities in my life to not make myself look ridiculous. My kids would be begging me not to do that. They'd be ganging up on me and saying, "Dad, please!"'

His mother Carmen had designs for little Quique to follow the showbusiness path. Flores, however, set his heart on a more introverted art form. 'Mum told me that I had a sweet and beautiful singing voice. But I never wanted to do that. When I was younger, I actually wanted to study as a journalist. I love all sports and what better job than talking and writing about sports. Over the last few years, while I was not working as a coach, I had a media career. I wrote more than a thousand articles over five years for *El Mundo, El País, Marca, AS, Diari Valencia*.

'I started to read a huge amount every day. From a literary point of view, I loved the South American writer Gabriel Garcia Marquez. My biggest inspiration as a coach is Phil Jackson, a basketball coach. I have read his books, *Eleven Rings* and *Sacred Hoops*. It reminds me – I must buy Sir Alex Ferguson's new book. Everybody should be rushing to the shop to buy this kind of book. If you want to read about how to lead a group, these guys know better than anyone. I started writing my own book two years ago but my story keeps changing! I prefer to talk about my life as a teenager, 30 years ago as a player, 40 years ago when I started playing with my father on the streets. I never wrote a diary but my experiences are fresh in my mind.'

Before heading to England, he had taken counsel from his old friend Mourinho. 'He said, "Quique, the Premier League is paradise for managers. It is where we all we want to be." Now I understand what he means. It's the atmosphere, the feeling in the stadiums; it's the passions of the players, how they crash into one another, fight until the end, how the referees understand the game. As a coach, it is simply a dream.'

For the first few months at Watford, Flores belied all expectations. If it had not been for Leicester City's remarkable title push, Flores would have received greater acclaim. After 17 games, Watford were on a run of six wins in eight games, and seventh in the Premier League after a 3-0 thumping of Jurgen Klopp's Liverpool. Flores had a disarming charm; a likeability that integrated him rapidly into London life. Gary Lineker greeted him in Spanish on *Match of the Day*, his teenage son Quique began to play in the Watford academy, and Flores set up a seven-a-side team with the club's staff that competed every week against local sides.

In his first press conference at the club, he had spoken of a long-term ambition to create a legacy at Watford, comparing the club's size and resources to Villarreal, an upwardly mobile side that also wears a yellow kit. He spoke excitedly about a phone call from Watford's celebrity fan, Elton John. 'He is an idol. Oh my God – "Sorry Seems to Be the Hardest Word" – I don't know how many versions I have heard of this. He did a rendition with Ray Charles that was just amazing. I have not been to a concert but I would love to. I read about the history of the club and saw he was president and I was like, "Wow!" I was walking in London with the kids and I answer the phone and it's Elton John wishing me good luck. Amazing!'

He set up home in Hampstead Heath, going for long runs in one of London's more picturesque areas. There is certainly evidence that Flores perceived it to be a long-term project. He talks with pride about his four teenage children, reflecting that it is as important to be remembered as a 'good father' as it is a 'good coach'. His ex-wife Patricia and the kids joined him in England's capital, the children attending local schools and cheering on their dad's team at Vicarage Road. After a last-gasp 2-1 defeat at home to Tottenham, his son Paulo was in tears in the players' lounge. The children's English was already excellent after attending British schools in both the UAE and Madrid.

'The boys love it. They enjoy mixing with the players; they love to know the ins and outs of the squad, who I'm signing. They drive me mad in the lead-up to a game. They want to know the line-up before the players! They come home and say, "It's Champions League tonight – we have to watch it together." They ask questions throughout the game, they are desperate to learn more.'

Flores concedes that he is wary of the impact on his children. 'I have been sacked once, by Valencia. I learned nothing from it really because it was not fair. We were in fourth position. We had 18 points from nine games, we were in the Champions League. We were just behind Real Madrid. It was ridiculous. I could not take any conclusion from it. I went home thinking: "What is happening with football? It is crazy." You feel ridiculous. I was trying to work out what I did wrong. It is difficult for your children, too, when they go to school and their dad has lost his job. I have to bear that in mind. My kids now are later into their teenage years and of course people at school know everything.'

Flores sees the connection between sport and art, the theatre and the performer, but, unlike Mel, he has a greater inclination towards pragmatism. Self-preservation matters, too.

'One of my reference points will always be the Argentine world champions of 1978. Then I loved the amazing Liverpool team in the 1970s and 1980s, with John Barnes raiding the wings. Spanish coaches are preparing to come to England. It is very important to adapt. You must respect where you are working and you have to open the mind to new ideas. I maintain my organisation of the team because the system is important. Whether you play, 4-2-3-1 or 4-3-3, football is in the transition. I am thinking as much about what happens when we have the ball as when we lose the ball. This is very important. I have always admired Rafa Benitez's defensive work and wanted to organise my Benfica, Atletico and Valencia teams in this way.

'Now the dynamic is a little bit different. Guardiola has altered the narrative around Spanish football but you have to be sensible with the players you have. The formula at Watford is the same that I have used at other teams over the years. We move as a block when we defend and attack, to restrict the space for the opposition. We are coming up against amazing players. We have to work incredibly hard and be hugely organised. It is the start of the idea and, little by little, we will improve and add more flair.

'I don't want it to be boring for the players. During the week, I will create a specific task and we will work hard on that for the defensive side of the game. For me, the players have to enjoy the session and be happy. It's not a case of putting one bib there, another there and working like robots. I want them to work hard but smile. They are footballers. It's a great job. Players should go onto the pitch happy and with a smile.'

At Watford, however, concerns developed as the season evolved. Flores was not naive to the realities of life under Watford's more continental approach to hiring and firing head coaches. He said the right things early on but this was also his eighth appointment in 11 years. Yet for all that, Flores had also ensured Watford would play consecutive seasons in the top flight of English football for the first time since 1987-88. His reputation in England was enhanced, underlined by Stoke City's attempt to prise him away from Espanyol in January 2017. Stoke sent an entourage out to Barcelona, offered a five-year deal and promised a hefty salary to Flores, but the coach eventually stayed loyal to the Spanish side. At Watford, his team did not flirt with relegation at any stage and the club reached the semi-finals of the FA Cup, where they lost 2-1 to Crystal Palace at Wembley. In the quarter-finals, amid a slump in the Premier League, Watford went away to Arsenal and pulled off a stunning 2-1 victory.

'Our preparation was meticulous,' Dean Austin says. 'Arsenal dominated for the first half-hour, we were low on confidence. If they had scored early, they could have hit us for a few. Yet we then had a couple of counters just before half-time and we came in thinking we have half a chance. Hold on, we are in this, we have a real chance. Quique changed things tactically, closing down certain spaces, noticing that a lot of Arsenal's stuff comes through the same couple of players. Quique's best quality is identifying the lock-picker in a team and coming up with a plan to eliminate that player's influence in a game. It's about blocking the lines, not man-marking.'

Yet Watford became concerned by statistical trends and curves, noting that the team took 29 points from the first 19 games (an average of 1.52 points per game), compared with 16 points from the final 19 games (an average of 0.84 points per game). The team also conceded 20 goals in the first 19 games, compared with 30 in the second half of the campaign. Some observers within the club felt that training-ground discipline had slipped and alarm bells began to flash.

Others felt he had overindulged in the London nightlife. In the *Daily Telegraph*, Sam Wallace made a compelling case: 'Consider the warning in the fall of Newcastle United and the rise of Leicester City over the last two seasons. In 2014–2015, Newcastle gathered 26 points from their first 19 games last season at a rate of 1.36 per match. In the second half of that season they accumulated half that, 13, at the rate of 0.68 per match and avoided relegation by three points. They have carried that form into this season and are currently 19th and one point from safety. Conversely, last season Leicester City took 13 points (0.68 per game) from the first half of last season and then 28 (1.47 per game) in the second half. Their rise this season has been astonishing but there is a lesson there that is not lost on Watford: if you finish the season a certain way, there is a good chance you will start the next season the same, unless radical change is made.'

Flores first caught wind of trouble as the spring set in. He had been alerted to some whispers. Assistant Austin explains: 'I honestly thought, and felt up until the end of February, he still felt he could be here a period of time. Then things were maybe going on behind the scenes, he sussed it out and he's a clever man. I always refer to football players in three groups: the ones who love the manager, good lads, good players, happy because they are playing. One-third who waver either way, yeah they're happy, they're in or out. Then you have the other third, maybe not too happy, down on their luck, think the manager should be picking them, they want him out and don't give a monkey's.

'You will talk about that scenario at every single football club where a manager is under pressure. Let's not beat around the bush here. Forget about Quique as a manager, he's a top person. Such is the class of this man and how he carried himself and been around it so long, this was football and he was happy with the decision. It was the right thing for him and right for him at the time. He did only good things for Watford.'

Juande Ramos is a man in the headlines. It is mid-December 2015 and Chelsea have sacked Jose Mourinho. A date has been in the diary for some time for this interview but, as I board a flight to Alicante, *The Times* is reporting that Ramos is in serious contention for a return to the Premier League. Chelsea require a fire-fighter to extinguish the divisions and loathing that have manifested during Jose Mourinho's rancorous final few months at Stamford Bridge. Ramos fulfilled a similar role at Real Madrid in the 2008-09 season, winning 16 La Liga matches and drawing one after replacing Bernd Schuster midway through the season. Now he is a candidate at Stamford Bridge, along with Guus Hiddink.

'We aren't here to talk about Chelsea,' he says, before we've even taken our seats at the table of a tapas bar. 'But look, maybe you can take something away from the fact I'm sat here sharing *patatas bravas* with you . . .'

Still, Ramos continues to hint and tease during the interview. He refuses to allow a photographer friend of mine to join us in case he is snapped. Ultimately, Chelsea plumped for Guus Hiddink to stem the tide, but it was remarkable in itself that Ramos came under consideration. Surely not this Juande Ramos, the Juande Ramos who stuttered and spluttered his way through one year at Tottenham Hotspur?

Ramos had arrived as one of the hottest properties in European football. At Sevilla, he won five consecutive cup finals. In May 2006, the Spanish club defeated Middlesbrough 4-0 in the UEFA Cup final. He repeated the achievement the following year, on penalties against Spanish rivals Espanyol. There was a European Super Cup success in August 2006, as he oversaw a 3-0 demolition of a Barcelona team featuring Ronaldinho, Lionel Messi, Xavi Hernandez and Deco. Add to that, in 2007, a Copa del Rey victory over Getafe and a 6-3 aggregate Spanish Super Cup triumph over Real Madrid and it was quite the set.

So when he arrived at White Hart Lane, with the club 18th in the Premier League and only seven points on the board from the first 11 top-flight games, expectations were high. He was flown into London by private jet, a far cry from the London Underground tube ride that the Swiss coach Christian Gross had taken a decade earlier from Heathrow to White Hart Lane.

Ramos says: 'There had been some contact from Tottenham previously and then the second approach came in and I decided to go for it. I'd been obsessed with English football for many years before arriving at Spurs. I knew very well why I liked to watch the games, but I wondered whether I would be successful as a coach in England.'

Immediately, he sensed a need for change. He was caricatured as a disciplinarian and was unimpressed by the absence of nutritional awareness in English football. A couple of months into Ramos' tenure at the club, Manuel Alvarez, the new fitness coach, delivered a scathing assessment on Spanish radio: 'When we arrived we realised the team was carrying excess baggage. I made a comparison with the Seville team that we had been working with, bearing in mind the size of the players, and the team was one hundred kilos overweight. So I immediately talked to our nutritionist, Antonio Escribano, and set the wheels in motion. The players have now lost between 40 and 50 kilos. Getting the rest off is the most difficult part but we have also turned a lot of fat into muscle. The truth is, the first buffet I saw, I photographed it because it was very interesting: sauces over everything, cakes, chocolate muffins, a box full of sweets. We tried to put things right.'

Ramos smiles when I remind him of the *Independent*'s head-line: 'Who ate all the paellas?' But the grin soon turns to a frown. 'I have to say it surprised me a lot that there was no real diet or regime for the players. It was a total shock. The impact on me was huge. I tried my best to make changes. The way I see it is clear. Players are being paid a fortune, fans pay to watch them, and the least they can do is be in the right shape to perform their best. It's not asking much, is it? People say I'm severe but all I did was try to implement professionalism in the physical side to improve the performance on the field. To their credit, the club never disagreed. They let me bring in people I wanted and make the changes I wanted. Sweets, cakes and whatever else were out. The improvement was clear straight away.'

That is not to say there was no resistance. 'Players were used to their treats and their way of doing things. Nobody had ever imposed rules upon them. When someone comes strolling in and says, "You must do x, y, z", obviously there is resistance and they don't like it one little bit. I felt a bit of rejection but I do think deep down those boys knew I was right.'

Ramos' methods provided an upturn in form. Players sup-ported their manager publicly. Jonathan Woodgate, the English centre back, said: 'The manager has won silverware, he looks the part and he knows what he's doing – he's a proper manager.'

Ramos sold striker Jermain Defoe to Portsmouth, but in an interview with *The Times* in 2017, the forward underlined the coach's forward thinking. 'Ramos was probably the reason I left Tottenham, but there were certain things, like how he got the team to counterattack with intensity. He didn't want too many passes. He said that when counterattacking "within three passes I want you to finish the action, either a cross or a finish or I'll stop the session". If you watch Chelsea now, they counterattack with one, two, three, four passes and the fifth [touch] is a shot at goal. He had that sort of quick intensity like Liverpool [under Jurgen Klopp].'

Within four months of taking over, Ramos won a sixth consecutive final, after defeating Chelsea 2-1 in the Carling Cup final at Wembley through goals by Dimitar Berbatov and Woodgate. It was the club's first trophy since 1999. A feature interview by the Spanish newspaper *El Mundo* makes for surreal retrospective reading, highlighting the flip-flop nature of the sport. In the piece, journalist Elena Pita joins Ramos for a day in north London shortly after the Wembley triumph. She writes: 'We walk into a pub, midway through the afternoon, and he is immediately inundated: photographs, autographs, hugs and kisses. A hero in Great Britain.' Ramos was idolised around the North Circular and cherished in the small town of his birth, Pedro Muñoz, some 150km south of Madrid, where the local authorities christened the municipal stadium in Ramos' name.

Ramos had made remarkable progress as a coach. A crippling knee injury undermined his playing career at the age of 28, bringing down the curtain on a modest existence as a midfielder for teams such as Elche and Alicante. He then managed ten different teams between 1990 and 2005, beginning in the third division of Spanish football with teams such as Ilicitano and Alcoyano, before working in the youth set-up at Barcelona, and then managing La Liga sides such as Real Betis, Espanyol and Sevilla.

'The first teams I coached were always fighting in the bottom half of the table. The challenge was tough. Every result felt terminal because there was such a sacking culture in Spain. I suffered a lot and worked crazy hours to move teams forwards. It was the best possible preparation for when I was then coaching bigger teams. To work as Barcelona's B-team coach was an education. I gave Carles Puyol his debut and had Xavi in midfield. I was working with young kids and the big distinction there is that the results don't really matter. It's all about the development of the players. We produced footballers fit for the elite of the game. The result was secondary. The principles of my coaching remained the same. I've always wanted to be very direct and very straight up with the clubs and players I've managed. Honour, dignity, pride: they are the values that guided my career.'

These characteristics yielded results at Tottenham, yet within six months of the cup triumph, divorce proceedings were underway. The second season began terribly, as Tottenham made their worst start to a campaign since before the First World War. Ramos attributes the traumatic slump to two key decisions: the sale of strikers Robbie Keane and Dimitar Berbatov, who had each scored 23 goals the previous season. His verdict on the club's chairman Daniel Levy makes for enlightening reading.

'Levy is a magnificent businessman,' Ramos says, with a shrug. 'He is excellent at bringing in income. He oversees huge sales. He is a good negotiator. He signs good players and then he sells them. With me, it was Berbatov and Keane. I signed Luka Modric in my first summer with the club and then they sold him to Real Madrid. It was the same with Gareth Bale. If you always sell your best players, you are never going to get a side capable of winning the Premier League, against Manchester City and Chelsea. Tottenham is a wonderful club and I was very proud to work there, but I always felt it was a club that thought far more about economics than sporting success.

'With regard to me, I just thought it odd. You bring in a coach who has a track record of winning European titles, and I had the dream of developing a team capable of competing for the top four and winning titles. I realised very quickly that it is an enormous club, but the primary work of the board was to generate funds for the shareholders and balance sheet. Keane and Berbatov had scored nearly 50 goals between them the season before. A team that loses their two best players and signs Darren

Bent, who had hardly played the year before, is always going to find it difficult.

'In the winter, once I left and Harry Redknapp arrived, they had to spend £50m and sign five or six players to sort out the mess. They knew the team needed major work. The biggest problem was Berbatov, who we sold at the end of the window. It was really typical Tottenham. Then I was told, "We don't have the time to sign great players." Fraizer Campbell came on loan from Manchester United as part of the deal but he was not ready for the Premier League. He was an 18-year-old kid. I think that is the reality and truth of my sacking at Tottenham.'

Certainly, Ramos felt personally hurt by Berbatov's departure. The Bulgarian forward told *The Times* in 2017: 'When I left, Ramos said, "Berba, when you go the beautiful football will go with you. I was like, fucking hell. Sitting there, really uncomfortable, don't know what to say. I said, "Thanks boss." It was funny, no one saw, it was between us. It was a great compliment to me. This is what I wanted to do in my career, just play beautiful football, entertain the people who watch.'

Ramos had requested stellar names in the event that Tottenham decided to sell their two main forwards. He did not always see eye to eye with sporting director Damien Comolli, who oversaw Spurs' transfer dealings. 'David Villa was the footballer that I asked the club to sign if we sold the strikers. He was in Spain with Valencia, before signing for Barcelona. There was a clause that we could have triggered. We also spoke about Samuel Eto'o. When you think about reinforcing the team, you give options. I was able to give suggestions but ultimately the club made the decisions.'

Instead, the Russian forward Roman Pavlyuchenko arrived at the end of the transfer window. 'Yes,' Ramos concedes. 'He came but he didn't know the language, the culture, he didn't know anything. Pavlyuchenko needed at least a month to six weeks at best to grasp the situation.'

Perhaps unsurprisingly, Comolli's recollections are rather

different. In an interview with the *Daily Mail*, the Frenchman said: 'One thing that worried me straight away after we appointed him from Sevilla was something their sporting director Monchi told me. He said that the coach from their reserve team was probably better than Ramos and that we'd soon find out he's not the reason for the club's success.

'We made it clear to him we couldn't afford to buy stars, we wanted to make them. We couldn't compete with Chelsea or Manchester United like that. He said, "No problem, I'm good at that." He mentioned he was the coach of Barcelona B. Then as soon as he came in, he said, "I want Samuel Eto'o and David Villa." He wasn't interested in young players at all.

'Eto'o was already on four times what our biggest earner was on and his agent said he wanted more. It was impossible with Villa as well. Tottenham just couldn't sign players like that. It started to become a nightmare. Training died, the relationship with players was gone, there was no dialogue with them.'

Ramos encountered problems with the players he did manage to sign. In July 2008, he recruited a 23-year-old David Bentley from Blackburn Rovers for over £15m. Bentley is one of the sport's more peculiar characters. At Blackburn, he drove into the training ground every day in a baby blue Ford Mustang, inspired by Steve McQueen's movie *Bullitt* and, along with Jimmy Bullard, referred to England manager Fabio Capello as Postman Pat. Yet he had emerged through Arsenal's academy, captained England's Under-18 side and was considered to be one of the nation's brightest hopes.

Ramos, however, was immediately disappointed. 'The club made a huge investment and there was a perception that he therefore had to start every game,' Ramos explains. 'I didn't agree – because there were players who worked harder. Simple. As far as I was concerned, if a player wasn't in the right condition physically, he wouldn't be near my teamsheet. It was a shock to me. He was a £17m investment. I train the players and I told the club's hierarchy I didn't believe he was in the right shape.'

Bentley's career did not recover and, at the age of 29, he retired. In a subsequent interview with *FourFourTwo* magazine, Bentley said: 'It was such a strange time. I joined him there, thinking he'd be another [Arsene] Wenger, but it was a nightmare. I was so excited to be there and it all went wrong. All my mates are Spurs fans and they were like kids, so excited that I was going to be playing for their team. I'm not sure I ever got over that bad start. I wanted to be part of something great at Tottenham, but it wasn't happening.'

Ramos is irritated by perceptions in England. It is clear that he endured difficulties without a firm grasp of the language and at times resembled a conductor without a baton, as his assistant, the former Tottenham midfielder Gus Poyet, often passed on instructions. He bristles: 'Within four months of me arriving, we'd won a title. Spurs hadn't won a title for ten years and haven't since, yet there I was, apparently unable to speak English, winning a title. We saved the season and won the Carling Cup. A few months later, the problem is I can't speak English. I mean, really?

'The problem was that we had no strikers. The next season starts, the team's a disaster, no strikers and it's all because the manager doesn't speak English. It's frustrating, of course. The press was sensationalist. It's the same in Italy, Spain, everywhere. In this world, I know that I am putting myself out there and you accept the criticism. What annoyed me was, after four months, I'm being hailed for revolutionising the diet, the team's playing well, a trophy is in the cabinet. Then, five months later, I'm on the scrapheap and worth nothing. We sold 46 goals. That's why the team stopped working.'

I make the point that for all the failings of the board and the players, two points from eight games and defeats against Middlesbrough, Sunderland, Portsmouth, Hull and Stoke do not reflect particularly well. Does Ramos share any blame? 'Yes, yes, of course,' he insists. 'At a football club, every person has a responsibility. Of course, the coach has a big part of that.

My responsibility, looking back, was my decision not to quit at the moment we sold the strikers. My mistake was accepting that situation. My error is to have continued going along with a situation where I did not agree with the club.

'We had some fantastic players and that was the frustration. We had Ledley King and Jonathan Woodgate in defence and the makings of a proper side. That's why I say they thought too much about business. I signed Luka Modric at the age of 20 and he went to Real Madrid. If they don't change the strategy and politics, they will always just fall short. If you have some of the best players, keep them, add to them, complement them and go and win things. Fight for titles, give the fans memories.

'Look at Manchester United around that time. They had won the Premier League and Champions League in the summer of 2008 and then Fergie goes and gets Berbatov to add to it. It is about stability and reinforcement. You cannot compete if you sell to the top-four rivals. I look at Tottenham now under Mauricio Pochettino, a brilliant coach, and it would be the ideal for Tottenham to gamble. They have a strong squad, close to the top, they need to keep the core together and build on it. Why not go and win the league?

'Despite everything, I still love English football. One of my first memories, as a 12-year-old kid, was the 1966 World Cup, where I remember a powerful and skilful England team that lifted the trophy. I'm always grateful to Spurs supporters. In Spain, all the fans care about is winning or losing, and feelings and emotions barely come into it. The Premier League is unique. Supporters carry teams in their heart, it dominates their lives entirely. It's far better because if the team is struggling or if you lose, the fans remain with the team. They don't get properly angry with you in the same way. I never felt the fans turn on me despite the bad results.'

It is sometimes tempting to wonder whether overseas managers are engaging in lame platitudes, but there is a consistency to this theory. Towards the end of his debut season in English football, Pep Guardiola produced a moment of rare humility to express his gratitude to the supporters of Manchester City. It had been his worst season as a manager. He went six games without a win for the first time, as City toiled between September and October 2016. He was knocked out of the Champions League at the final 16 stage for the first time in his coaching career and lost more matches in a single season than ever before.

Deep in the bowels of Southampton's St Mary's Stadium in April, Guardiola paused for breath. City had produced one of their more impressive performances of the campaign to win 3-0 and Guardiola opened up. 'We were out of the Champions League in Monaco and we played three tough games against Liverpool, Arsenal and Chelsea. We drew two and lost one and then we played Hull City at home. I was a bit worried but, as I walked out, our supporters clapped and supported us. In Italy, Germany and Spain, that does not happen. That is why I am so glad for the fans we have because it is the first time in my life I have experienced that.'

Sadly, it does seem that Ramos lost the trust of his players. Midfielder Jermaine Jenas, speaking on Radio 5 Live, recalled Ramos' final day in charge: 'We were on the training pitch. We were going through a bad spell, second bottom of the league. For Spurs at the time it was a catastrophe. [Ramos] is going through some team shape and he put Tom Huddlestone on the left wing. We were like, "What's going on here?" We'd look at assistant Gus Poyet, and he looked back as if to say, "I don't know what to tell you." We walked off the pitch baffled. Alan Hutton then knocks on my hotel room door at 11pm to tell us we had a meeting. You just think it's one of the lads having a laugh. So we go downstairs and the chairman said that Juande has been relieved of his duties and Harry Redknapp is coming in from tomorrow.'

Captain Ledley King had a theory that Ramos struggled with the intensity of life in the Premier League. 'I'm not sure he realised how tough the league was,' King told *FourFourTwo*.

'Maybe in Spain there were some teams you could almost just turn up and beat, but in the Premier League you've got to be on your game every week. We didn't prepare in the same way for the lesser teams as we did the big teams, and that's why we struggled in those games. He didn't speak great English so the translation was an issue. He had Poyet there to help, but I don't think the two of them were completely on the same page in terms of the way they believed the team should play. Obviously things were bad in those last few months, but it wasn't through lack of effort. If anything, the harder we tried, the worse things seemed to get. Under Ramos everything was very strict – the training, the diet – but Harry just took things back to basics and told us to enjoy ourselves.'

After Tottenham, Ramos returned to his home country with Real Madrid within a matter of months, before spells in Russia, Ukraine and back in Spain with Malaga. So, after a 26-year coaching career, who is the best player he has managed? 'Come on, in Madrid, I coached stars. You can't say names. If I leave one out, it will explode and offend people.' How about David Bentley? He grins. 'You'll get me in trouble!'

CHAPTER 10

Magic Men

One morning during defender Chico Flores' time at Swansea City, anti-doping officials headed down to the club's training ground. An administration error, however, led the testers to arrive on the wrong day, when the only players at the training complex were injured and going about their recuperation process. The fit and available players were on a day off. The testers came round to the view that they had come all this way to Wales, so the least they could do was a quick test on the recovering footballers. Flores was one such player.

The requirements of the drug-testing process meant he would need to hang around for a couple of hours but there was a problem. This request clashed with Flores' social plans. His response was explosive and he quickly declared his intention to gain revenge. The drug testers required a urine sample. So by way of retribution, Flores, who keeps a pet monkey called Willy that he regularly dressed in a Swansea replica jersey, resolved to force the testers to stay in Swansea for as long as possible. To that end, he refused to spend a penny in protest. He held it all in, from mid-morning until nearly midnight.

He called up his wife, asking her to bring a pillow and duvet to the training ground – you cannot leave the premises during tests – and he ordered in a takeaway for them both before settling down to watch a movie. Finally, late into the night, he provided his urine, coolly told the drug testers they had missed the last trains out of Swansea and now they knew how it felt to be inconvenienced.

Swansea have enjoyed a Spanish influence for much of the past decade and, for the most part, this process has been a far more pleasant and straightforward experience than that day with Flores. Between 2007 and 2009, Roberto Martinez introduced a more expressive style of play and bold coaches such as Paolo Sousa, Brendan Rodgers and Michael Laudrup followed him. While Laudrup was at the club, Swansea also decided that they wanted to improve the club's academy. Mostly due to the proselytising work of Martinez, Swansea were ahead of the curve and they skipped up the divisions from League One in 2007 to the Premier League by 2011. Spanish journalist Pablo Gomez even wrote a book, called *Los Cisnes* (*The Swans*), which charts the club's rise under Martinez and beyond.

Swansea were a little more advanced in their methods but much of their development corresponds with the most profound influx of Spanish talent into England. After Spain won the European Championship under Luis Aragones in 2008, English clubs began to look more seriously at the Iberian market. In the Premier League era, 125 Spaniards had featured by November 2017, and fewer than 40 of those players arrived before the national team's 2008 triumph.

We are living through the reign of Spain. On the international scene, Spain won three consecutive tournaments between 2008 and 2012. After Real Madrid's Champions League triumph in 2017 leading Spanish club sides have won 11 of the last 18 Europa League or Champions League crowns. Spain won the Under-21 European Championships in 2011 and 2013, while they reached the final in 2017. Spain have won three of the last seven Under-19 European Championships. The hegemony has created a romantic stereotype of a Spanish footballer. The modern Spanish footballers lighting up the English game are often professionals blessed with technique and invention, more often than not the midfield metronomes who always want the ball and possess the supreme football intelligence to know what best to do with it.

Yet it is not only their football ability that impresses so much. It is often their humility and love for the game that stands out above all. Arriving in England in recent years, David Silva, Juan Mata, Santi Cazorla, Xabi Alonso, Cesc Fabregas and company have captured the imagination and inspired a generation to see the game in a more inventive, more creative and, perhaps most importantly, a more fun manner. In the 2016-17 season, the Premier League featured 36 Spaniards, a figure higher than any other nationality except for English players. There were over three times as many Spaniards as Germans, more than double the number of Welsh or Scottish players and over a dozen more Spaniards than Dutch or Belgian players. The French came in third place with 28 representatives. The Spanish trend has filtered down the leagues and, at the start of the 2017-18 season, Thomas Christiansen began the campaign in charge at Leeds United and Pep Clotet was the manager of League One Oxford United.

Yet identity is a complex issue. Perceptions of Spanish football both within and outside of Spain have radically transformed in recent years. French journalist Henri Desgrange coined the term '*la furia roja*' to describe the Spanish national team during the 1920 Olympic Games in Belgium. During the Franco era, the term took on a political edge. In the aftermath of the Civil War, the Falangist newspaper *Arriba* wrote: 'In sport, the *furia* best manifests itself in football, a game in which the virility of the Spanish race can find full expression, usually imposing itself, in international contest, over the more technical but less aggressive foreign teams.'

These days, it sounds more like a description of a Tony Pulis team than a vibrant and expressive Spain team. The new perception of Spain is that of tiki-taka, the tippy-tappy approach that favours brain over brawn, finesse over force. Yet we should be wary of concluding that Spain is a homogenous culture of virtuosos, where children enjoy idyllic conditions, playing out rondo after rondo before breaking out for stepover sessions.

Chelsea defender Cesar Azpilicueta does not fit the stereotype. He is a modern defender who is polished with the ball at his feet, but he is, first and foremost, a defender who defends. 'Everyone talks about Alonso, Cazorla, Mata, Fabregas and rightly so,' he says. 'And oh my God ... those training sessions! There are some things you see and you're like, "How the hell has he done that?" I just enjoy them. But think about it. Rafa Benitez and Quique Flores are very different managers to Pep Guardiola. It is often forgotten that a thumping header by Carles Puyol decided Spain's 2010 World Cup semi-final against Germany. He was a real warrior.

'Our greatest teams have had both character and finesse. Any identity requires variety. It's true that in the last couple of international tournaments, it has not been perfect. We have had a transition of players but we are not going to renounce the sense of what we are about at all. We will maintain and enhance our style of play.'

As Azpilicueta hints, there can, at times, be a suggestion of puritanism about the way we discuss tiki-taka and the Spanish vision of football. Consider, for example, that at the age of 14, Manchester City's David Silva went along to trials at Real Madrid. The revered scout Sixto Alonso had identified Silva's talent in Gran Canaria. 'I took him twice to Real Madrid and twice they rejected him,' Alonso told Spanish media. 'They liked the kid but said he had the wrong physical shape. He was small and thin. He returned three months later after intensive gym work for more trials. Again they said no. During those trials, he played in a tournament against Valencia, who went on to sign him instead.'

At Valencia, they admired Silva's talent as a teenager but

felt he needed a bit more toughening up. The solution was to send him on loan to Eibar, a Basque team with a 6,300-seater stadium in a town with a 27,000 population. The aim was for him to build character and gain consistency. There are certain consistencies in football, regardless of whether a player is born in Salamanca or Stockport. 'It was an apprenticeship for him,' says Jose Luis Mendilibar, who coached Silva at Eibar. 'It was competitive football, more physical and actually good preparation for England. David still didn't have his own driving licence so I often picked him up to training. We remain close to this day. When I came to Manchester City to observe Manuel Pellegrini's sessions and learn some English, David let me stay in his spare room.'

In truth, the cult of gigantism was only truly challenged following the extraordinary success of Barcelona and Spain. Sitting outside a restaurant in the town of Oviedo, Julio Lamuño lights up a cigar. In Asturias, the drink of choice is cider. Food portions are hearty, with *fabada asturiana* (a bean stew) the most homely of the local dishes. When waiters serve cider in bars and restaurants, they pour the bottle from over their heads so it nestles into the glass fizzing and at pace. At local club Covadonga, Lamuño was one of Santi Cazorla's first coaches.

'He was always pint-sized,' Lamuño said. 'Back then, everyone was looking at small kids with suspicion. Pep Guardiola has altered perceptions. I think you guys come over from England and imagine we were always enlightened. Twenty years ago, we were the same as England. Guardiola altered everything with Xavi, Iniesta and Messi. In Asturias, the weather is often rainy so forget the idea that the pitches are pristine. Nonsense. When Santi was playing, the weather could be so bad he'd lose his boots in the muddy ground. Some days the pitches could be sandy like a beach at times. Local councils have made big investments recently and now we have more synthetic grounds. But as a youth coach on a rainy day, you have to be strong because the temptation is to get the ball off the ground.'

Serious injury has devastated Cazorla's career in recent years but, at his best, he is a magnificent midfielder, adept with either foot and unique in his capacity to control the tempo of a game. Growing up in Lugo de Llanera in the north-west of Spain, Cazorla mostly played indoor five-a-side football until the age of 13, which explains his immaculate close control and his manner of bamboozling opponents. Spanish World Cup-winning defender Joan Capdevila once said of Cazorla: 'I played with him for five years and I still don't know if he is right-footed or left-footed, even from corners and freekicks – it's insane.'

Lamuño smiles: 'Santi saw me in the street recently and came running over. "Are you still telling the kids to use both feet?" I have always been obsessed with getting our kids to be strong with left and right. It annoys me when I see professionals only confident with one foot. It is a fundamental basic that coaches should teach children and absolutely insist upon. In real life, do you use one foot or two feet to walk? So why should it be different when it comes to playing football? It's not rocket science and there is no big secret to the method. He would do things like passing the ball repeatedly against the wall using both feet. We would do drills, controlling the ball with the weaker foot and passing with the stronger one, therefore getting the body position and balance up to speed.

'It takes a lot of dedication. If a kid really loves football, they will do it. Some kids couldn't cope with my demanding style. It's my work. I told dads and grandads how I would work and, if they didn't like it, they could take their kids elsewhere. His family was amazing. Normally just the dad comes along to games. But with Santi, there was mum, dad, auntie, uncle, grandmother, the works. His father, who sadly passed away several years ago, was a friend of mine. The secret of success for a young player is talent, dedication and surrounding yourself with the correct people. That is the same in England as Spain.'

For Juan Mata, who hails from Burgos, it was a similar story. He remains extremely close to his father, Juan Sr, who has opened a tapas restaurant in Manchester. He and his girl-friend, the osteopath Evelina Kamph, launched the Common Goal project in 2017, where Mata became the first player to commit to donating 1 per cent of his wages to charitable causes. Many more have since followed, including German and Italian defenders Mats Hummels and Giorgio Chiellini.

Mata has worked towards two university degrees – one in sports science and one in marketing at Madrid's Universidad Camilo Jose Cela. His depth of character has charmed English football supporters. 'I loved my two and a half years in London on a personal and sporting level. I mastered the language, I discovered the city. I thought I could speak a bit but I got here and very quickly realised I needed to work on it. I had classes at school. London is like a thousand mini-cities all in one wonderful place. My days off were adventures. I went to Camden and browsed the old record shops. I went walking near Primrose Hill, visited cafés in Soho, practised photo-graphy around Regent's Park. Manchester is different but you have the Northern Quarter, which I love, and wonderful museums too.'

'My father was a footballer and my grandfather was so dedi-cated to transporting me everywhere,' Mata says. 'From a little boy, I always had a ball in my hands. My grandfather ferried me, whatever the time, whatever the distance, nothing was too much to see his grandson play football. When I was 15 years old, I went from Real Oviedo to Real Madrid and that was the first time the lightbulb switched on that I might really make it. My grandfather would sometimes make the 560-mile round trip from Oviedo to Madrid to watch my games. He sadly passed away in 2017, just a day or two before our EFL Cup final against Southampton. He was always so proud of me. When I scored two goals at Anfield, including that scissor kick, he went out of his house, to the bars and said to everyone, "Have you seen what my grandson did today?"'

At the Real Madrid academy, Mata made progress but he was

competing with *Galácticos* for a first-team place. 'There were no guarantees and I wasn't sure. I went from Real Madrid Castilla to Real's B team when I was 18 years old and that's when it felt really close for me. It was the hardest decision of my life to leave Oviedo at 15 for Real Madrid. Every major Spanish club came calling. My parents liked the schooling and educational programme that Real Madrid offered and we decided it would be best. My parents insisted a lot that I saw through my studies. I committed everything to it. At the start, it was really very difficult. Oviedo is a very distinctive place and I left family and friends behind. We all stayed together as kids in the Madrid academy residence, with players such as Jose Callejon and Alvaro Negredo, and my parents and sister regularly came to see me.'

Joselu, the former Stoke striker that moved to Newcastle in the summer of 2017, emerged through the Celta Vigo youth system but joined Real Madrid as a prodigiously gifted striker at the age of 20. He played in the Real Madrid Castilla team in the third tier of Spanish football and regularly trained with Jose Mourinho's first team. As we meet in the Cheshire suburb of Alderley Edge, his insight into both Mourinho and Madrid's identity is enlightening. 'I scored on my debut under Jose Mourinho at the Bernabeu,' Joselu grins. 'I have no regrets. I scored a load of goals for the Castilla team, in a partnership with Alvaro Morata. Madrid wanted me to bide my time and stay. But I took the decision to leave the club and head to Germany with Hoffenheim because I wanted top-level football.

'I loved it at Madrid. I spent two years with Mourinho. He opened his doors to us kids, gave us high-intensity experience of first-team training and provided huge exposure by giving us debuts. Every time I see him, I give him a big hug and we catch up. He is simply one of the best. Never forget what he did with Porto, back when nobody would have expected that team to win the Champions League. Inter Milan, the same. He wins titles and makes footballers better. What more could you want from a manager? His personality is difficult, but everyone knows who he is and what they are getting themselves into when they make Mourinho their manager. There are no surprises. He stands out in football these days because of his directness. He can be sharp and abrupt and some people can't handle that. The challenge is how such directness translates to modern players. There are some who cannot cope with it. But you have to accept criticism. Mourinho is fair. He praises you for good things and rightly criticises when it is necessary. Nobody is perfect all the time; even Messi and Ronaldo have off days. So you have a manager, to guide, inform and improve you.'

As for comparisons between Barcelona and Madrid's academy philosophy, Joselu says: 'It's true that Real Madrid does not have the same productivity. I can tell you, though, that from our Castilla team that earned promotion to the second division, many went on to play in the top flight of a European league. Madrid products are distributed more broadly, whereas Barcelona had an incredible generation that went into the first team. But Madrid's academy still makes an enormous contribution to Spanish football. Alvaro Morata, Pablo Sarabia and Lucas Vazquez are recent examples. But I don't dispute that there is something special, something unique about one of your own making the first team.

'Rafa Benitez, in his short time at the club, had the idea of introducing more Spaniards into the Real Madrid team. This is not the philosophy of Madrid. The club's identity is clear: sign the best players. If they are Spanish, OK, but if not, whatever. Beckham, Figo, Zidane, just sign the best. If Jamie Vardy scores 50 goals, Real Madrid will sign him. That's the philosophy. It's the club where the stars come to shine. And they have the most Champions League titles, so it clearly works.'

Mata left Madrid behind at the age of 19, as he linked up with Valencia, where he scored 46 goals and made 52 assists in 176 appearances. 'When you are in the Real Madrid academy, your dream is always to get into the first team. However, as you get closer, you see a very competitive squad and big signings every summer, particularly in the forward positions. It is very, very difficult to break through. Barcelona have a very clear identity and the promise of first-team opportunities. However, at Real Madrid they have produced a huge number of first division footballers in Spain and also in the Premier League, so we shouldn't knock it.

'I trained once with the first team! I went to a Champions League game in Ukraine against Dynamo Kiev but I didn't play. Fabio Capello was the manager. It was unbelievable. I was 18 and five or six of us went on the trip. I sat in the dressing room, staring open-mouthed at Raul, Ronaldo, Casillas, Beckham, Figo, Roberto Carlos. They were the biggest names, the guys I'd grown up watching and imitating. I remember Ruud van Nistelrooy made a real effort with me. We had a long conversation on the flight home and he seemed incredibly humble and keen to help the younger players.

'By 19, I was playing for Valencia under Ronald Koeman and Quique Flores. That was a master's degree, a real finishing school for me. When I arrived in England, people in Spain were saying it will be too rough and ready, you will find it hard, all this. Thanks to the success of the international team, the Spanish vision for the game has been transplanted into England. We now appreciate the values and principles of the Spanish football. This is the crux of it. We have talent but also the mentality to adapt ourselves.'

So how have Spain done it? How have they created this cohort of talent? Former Real Madrid captain Fernando Hierro was the Spanish FA's sporting director between 2007 and 2011. 'The academies are outstanding,' he says. 'Valencia, Real Zaragoza, Barcelona, Athletic Bilbao, Villarreal, Sporting Gijon, Celta, Deportivo and Espanyol. Let's put this simply: Barcelona have defined an era of Spanish players in their way of understanding football and how they play the game. The quality of their play has impregnated the national team. There is extraordinary work going on.

'So what do we do differently? What is the big thing? We coach the coaches properly. The training the coaches get is beyond anywhere else. The structure of competition through the young age groups is now excellent in each region of the country. We have clear pathways. There is room for variety but it's monitored. There are so many young coaches coming through, now working all over the world. I see in England that people are obsessed with forming footballers. But what about forming the people who form the footballers? If you do that, then you get a better consistency.'

The English Football Association is aware of this critique and it was one of the motivations behind the St George's Park project. UEFA data in 2013 showed that England had only 1,190 A Licence coaches compared with 13,070 in Spain, and just 205 Pro Licence coaches compared with Spain's 2,353.

During a visit to Sporting Gijon's training ground, their B-team head coach Jose Alberto explains to me: 'People talk about Pep Guardiola being the best coach in history. He is very good but the gold is found in the academies. I have observed every club in Asturias. I have been to Real Madrid, Atletico, Villarreal, Espanyol, Barcelona, Athletic Bilbao and Celta Vigo. There is a unity in the vision from the lowest age group to the top now.'

At Milton Keynes Dons, Eduardo Rubio is one of those highly qualified Spanish coaches. He is the head coach of the Under-23 and Under-18 teams, as well as the man entrusted with the transition between youth teams and first team. He worked at Valencia during Rafa Benitez's period at the club, and has previously fulfilled different coaching roles at the English FA and in the Chelsea academy. He first came to England as an Erasmus student at the University of Roehampton and, in 2004, he made the bold decision to leave secure work behind.

'I was 23. People thought I was crazy to leave Valencia. I left a well-paid job in a good academy to coach a grassroots club, Hampton Rangers, twice a week for £30. One of the differences between coaching in Spain and England is the public respect for the profession. In Spain, the profession is linked with a sports science degree or what we call *magisterios*. Sports science is a four-year degree and *magisterios* is three years. The latter allows you to be a qualified teacher in school or college. This feeds a huge amount of qualified people into sports coaching. Football is popular, maybe 50 per cent go into it that way, but lots go into swimming, tennis, jujitsu, handball and basketball.

'The foundations were laid in the 1992 Barcelona Olympics. There was a massive boom from the late 1980s in terms of investment in sport and interest in sports science. It was recognised as a degree on a level of respect alongside law and medicine in Spain. Academics opted to go into it, rather than just people who are crazy about sport or overeager dads scrambling to coach their kids on a Sunday morning.

'I don't get the same impression in England. Maybe the Olympics have not had the same legacy yet. Here, if you want to become a coach, the FA is doing it better these days. In Spain, you needed your coaching badges but you also need your degree in sports science and teaching. It gives a different profile; these people had invested three years in university and really want it.'

As part of English football's modernisation, some youth coaches have begun to emphasise taking part over success, focusing on nurturing and honing talent rather than results. Rubio insists Spaniards do not share this approach. He explains: 'Spain was influenced by Rinus Michels and then Johan Cruyff. If you go back to just before 2008 when Luis Aragones was in charge, the essence was there but it had not flourished. This was the breaking point to say we know who we are and how to express it. The Spanish model is clear: football based on possession, technique and intelligence rather than aggression. It's "Are you clever enough to see this space?", and "Are you clever enough to break lines?" The coaches must be geared towards teaching our players how to do these things but we must maintain our character, too.

'We had a great weekend here recently. We convinced Barcelona to bring their Under-15 team for an academy game. I know their academy head, I sent them a few clips and they could see our possession game. We had a workshop with their coaches and there was a games room for Barça players and our players to mix and learn a bit of one another's language. That is crucial. We talked with them about coaching methods but also mentality. To distinguish modern England from the perceived "bad old days", people make a point of saying winning and losing is not important. It's their way of separating themselves from the past.

'It is true that I want our youth teams at MK Dons to play out from the back, exploit the pockets of space, use the flanks and have a possession-based game. That is non-negotiable. But we also implement a competitive edge. In England, there is this break that divides coaches into being either a winner or a developer. If you are a developer who likes winning, you are not seen as a true developer. And then if you are a winner, you are not developing. I want to be both. We should not have a complex about wanting to win. The first-team gaffer does not want a loser. However, it's not winning at all costs or damaging a young person.'

He says English methods are changing but there are still moments that make him shudder. 'I've just come back from a game and well ...' He blows out his cheeks. 'In the final 20 minutes, the opponents were holding onto the result by launching it into the corners. I'm thinking, "Really?" In this age group, in modern football, the best way to defend is to keep possession. I get really cross thinking these guys are only 17 years old and they are being made to perceive football in the way we did 50 years ago. It still happens with certain teams and in lower leagues. But things are improving. England is more open to new ideas.'

The evidence of England's progress came during a glorious summer and autumn in 2017 in which England lifted the Under-20 World Cup by beating Venezuela, and then won the Under-17 World Cup, defeating Spain 5-2 in the final. Only Brazil had previously won two lower-age group World Cups in the same calendar year. England also won the European Under-19 Championship in 2017. For the first time in a long time, signs of real promise emerged. But consider this statistic: on the October weekend that England won the Under-17 World Cup, only 15 of the 245 players who featured in the Premier League were English and aged 21 or below. The following week, this dropped to 13.

The further we look, the more distressing the figures become. After England's team impressed in the 2017 European Under-21 Championship, it was hoped opportunities for home-grown talent might follow. Yet on 3 October, a BBC study detailed the number of minutes played by squad members of the four semi-finalists. They looked at how many minutes of top-flight action had been enjoyed by players in the squads of England, Germany, Spain and Italy in the opening couple of months of the 2017-18 season. The study found that the English players, with just 4,462 minutes under their belt, had played 49 per cent of the total top-flight minutes of their Spanish rivals, 58 per cent of the Germans and 67 per cent of the Italians.

Now set this against some research carried out by Manchester City's head of football services Brian Marwood. In an interview with the club website, Marwood revealed: 'We discovered last year that in the last ten years 83 per cent of players who featured in the quarter-final stage of the Champions League had all played first-team football at 17.' This, therefore, underlines the significant issue. It may be that England's coaching or talent issues have to a large extent been rectified, but now the players are being inhibited by a lack of opportunity.

The problem is exacerbated as clubs now scour the world for talent in the younger age groups. Eric Garcia, a central defender, was a member of Spain's Under-17 World Cup squad in 2017 and already on Manchester City's books. Jose Alberto, the Sporting Gijon B-team coach, admits his club must now contend with prying eyes from not only Spain but also beyond. 'We have a lot of interest from leading Spanish clubs and it is difficult to keep your best talent. We have seen in the last ten years that English clubs are very strong and aggressive. I would say English clubs are across our talent from age 13 or 14. Before, it was impossible that a player that age would even know what an agent is. Now they all have them. I have seen 11-year-olds with agents. We have entered into a market where agents want to take players away and cash in. It's hard at Sporting. We have the fortune that we are a bit like Athletic Bilbao. The kids here have a real affinity with the area and with the club.'

The English interest in young Spanish talent first came about when Arsenal stunned Barcelona by poaching Cesc Fabregas. He was identified at the age of 15 when Spain beat England in a youth-team match in Darlington. Fabregas had won the best player and Golden Boot awards at the 2003 Under-17 World Cup. The Arsenal scout Francis Cagigao organised a meeting between Fabregas' parents and chief scout Steve Rowley. The club made the most of a loophole that meant Spanish clubs could not sign players on professional terms until the age of 18 under Spanish law, while English clubs, according to European Union and FIFA rules, could make their move at 16.

For the Catalans, this was unthinkable. Fabregas grew up in a family of fanatical Barcelona fans and his grandfather took him to the Camp Nou for his first game at only nine months old. As a child in La Masia, he slept in a dormitory overlooking the club's pitch. Barcelona hoped that Fabregas would one day be the heir to Pep Guardiola in the midfield, and the sense of outrage was palpable. Johan Cruyff said: 'European football is turning cheating into an art form. OK, I don't know every detail of Cesc's move to Arsenal but I do know that the English club's behaviour is what I count as underhand.'

Fabregas, however, relished his chance, becoming Arsenal's youngest first-team goalscorer and youngest player in the Premier League era. He became Spain's youngest debutant for 80 years when he played against Ivory Coast in 2006. The Highbury faithful hailed Fabregas with the chant: 'He's only 17, he's better than Roy Keane.' Rival clubs strived to find the next Fabregas, who revelled in English lessons three times a week and enjoyed the physical challenge.

As an 18-year-old, he told the *Sunday Times*: 'Even if the opponent's Roy Keane, and I've been watching him on television since I was 14, and I know he's got a bad tackle, I want that. I'm never scared. I never trained with the Barcelona first team but I've spoken to Lionel Messi and he trains with them. He says if you do something wrong, everyone says, "He's young, it's OK." It's not like that here. In my first session Kolo Toure kicked me. It was a terrible tackle. He knew I was 16 but it was, bang! Welcome to England.'

Premier League clubs built up strategic systems to tempt the world's best at the youngest age for the least money. Yet it has rarely worked. Arsenal struck gold once more when they signed Hector Bellerin from Barcelona, but he is among the exceptions. Manchester Untied saw off Arsenal and Chelsea to sign Gerard Pique from Barcelona at the age of 17 but despite maturing in England, he could not break the Rio Ferdinand and Nemanja Vidic stronghold. He returned to Barcelona to become a global icon for club and country.

Recent Premier League history is littered with young Spaniards who came early to England and failed to break through. Suso, Dani Pacheco and Daniel Ayala may regret early moves to Liverpool, while Fran Merida and Jon Toral may reflect that they would have been better off remaining with Barcelona rather than taking an early plunge at Arsenal. Foreign teenagers, however, remain a minority within most leading clubs in the youth age groups. When I joined Patrick Vieira and Jason Wilcox on Manchester City's pre-season tour of Croatia for their Under-21 and Under-18 sides in 2014, it was encouraging to hear that over 90 per cent of City players below the age of 18 were English. The issue, therefore, appears to be at the top, where managers facing demands for instant results fear risking their reputation and careers on the development of local talent.

'It is very difficult,' Roberto Martinez says. 'A solution does not exist at the moment. You would have to change the structure of English football. The evolution of a footballer between the age of nine and 18 is outstanding. The area where you are losing players is between 19 and 21. It depends on the manager of a club and they are often under pressure for immediate results. In Spain, there are B teams in the second division and players develop their tactical understanding. Those three years are the difference between the progression of Spanish and English players.

'The Under-23 Premier League works for players for a few months, both on a technical level and in terms of the teams you play. But there's nothing competitive about it. Then you have loans, which are unpredictable. Sometimes they are excellently managed and sometimes they are a waste of time. What is the solution? To introduce the B teams, but British football is too well organised for it. We have 92 well-supported clubs in the Premier League and Football League, plus many more beyond that, so it is not easy to introduce this. I almost had an agreement with a Scottish team to lend them seven or eight players for one season. English players are at a disadvantage. We had chances to develop players at Wigan and Everton but it's not the norm. At Swansea, Joe Allen was playing for me age 16. Callum McManaman, he progressed hugely at Wigan. They need personalised programmes to get results.'

Guardiola shares Martinez's view. Asked why he had afforded so few opportunities to young talent during his first season at Manchester City, he said in a press conference: 'The second teams in Spain, at Barcelona or Real Madrid, play in front of

40,000 people and every weekend in the second league. In Italy or Germany, they are so tough, so demanding, they are playing with guys who are 28, 29 or 30 and that is the best way to improve, not training with the first team sometimes.'

Martinez continues: 'The other issue is that we have created an atmosphere that is totally unrealistic. Who is to blame? All of us. We are all complicit. There are young players nowhere near first teams with salaries that you wouldn't believe. A group have been created in that age range where it is too much, too soon, and now it is very complicated. This is not only football. There's been a social change, more players are better educated and that's a good thing but they don't have the same struggle. You get a South American player and it's the fight of their life to get to where they are. To achieve their dreams can be massive for their family.'

Rubio was at MK Dons when Dele Alli emerged through the ranks, and he previously coached Chelsea's Under-15 side. The Chelsea academy has received stinging criticism due to the club's failure to promote home-grown talents to the club's first team and a perceived stockpiling of young talent. 'I didn't get frustrated at Chelsea,' Rubio says. 'You only get frustrated when your expectations are not real. Chelsea have a really good coaching programme but it's important to recruit the ideal manager who adds value to that culture. If you have loads of youngsters but the manager doesn't get the support from the club and doesn't have the ethos of buying into it, then what's the point of having a very successful academy? Of course, it was a frustration in a way but you knew the expectation was not for them to play for the first team because it was not set up in that way. So as a coach, the expectations change.'

Do players in the system believe they can make the first team? Rubio explains: 'I would say to players, "Listen, I'm going to help you become a professional player. You may get a loan elsewhere and you see Nathan Ake and Dom Solanke, who I worked with, have forged careers elsewhere." What is my job?

To develop professional players. If a club doesn't have the right pathway or the right manager for our first team, it just means they have a career elsewhere.'

Is it better, therefore, for young players to choose more carefully and head to a club like MK Dons, where Alli was in the first team at the age of 17? 'There is no ideal pathway. What I do believe is that you need to be faced with certain challenges and experiences that help adaptation. We need to develop resilience and flexibility. Sometimes, lower academies with lower resources can offer better challenges. Pitches that are not ideal or different-sized pitches can provide real experience of what you will see later on in senior football. We give flexibility by asking players to train with a higher or lower age group, which gives a different speed of game. Sometimes we do an international tournament and sometimes we do friendlies against grassroots teams. In development, you must encounter different things and this is missing in certain academies.'

In spite of their outstanding facilities, some of the larger Premier League academies have taken to old-school methods to bring their kids back down to earth, such as youth-team players only being allowed to wear black boots before making the first team. 'I don't believe black boots are a challenge,' Rubio says. 'Then I see some coaches who think they are making challenging sessions because there are loads of rules. The beauty of football is simplicity. If you put too many rules, they end up playing the rules rather than the game. Black boots, red boots, whatever. Same game, same principles, but go and play against a conference team or grassroots team, train with the first team, play a game against a team from France or Greece. Pair up a striker with a different defender. These are real challenges rather than superficial ones.'

Spain's winning mentality has cut across the sporting landscape. Tennis star Rafael Nadal is a serial Grand Slam winner and his female Spanish counterpart Garbiñe Muguruza won at Roland Garros in 2016 and Wimbledon in 2017. There were three different Tour de France winners between 2006 and 2009, and Alberto Contador had his 2010 title stripped after the Court of Arbitration for Sport found him guilty of doping. The charismatic Sergio Garcia charmed the world as he finally won a Masters title to claim his first major in April 2017. Garcia had previously finished in the top two on four occasions and in the top ten on 22 occasions in the past 18 years. Fernando Alonso won 32 Grand Prix races as a Formula One driver.

The irony of Spain's international sporting success is that much of their unbridled joy has arrived in the nation's most vulnerable decade in the post-Franco era, when the question of Spanish identity feels ever more complex. On 1 October 2017, the Catalan regional government, headed by Carles Puidgemont, held an independence referendum, which the Spanish courts declared illegal and unconstitutional. The majority of those who turned out voted to break away from Spain. The subsequent chain of events saw mass protests, state-endorsed violence by the police, a declaration of Catalan independence and the detentions of the Catalan ringleaders. The Spanish King Felipe made a rare televised speech in which he criticised the Catalan leaders for dividing Spain and warned that Spanish democracy faced 'very grave times'.

Catalonian nationalism is, for many, a seductive and optimistic vision of change. As an outsider, it is easy to sympathise. We associate Catalonia with the paintings of Picassso, the artwork of Salvador Dali, the culinary skill of Ferran Adria, the architecture of Antoni Gaudi and, of course, the football of Pep Guardiola. Catalonia is shorthand for a high point of cultural expression. Barcelona, as a club, have demonstrated signs of a sharper political edge in recent times. In 2012, they introduced an away kit that featured the red-and-yellow stripes of the Catalan Senyera flag. The club proudly announced that sales of its Catalan shirt overtook the first jersey a year later. During home games, supporters chant for independence on 17 minutes and 14 seconds – 1714 being the year the Catalan state was officially abolished, when Barcelona fell to the Bourbon King Philip V in the War of the Spanish Succession.

Guardiola, the iconic Catalan figure, has rarely hidden his own views on independence and he joined a 40,000-strong rally at Montjuic earlier in 2017. After the referendum violence, he said: 'The images don't lie, there were people who wanted to vote and they've been attacked. There are more than 700 hurt – people who were going to vote, not rob a bank. Spain will try to hide the reality, but the rest of the world's media will show it. The images are clear and everybody knows what has happened.' Yet curiously, he admitted only a couple of weeks before, in a BBC interview with Gary Lineker, that he would like to manage the Spanish national team one day.

So the quest for identity in Spain is ongoing. On an autumn afternoon, it is rush-hour in Oxford city centre and Pep Clotet, the football club's new manager, pulls into a petrol station.

Clotet is a fascinating case study. The tempting conclusion of a Catalan Pep working in the third tier of English football is to suspect Oxford of keeping up appearances. Yet Clotet has a hodgepodge identity. After suffering a career-threatening injury in his early twenties, Clotet swiftly decided to pursue the coaching route. At different times, he has considered leaving football behind. 'Yes, always,' he says. 'I always have the feeling I give a lot to football but it's because I love it. It's a way of life. There are times I've wondered because you really need huge self-discipline and focus to cope with today's football. I've no idea what I'd do otherwise. Nothing else that gives me the same drive.'

After earning his coaching badges and gaining his UEFA Pro Licence qualifications by the age of 26, Clotet began working locally in Catalonia. He studied education at university and, by his late twenties, he was coaching Espanyol's Under-19 and B teams. He was part of the Espanyol coaching structure during Mauricio Pochettino's period in charge of the club. Clotet says: 'We were promoted to Segunda B and we put a lot of players into his first team. He took over 20 young players up at different stages. You could see even then his trust and faith in young talent, which has since been replicated at Southampton and Tottenham. I had been there five years and I felt I reached a point of maturity.

'I had always travelled to learn about players and coaches. I felt Scandinavia was a good reference point. In the later 1990s and early 2000s, I was fascinated by that part of the world. I wanted to understand how it was possible that small countries had strong teams like Helsinborgs, Rosenborg and such good national teams. What were they doing? I wanted to find out. It was time to spread my wings. So I went to Malmo as assistant coach to Roland Nilsson and we won the title in 2010. Then I worked as a coach at Norwegian team Halmstad and after that it was Viking, where I rented the same property that Roy Hodgson used during his time in Norway.'

Many in football claim to be dedicated but few have shown the commitment of Clotet. When Louis van Gaal managed Barcelona, Clotet took up a daily routine. Every morning, he would make his way to the club's training ground, where he had located a small gap in the fencing. Van Gaal's sessions were not open to the media or fans but Clotet would not be deterred. 'I did that ritual close to 200 times. Most of the training sessions were behind closed doors. I found my little gap where I could peek through. I was there every morning, taking notes and learning for a whole year. I was clandestine! He never found out while he was there.

'When Van Gaal went to the Dutch club AZ Alkmaar, they let me in and I told him what I used to do. Van Gaal is a great influence because he was the first one who took what Cruyff was doing and started to talk about the positional game and how to expose the free man during possession. This was a huge influence for the football that Guardiola is producing now. This also shaped my offensive style. Marcelo Bielsa is an influence for his approach to individual player development. His offensive play is more aggressive, especially the way he develops the individual to impose himself on the opposition. I was able to watch his training sessions when he managed Argentina and they had a training camp in Barcelona.

'I have lost count of how many people I have been to see coach. When Ottmar Hitzfeld was at Bayern Munich, I spent three months living in a cabin because I couldn't afford a hotel in 2002. He let me in to watch and was amazing with me. I saw Claudio Ranieri and Rafa Benitez at Valencia, Jupp Heynckes; I saw Marcelino, who is now manager of Valencia, when he was at Gijon and Villarreal. I saw Unai Emery at Sevilla during a trip with Garry Monk.

'I never came to England because I was driving through Europe on a road-trip at that time. I could've barely afforded the plane ticket. I put all my money into learning. I went all around Catalonia and saw the best local coaches. It became my way of living. I stay in touch with many of these guys. When I was at Swansea and Leeds, I made a lot of calls to people I have visited for information about a player.'

Clotet returned to Spain with Malaga, where he prepared young players for Manuel Pellegrini, who would go on to coach Manchester City. Then came the call from England. 'Michael Laudrup phoned me on a Friday afternoon when I was in Malaga. He said he wanted to meet me. It was the first time we'd ever spoken. He was my idol growing up, a fantastic player. He said, "We will be in London tomorrow, meet us there." I booked flights straight away and met with Mr Jenkins [the Swansea chairman] and Laudrup. The role was to try and take the academy from Level 2 to Level 1 status. They challenged me to change the structure. It was a good way to land into English football and learn how things are rather than tear the house down straight away. Laudrup had a Spanish way of training and previously there had been Paulo Sousa and Roberto Martinez.'

When Laudrup was sacked the following February, Clotet

was promoted to be Monk's assistant in a new managerial team. The pair saved Swansea from relegation and then led the club to eighth place in the Premier League in 2014-15. Most satisfyingly, Swansea won three consecutive Premier League matches against Van Gaal's Manchester United and also won away at Arsenal. Monk was especially praised for adapting Swansea's style from a fluid passing system into one more capable of competing and grinding out results. It was, in some ways, an admission that *Swansealona* may have gone a little far.

Clotet explains: 'We looked for a different brand of players while trying to maintain our tactical focus and speed. It was a team that was much more prepared to adapt to the opposition than in Brendan or Roberto's era. We were quite pragmatic and had our feet on the ground. We wanted to stay in every game. We focused heavily on defensive training and the transition. We highlighted ways to attack that would help us defend. The team improved immeasurably. We would pore over videos, watch at least ten games of opposition teams to spot trends in their attacking and defensive strengths and errors.'

A poor start to their second full season saw Monk sacked, and Clotet followed. They then went to Leeds United, where a season of huge promise fizzled out towards the end and the club missed out by a whisker on the play-off places. As Monk headed to Teesside with Middlesbrough, Clotet decided to go it alone.

'It didn't bother me to go down to League One. I turned down other jobs previously in a higher league. The project and plan was more important to me. We have to play the right way. The difference is that the higher you go in the leagues, the less individual mistakes you see and the less teams are affected by individual mistakes. There are teams in this league who build upon the mistakes of the opposition but you will find that harder in the Championship and it is impossible in the Premier League.'

Is capitalising on errors by opponents not the Mourinho model? 'No, no! Mourinho teams force the mistakes from the opposition; they don't just happen by themselves. His teams work very hard to identify weaknesses and brutally exploit them. His teams also have big strengths for the opposition to worry about.'

At Oxford, Clotet was concerned by identity. He is not a preacher. He does not want to be seen as exotic or a tiki-taka visionary. He speaks a lot about immersing himself in the culture of the town. His buzzword is *humility*. His English is outstanding; he is qualified to teach the language in his native Spain. Upon joining Oxford, he was realistic about the club's financial means. There were no prima-donna demands for an ample coaching staff. Rather, he respected that Oxford are on an upward curve following a recent promotion from League Two and he came alone. He spoke quickly to the existing staff, insisting he wants to learn from them and he hopes they will reciprocate. 'They did a lot of hard work and I felt I should be humble and respect that. It gives me the opportunity to know and show everyone here I value them.'

He noted that the club has a strong relationship with the Gibraltar Barracks in Surrey. The England women's rugby team had previously been visitors. The stereotype of players going along to a boot camp to be drummed into shape by army generals may make many Spanish coaches wince but Clotet embraced tradition. 'It was a good experience for all of us. Oxford has a lot of army links and they have done things like this for years. I did a lot of digging, I went to visit and meet them. The army in Great Britain is based on service to people, teamwork and duty. I felt that these things could be relevant to a football team. We stayed in the barracks and used their fantastic facilities. We used their recovery techniques, and their swimming pool is excellent.

'The army men organised team leadership exercises. We had little groups of problem-solving issues and then the players wanted to play soldier for the day. So one afternoon we let them have a shooting competition. On a more serious note, the soldiers gave talks about their experiences. All of them served in Afghanistan and they shared their powerful experiences. It was about teamwork and coping in stressful situations and managing new situations in adversity and adapting. There is a difference in terms of the gravity but there are similarities in the principles to football.'

Clotet is a rapid learner. He knows that in Oxford, Cambridge should be called 'The Other Place'. He went on several walking tours of the university town and gratefully embraced a fine-dining occasion at the historic St John's College. 'Lionel our board member works in engineering studies at Oxford University. I have been to St John's College twice. They tell me it is over 460 years old! The meal was very formal with grace said before we sat down. I was dressed up to the nines and not quite sure when to sit down and stand up. But what an experience! In Spain, everyone grows up hearing of Oxford and I am completely impressed by the university, by the colleges and by the culture they are preserving. It is a huge asset for England to have Oxford University.'

Clotet may be a traditionalist but he is also highly progressive. Having travelled all over Europe and immersed himself in English football, he concedes he is unsure how to define himself. In January, he was sacked from his position after a bright start gave way to a slump in form that included a 7-0 home defeat against Wigan and a loss against bottom-placed side Bury. The side fell away from the play-off places and the club said they made the decision 'in the best interests of Oxford United'. Clotet had made compromises on some of his principles but at a traditional club, it may not have been enough. His methods, however, share many traits with Spanish coaches. He insists heavily on nutrition and conditioning. He shares with Guardiola an insistence that players eat breakfast and lunch together at the training ground every day. He speaks of the 'metabolic window', where glycogen must be restored to the muscles within a certain timeframe. 'Eating is part of training. It's very important when you train that you refuel. It's a physical cycle. We know training is completed when they eat so it's not just a social thing for players to eat together.

'We have Jasmine Campbell, a dietician. She gives knowledge to the player on what is good and bad to eat. We prepared two cooking classes, especially for younger players. We felt around a dozen of them would benefit. We showed them how to prepare healthy food. Jasmine then took them to the supermarket to show what is good and bad. In their career in the long term, it will help. At this level, players are sometimes on a one-year contract, but we have a duty to pass on our knowledge and improve them as much as possible. We want them to train well and play well but enhance their whole career.

'I don't go to extremes of control. I am respectful of a player's life and build a relationship of trust. I let people regulate their environment. The players have come up with their own rules and fine system. It's a form of self-discipline. As a manager, it's important not to be banning things. I prefer to educate people and respect them.'

So, Pep, how would you define yourself? 'I used to be director of the Catalan School of Coaching. I took my badges and studies there, but that is where I made most of my mistakes. Mistakes configure your football. So if I was making an identity pie chart, the Catalan influence would still be the biggest section, but I am open to the world.'

CHAPTER 11

David to Goliath

David De Gea is sitting down, concentrating his steely gaze on a computer screen in a small room at Spain's Las Rozas training ground in Madrid. He is watching a clip from his first game in the Premier League. His new team, Manchester United, won the game 2-1 at the Hawthorns, but for a 20-year-old boy, it was an unsettling, demoralising experience. A tame Shane Long strike crawled under his body. Within the first hour of his Premier League career, rival supporters were teasing him with cries of 'dodgy keeper'.

In his role as a Sky Sports pundit, former Liverpool midfielder Jamie Redknapp commented that De Gea 'looked like he needed to grow into his clothes', and rarely has a segment of television analysis seemed more accurate. 'Oh my God,' De Gea says, rolling his eyes. 'The headlines, like "Jeepers-Keepers!" I had a bad start. We played at West Brom and they saw this 20-year-old Spanish kid in goal. So they did the sensible thing – they launched high, long balls and they challenged me physically. The truth is, it was a brutal start.

'They were hard moments and I knew I had to improve quickly. I knew the changes I needed to make but I needed time and experience. It was really, really hard. You arrive into a new country, a dressing room where I didn't know a soul, and a language that I could barely speak a word of. It was a huge challenge. I was still really young, too. Most kids are just starting university and I was in a dressing room of people who expected to win every single game. We had this hugely experienced defence, full of icons like Rio Ferdinand, Nemanja Vidic and Patrice Evra. They expected to win not just every game but every match in training. They were very demanding with me. I remember Rio and Paddy telling me, "OK, fine, you're young but this is Manchester United. We only accept the best."

'Ferguson took a huge risk on me. I was so young and he had the courage to give me that jersey. Ferguson was blunt and honest. He told me I had to adapt; it was going to be hard and there would be bumps in the road. There was no delusion. He made it abundantly clear that playing in the Premier League would be fundamentally different to life in La Liga. I remember reading about United's interest and I didn't believe it at first. They were looking for a replacement for Edwin van der Sar, who had such experience, and there was me, just a kid. We knew there would be challenges.'

Challenges presented themselves at every turn. After signing in the summer of 2011, errors followed in the Community Shield against Manchester City and a victory over Arsenal. Uncertainty pervaded his play. He was the goalkeeping equivalent of Dracula – terrified of crosses. A peculiar episode in a supermarket led to the *Sun* newspaper running the front page story: 'United goalie caught nicking £1.19 Tesco doughnut'. By 20 August of his first season, *The Times* were publishing an interview with the notorious Manchester United goalkeeping flop, Massimo Taibi, who assured the world that he could see parallels between himself and De Gea.

By the time we meet, however, in September 2016, De Gea's transformation is complete. He is by now among the world's greatest goalkeepers. He was United's in-house Player of the Year for three years in a row, 2014-16. He has made the PFA Team of the Year as the goalkeeper four times in five years, between 2013 and 2017. De Gea is a rare example of a Spanish player who has overcome teething problems in England to emerge as a global superstar.

So, David, are you now the best in the world? 'It's not for me to say,' he begins, smirking diplomatically. I suggest that not many goalkeepers are Player of the Year at a club like United for three years in a row. 'That's true ... I'm playing well, I'm confident but I have to maintain it and, crucially, I have to win trophies. That's what world-class players do.'

United chose De Gea over some of the best goalkeepers on the planet, including France's Hugo Lloris, Holland's Maarten Stekelenburg, Germany's Manuel Neuer, Portugal's Rui Patricio and Argentina's Sergio Romero. Ferguson's goalkeeping coach Eric Steele had made the recommendation, having spotted De Gea as a 16-year-old. 'I was at Manchester City when I first saw him,' Steele said. 'I wasn't really looking for a goalkeeper because we had Joe Hart coming through and Kasper Schmeichel as well.

'I went to the European Under-17 tournament and I watched the semis and the final. Spain beat England 1-0 and David was doing things in that game that made me mark his card. It persuaded me to write a report to keep on file. He stood out because of his frame. He caught my eye, first of all, because of the way Spain play. He fitted into that; his use of the ball was excellent. His calmness and assurance were what really struck me. In any situation he was in, he was calm. That was what I marked on his report and that was what I kept. When we began the search for Edwin van der Sar's replacement, he was one that I highlighted very quickly.'

United's scouting process was extensive. 'Oh, crikey me,' Steele says. 'It was not short of 20 times for myself alone. We had European scouts covering his league games; I went to live games against Barcelona and Valencia. I followed him in the Under-21 tournaments. For me, midweek would be on the road checking out his performances. People forget that he went into the Atletico team at only 18 – extraordinary, really. Once he made his debut, that ticks the box and we could say, "Wow, a young goalkeeper playing in La Liga for a top-four club."

'We then collated all the facts and information and the decision was made. The chief scout Jim Lawlor watched him, and then his European scouts did the same. We sat down and presented all the facts to Sir Alex and said, "Now we need you to come and see him play." He watched all the DVD clippings and read the reports thoroughly. He watched him live, as did Mike Phelan. The age factor wasn't a concern because he has always been a manager who gives opportunities to young people. It never entered his head as an issue to take him on as a teenager.

'He did not come in with little experience. He had won the Under-21 tournament and the Europa League with Atletico. We saw him in a semi-final against Liverpool in front of the Kop. The whole stadium was red and white, volatile and hostile. You wouldn't have believed you are watching a 19-year-old boy. Of course we knew the senior players are going to look and going to judge. When he came in, naturally people were saying, "Wow, he's tall but he doesn't have the biggest frame." The only way to convince those players is with your ability; that would take time but he came in after beating AC Milan in the Super League and making a penalty save. He wasn't a raw recruit. He had played in Madrid derbies and against Barcelona. We knew it could be a slow process.'

As United shipped goals and threatened to lose ground to neighbours Manchester City, observers wondered whether Ferguson would remain faithful to his young goalkeeper. Indeed, De Gea could often appear haphazard in his personal preparation. He is long-sighted and wears contact lenses during games, but in those early days there were several sessions where he forgot to insert his lenses before training began. The United manager had previously indulged growing pains in young outfield players, such as the Class of 92, Cristiano Ronaldo and Wayne Rooney. Some tested his tolerance rather more.

Luis Nani, the Portuguese winger, was a case in point as his inconsistency baffled the manager. Ferguson became more irked when the player moved into the same street as him and brought with him a dog with a bark that could keep the neighbours up at night. Ferguson was patient with his outfield talent, but would he show the same endurance with a goalkeeper, where every mistake can have such grave consequences? De Gea was, after all, the goalkeeper on the day United lost 6-1 at home to Manchester City in October 2011.

De Gea is able to highlight two turning points. In his debut season, Ferguson demoted his goalkeeper to the bench after a mistake at home to Blackburn in December. Anders Lindegaard came in and, when the Danish goalkeeper then became injured, De Gea even faced a challenge from United academy prospect Ben Amos. In the lead-up to a trip to Chelsea in February 2012, column inches were filled with a debate as to whether Ferguson could afford to risk putting the Spaniard back in his goal ahead of Amos [who started the 2017–18 season on loan from Bolton at third division side Charlton Athletic].

De Gea started and, although the game ended 3-3, his reputation was enhanced by an extraordinary save to deny Chelsea's Juan Mata, who would later become a teammate at Old Trafford. Deep into stoppage time, Mata could not have placed his 30-yard free kick any more accurately, and sent it searing towards the top corner to De Gea's left. The Spaniard, however, launched himself across his goal and somehow diverted the ball past the post with his right hand. 'I've seen this one a thousand times . . .' he laughs, clicking on YouTube. 'This might have been the defining moment of my United career. The week leading up to it, the third-choice keeper Amos had been in the team ahead of me. From there onwards, it got better and better. Juan is still pissed off about that one.

'The second big moment was midway through my second season. Ferguson was amazing with me. I had been under pressure after a game at Spurs, where Gary Neville criticised me on Sky Sports. I made a mistake late on but I'd made a hatful of brilliant saves that day. It doesn't bother me, that. Neville was right. It was snowing and I misjudged a cross. Not long after, we were playing Real Madrid away from home. Ferguson brought me into the press conference in Real Madrid's stadium. He told everyone, the British media, the Spanish media, that I have a special talent. I remember what he said exactly. He compared me to a young toddler taking their first steps forward. You wobble, get up, wobble, get up again and then you walk. Ferguson ended that press conference saying: "The boy is walking now." Ferguson sat next to me and told the world how much he believed in me. I felt emboldened. Ferguson was very patient with me. He did not shout and was never too harsh. He knew I needed time and trust.'

It was wonderful imagery and De Gea responded with one of the more impressive performances of his young career, as he made save after save to repel Real Madrid and helped United earn a valuable 1-1 draw. Ferguson was angered by Neville's analysis in which he said United players would admonish De Gea in an unforgiving dressing room. He privately rebuked Neville and sources from the dressing room insist that his senior team-mates rallied round him, recognising that the goalkeeper's many saves earned United a draw. He started to feel the benefit of his intensive gym work. In Spain, the focus for goalkeepers is on technical awareness and development. As a youngster, De Gea was schooled in *fútbol sala*, the Spanish answer to five-a-side or seven-a-side indoor football. 'At school, I played as a striker until about the age of 14. On a Saturday, at a nursery team affiliated to the Atletico academy, I was in goal from the age of eight. *Fútbol sala* is a huge part of my development. I was playing out of goal, in tight, confined spaces, one or two touches – and they had to be sharp and accurate passes. It made me technically stronger, confident with the ball at my feet and, in this day and age as a goalkeeper, it's essential.'

At Colegio Castilla in Toledo, De Gea played football,

basketball and tennis. Manuela Infante, his PE teacher, recalls: 'Every sport he tried, he seemed to master. His mum Marivi was always right on top of him. She'd call up every week, three or four times, saying. "I'm very worried about David." We are still in touch now. She had concerns as well about the balance between his studies and his sports. When he was jetting off to tournaments with Spain, he'd miss a lot of school and it reached the point where he had to choose whether to prioritise football or studying.

'Of course, that would always be a no-brainer. He was going to European and World Championships. I would always compare him with Peter Schmeichel; the blond hair and the agility and the height. In class, the kids would write down their plans and David would write, "I want to be like Peter Schmeichel."'

De Gea has imitated Schmeichel in United's goal, although the two players' methods are contrasting. Schmeichel's sprawling, spreading saves were more conventional than De Gea's approach, as the Spaniard's telescopic legs often come to his aid. Considering their differing frames, it is a surprise when Steele points out that De Gea's glove size (between a size 10 and 11) is actually bigger than Schmeichel, who was only a size 9. He grins when I mention his unique propensity to make saves with his feet. There are numerous examples, none more eye-catching than a save in October 2017 to deny Liverpool's Joel Matip at Anfield. The Liverpool defender struck the ball from eight yards out and the speed of the shot was recorded as 58 miles per hour. De Gea's reaction time was 0.28 seconds as he jutted out a leg to make an astonishing stop.

Steele nurtured the skill at United, even introducing a training drill De Gea requested to enhance his reflexes with his feet: 'Edwin [van der Sar] was very good at saving with his feet and David had a different technique that we changed slightly. Edwin had a great phrase: "With the pace of this ball, the nearer that the striker gets to the goal, the narrower we put our feet." Edwin, at six-foot-six, was unbelievable at making saves with his feet. David uses the same philosophy now. He used to use his feet when he could have used his hands and it was a technical aspect that we worked on. Now he has the balance to do that. It doesn't matter what part of the body you use as long as you keep it out. With the pace of the ball now, if you can't get down in that split-second, then two good feet are a fantastic barrier in terms of shot-stopping.' De Gea adds: 'If the ball flies towards me, I just react like this. It's innate and really useful. Some coaches, I won't name names, have tried to change this about me but it's not happening. I like it; it's good to have a trademark. If a ball is coming towards you, it's just quicker sometimes to use your feet and legs. I can't change it.'

There were, however, certain things United could change. Diet and fitness became priorities. During the first two seasons, he was in the gymnasium at 9.30am three times a week. At the start of the week he focused on core strength using TRX bands with proprioception. In the two days before match day, it would be speed and power, involving box and hurdle jumps. Twice a week, there would be extra afternoon sessions. On top of that, there would be normal training sessions with the team and intensive English language lessons. Goalkeeping coach Steele learned some Spanish to hasten De Gea's development.

De Gea says: 'Chicharito helped me a huge amount with the language. I was learning words for the defence like "my ball", "push out", really the basics. And then I had to try and understand Ferguson's accent . . . not easy. That thick Scottish accent, it was difficult but by the end it was OK.'

Steele adds: 'So much was new to him. He didn't know anything about going to Stoke and dealing with Rory Delap's long throw – but that was my job. What did he say? He had his usual look. He raised his eyebrows, blew his cheeks out several times and goes, "Oof, oof" and mutters something to himself in Spanish. I say, "Can you translate that into English?" – and he repeats "Oof, oof" and blows his cheeks out again and smiles.'

Curiously, Steele saw positives even in De Gea's darkest

moments, such as that first afternoon at West Brom. 'I don't dwell on the negatives. He made a mistake on the goal and then second half, as you expect, the opposition sensed vulnerability and piled bodies into him. I showed him the goal and said, "That's not like you, technically." It was a simple, routine shot that went through his hands. We won the game and I said, "No problem – just you remember this." I talked him through a moment later on in the game and gave him a still image that he still keeps. Twelve minutes from the end, he comes for a cross and is above two of the players who had previously battered him and he claims the ball. His knees are high and he catches it – we say, "That's what you have to do, that takes guts, to keep coming."'

I wonder whether there was a time De Gea feared, during those early months, that it might not end well. He hesitates and frowns. 'Hmm ... I don't know, maybe. The truth is, I have always had big self-belief and it's true that was tested. I knew my best would arrive.'

At Atletico Madrid, his mentor was coach Emilio Alvarez Blanco, who became a close friend of De Gea and his father Jose, who also had a professional playing career as a goalkeeper. When De Gea began playing in the Atleti first team, he would look to Alvarez in the technical area, where he would demand a thumbs-up from his coach every time he made a save. Alvarez said: 'I remember telling him, "We cannot do this, with all the cameras, people will think we are mad." He is saying, "But it is perfect like this." It wasn't once during a match, it was constant. I explained to David that it had to be phased out.'

Alvarez formed part of Quique Sanchez Flores' backroom staff. Flores arrived in the summer of 2009 and, during the previous summer, De Gea had almost been loaned out to Numancia and Las Palmas. Roberto Martinez's Wigan also made an approach but an 18-year-old De Gea wanted to remain at Atletico. Alvarez explains: 'De Gea was the third goalkeeper, behind Sergio Asenjo, bought for €5m from Valladolid, and another called Roberto, who was older and experienced. On the first day of training at Atletico, where we had inherited a really poor situation, Quique asked me for some feedback over the goalkeepers. My first words were: "*El mejor de los tres es el niño*" [The boy is the best one]. Quique said, "Are you serious? He looks like a little boy." But he had something different. So Quique prepared him, working him hard for a month to get him ready to play. We put an 18-year-old in goal in an Atletico Madrid team that was a very different club to now under Diego Simeone. Every game put David under huge pressure.'

Flores explains: 'We needed the freshness that he brought us, his personality and sang-froid. Asenjo was nervous, over-whelmed by his price tag and under pressure. He was struggling with the attention from the press. After a few games, my mind was made up. It was clear from the analysis that De Gea had to be my first choice. He could dominate his area, he was an amazing shot-stopper, and he was athletic, tall, agile and fast. He jumped within a month from third choice to first choice at the age of 19. He got on really well with Kun Aguero. They were the two rising stars. They shared a room together on away trips, playing together on the PlayStation, and we worked a lot with the two on Aguero's movement. When David caught a cross, his first instinct would be a quick pass or throw to set Kun away. Every week, he was growing like a giant, with more recognition from the media and the fans.'

Upon taking over at Manchester United, one of Jose Mourinho's first moves was to recruit Alvarez to his back-room staff based on De Gea's recommendation. One of the methods he employed to improve De Gea's reflexes was get-ting the goalkeeper to wear a blindfold and respond to shots from close range. I met the coach in 2014 for an interview with the *Daily Mail* and he was enlightening in his analysis. 'I have a personal relationship with David and his family that is really very special. It is not normal. Usually, when you part ways, it is, "Good luck, see you again sometime." I helped

David a lot during his time with Atletico and I still do now. I would speak with him and we would analyse things together. His family were always on to me. "Emilio, help us with this – David had two great years working with you, now it's not going as well." I explained it's normal, with the change of environment, and to move to Manchester. It's a different lifestyle, language, weather, food and a club as big as United.

'Old Trafford, Manchester, Sir Alex Ferguson, that's something else. When you are so young, that's hard. David was feeling alone and he wasn't at his best in the first two years at United. He made some amazing saves, the odd brilliant match, but it was flashes of his potential. David showed his class but at Atletico he was brilliant almost every week. David suffered the effect of a "*choque*" when he moved and so did his family. They had a tight nucleus of friends and family and they left that for Manchester. It's another world.

'His parents have helped him and helped him and they do not stop. Amazing people. His dad is his best coach because he is very demanding of him. At Atletico Madrid, he was at every game, naturally, but every single training session as well, in rain or snow. It is allowed in Spain but he could not do this at United. Even when De Gea was with the *selección*, they came to watch him at training and pick him up. After training, in the car, he'd have a chat and David would say, "What did you think about that save?". They have a special, tight relationship, that is super-important. Even now, David is an international superstar, the best goalkeeper in the world, and Marivi is saying, "Oh, you forgot the boots or the gloves, I'll go back to get them now."'

De Gea admits his dad remains his harshest critic. 'My parents live in Madrid now, but they moved with me to Manchester at the start. They were my personal taxi service as a kid. Parents are parents. Without him, I wouldn't be a goalkeeper. He still gives me advice after every game. When I was a bit younger, he was probably the most honest with me. I knew he would say it as it is. Now he's softer on me, but that's because I am quite good these days, to be fair. He is still critical enough. He notices every detail, every little mistake. He has always trained me from a little boy; I have learned so much from him. It's special that you can have that bond with your dad.'

De Gea spent only two years under Ferguson's guidance and his best form has emerged in the subsequent years, under David Moyes, Louis van Gaal and Jose Mourinho. Following Ferguson's departure, a malaise set in at Old Trafford. De Gea has been the rare exception of a player who has excelled and improved. Moyes lasted one season as United slumped from champions to seventh place in the Premier League. Under Louis van Gaal, United finished fourth and fifth.

As De Gea stepped up, United deteriorated. For all De Gea's brilliance, it is not a particularly healthy reflection of a club's trajectory if a goalkeeper is the shining light for three seasons in a row. In the summer of 2015, following Van Gaal's first season at the club, matters came to a head. Real Madrid pursued De Gea, hoping to lure him back to the Spanish capital in a summer-long saga that went down to the wire on the final day of the transfer window. It ended in calamitous fashion, with De Gea waiting for news with his family in Madrid as the deadline approached and the deal fell through when midnight passed. The two clubs traded public relations blows, blaming one another for the failure of the transfer.

Ironically, the day we meet is exactly one year on, the day after the closing of the window. 'It's been a normal summer this time,' he sighs. 'People talk a lot. Were you writing about it?' I nod. He frowns. 'It's hard, I think,' he muses. 'In the digital age, there are literally thousands of things written about you. Every day, it was "De Gea this, De Gea that".'

During the month of August, De Gea's reputation in Manchester had suffered. Van Gaal repeatedly questioned his focus and claimed that a meeting took place between De Gea and goalkeeping coach Frans Hoek, in which the Spaniard stated that he did not want to be selected for United's opening two league games of 2015-16, against Tottenham Hotspur and Aston Villa. As United travelled to Villa Park, De Gea was made to train with the reserve team as Van Gaal isolated him from the first-team squad. De Gea has always denied the suggestion that he refused to play for United and insisted he told Hoek that he would be more than happy to play if selected.

Following the collapse of the transfer, he was restored to the team. 'My first game back was at Old Trafford against Liverpool. Obviously Louis had said what he said. The truth is, I wasn't sure how Old Trafford would react to me. I was nervous walking out that day. They have always been behind me but I did wonder that day. As it transpired, they were amazing. Everyone was singing my name. It was important for me.'

We meet a few weeks into Jose Mourinho's new reign as United manager and De Gea is enjoying working with the Portuguese coach. He senses a change in mentality. He has not enjoyed United's recent pursuits of fourth place and feels a title challenge may materialise under Mourinho, even if it needs a season or two to take shape. 'Yeah, it was odd. For me finishing third and fourth is not good enough. I want to win. We want to finish as high as possible. Obviously. It has to be more. Titles are what I crave as a player. It's huge for players and the club. We have to get United back to their best, back in the Champions League, back as the champions of England, back to the top.

'If you are at Manchester United, you need a manager with a winning mentality. We had that with Ferguson. Mourinho is that man. Mourinho wants to win every game and he is transmitting this to the team. We spoke during the European Championships and he told me he wanted me with him and that he wanted to win trophies. We've had a tough time since Ferguson retired; it's hard to diagnose what's happened. But we want to win the Premier League. Of course.'

When De Gea arrived at Old Trafford in the summer of 2011, he was the only Spaniard. In the subsequent years, as

United increasingly scoured the Spanish market, he was joined by compatriots Ander Herrera and Juan Mata, as well as Latin Americans Sergio Romero, Radamel Falcao, Angel Di Maria, Marcos Rojo and Alexis Sanchez. In the Cheshire suburbs, his friends and Potters trio Bojan Krkic, Joselu and Marc Muniesa also lived nearby as Stoke City recruited Spanish talent. Mata arrived in the January of David Moyes' only season in charge and, along with De Gea, he has witnessed the peaks and troughs of the post-Ferguson era.

I speak to Mata a few months into Mourinho's first season, when performances have improved but United are drawing too many games. 'When I arrived at United, it was really a very complicated time for the club. It was a period of restructuring. We won an FA Cup. I feel we are playing really very well under Jose Mourinho. The results have not been perfect but everyone is together and the fans can see the progress. The Manchester United supporters have amazed me during the past few years. At times, it has been traumatic in terms of the ups and downs but the support has been unconditional. I can think of the year when we finished outside the Champions League places and the fans still cheered us. I don't think you would find this anywhere else.

'There were too many moments where things weren't going well. We had a good run towards the end of Louis van Gaal's first season where we qualified for the Champions League and then we won the FA Cup, but they were two hard years. The media were very hard on Van Gaal and we found it difficult. Louis was an honest man and I admire what he achieved.'

Mata admits the scorching spotlight over every United performance can have an impact on morale. 'It's huge. It's one of the things I have really noticed. The repercussion of every little thing is amplified when it comes to United. I do think the level of scrutiny is higher on United than everywhere else in England. In terms of the column inches, the radio phone-ins, the airtime given to ex-players, it is intense. As players, it is just something we have to deal with, embrace and take as a compliment to the fantastic club we play for. You are dealing with something very emotional. People get too high and too low when it comes to United. It's become a mentality of extremes.'

In the case of Herrera, United's interest can be traced back to Sir Alex Ferguson's reign. In the 2011-12 season, United hosted Athletic Bilbao in the Europa League. Marcelo Bielsa's Bilbao were sensational, tearing through United with ferocious speed. The scoreline was 3-2 but only De Gea's brilliance in the United goal spared Ferguson's team a humiliation. 'This game feels like yesterday. Just over the water from here.' Herrera smiles, pointing out of the window at Gary Neville's Hotel Football and glancing across to Manchester United's stadium. 'I can't remember another team that has ever come to Old Trafford and made themselves the protagonist in the same way. We battered United. Not just United but Ferguson's United.

'I think Sir Alex Ferguson was the one who first tried to sign me. I imagine those two games made a difference. We won the second leg 2-1 in Bilbao and those games may have been crucial to my eventual move. The day before the first game, I had an injury. I was in terrible pain but then I woke up the next day and the pain had gone. Something out there wanted me to play. The team was brilliant. I think 12,000 people travelled from Bilbao. We deserved to win by four or five. I will never forget that game. I have heard Athletic fans say that it was the greatest performance in the history of the club.'

Everyone in football proclaims to be obsessed by the sport, but Herrera is unique in both his fervour and depth of knowledge. He is breathless and endearing company. 'I spoke a tiny bit of English before arriving,' he says in perfect English, having insisted on doing the interview in his second language. 'I learned quickly because I can't shut up. Antonio Valencia once asked me if my family didn't let me speak at home because I don't stop yapping at work, in the training sessions and dressing room. I want to make life happy for everyone. I don't understand when footballers are grumpy or miserable. We lead a life that everybody dreams about and we should be grateful for this every day. What's the point otherwise? If you aren't smiling, then you should be doing something else.

'We have the best profession in the world. I speak with Juan Mata about this a lot. We talk about life and the meaning of life a lot. I say to him: "What are we doing with our life if we are sad because we haven't won a game or because we are on the bench?" We have the best life, we have huge freedom and we get paid absurdly well. We can help our families and friends. Football is the best thing ever and I want to make the day good for everyone. Of course, everyone has his or her own problems and footballers are not immune to that, but I try to make the day better.'

On the day Herrera signed for Manchester United, Sir Bobby Charlton greeted him at the club's Carrington training complex. The Spaniard still keeps a picture of the two of them together on his mobile phone. Herrera first emerged at Real Zaragoza, where his father had played and later worked as a sporting director, and he remains a passionate supporter. 'Zaragoza is the city where I grew up, where I learned. Zaragoza is my club; I am a fan but that doesn't mean I don't see Bilbao as special. I want Zaragoza to be a bit more like Bilbao. But . . . I am still Zaragoza. You can change your wife – although hopefully that doesn't happen to me! – you can change your car, your hairstyle, your house . . . but the two things you can never change are your parents and your football club.'

Still, Herrera has rapidly bought into the United ideals. 'When I think about Manchester United, the first thing that comes to mind is that romance, that generation of the Class of 92. Ryan Giggs, Paul Scholes, Nicky Butt, Gary Neville, Phil Neville . . . the other one . . . David Beckham! How can I forget Beckham? United are a massive club and they have to keep that philosophy. You need a good mix. I always say that if a foreign player comes here, you have to accept there are players moulded here who would die for this club. They know and understand everything; I know I can ask Ryan questions about the history [Giggs was United's assistant manager at the time], I can learn from them. When I arrived, Tom Cleverley, Danny Welbeck and Ryan Giggs were here. It feels special, it feels different. Now we have the fearless Marcus Rashford and super Jesse Lingard coming through, too. The Premier League has four or five very strong teams but United for me will always be the most special. It is the romantic one; I feel very blessed to play for the biggest club in the country. The truth is, I was happy in Bilbao. Before United came in for me, I had a conversation with my agent. I held out my hand and said there are only five clubs in the world I would leave Bilbao for. Otherwise, I would have stayed for a very long time. If United did not come in for me, I'd still be there.'

United first made an approach for Herrera in the summer of 2013, as David Moyes attempted to make central midfield reinforcements towards the end of the transfer window. He had resisted a move for Barcelona's Thiago Alcantara, who instead signed for Bayern Munich. At that juncture, United were not prepared to meet Herrera's €36m release clause. 'I didn't know what was going to happen. I was just sat there waiting, the same as the supporters. I was very happy with Bilbao. I played very well the season before; we were in the Champions League. I wanted Bilbao to be happy with the transfer. I got my head down after the window closed. I knew they were watching me still and knew something would happen. Then Louis van Gaal became the manager and the following summer, three or four days before it happened, I was told United would trigger the release clause and of course I was very happy. I don't regret it. I am a United player; I love playing for this club and I feel the best is yet to come.'

At Old Trafford, it was not always a happy camp with Van Gaal in charge. The Dutchman was perceived to have stifled United's attacking instincts. Herrera rarely received a clear run in the team and it is interesting that he started more games in Jose Mourinho's first season than two seasons under Van Gaal. Herrera was not the only forward-thinking player to be repressed by Van Gaal's rigidity. In the 2015–16 season, Van Gaal's second campaign, United failed to score in the first half of 25 home matches. They had stopped resembling a Manchester United team, surrendering the cavalier spirit imbued into the club by Sir Matt Busby and Sir Alex Ferguson.

De Gea describes Van Gaal as '*pesado*'. It can translate in many ways. Its most extreme interpretation is, essentially, a bore. A more positive rendering would be heavy, thorough, painstaking or meticulous. Van Gaal's excessive attention to detail was out of tune with modern players. The cutting criticism delivered during post-match video analysis sessions diminished confidence. Michael Carrick and Wayne Rooney even went to the manager's office to ask him to ease up.

I met Herrera while Van Gaal was still in charge at United, shortly before the club won the first and only trophy of his reign by defeating Crystal Palace at Wembley in the 2016 FA Cup final. Early in his United career, Herrera had spoken of his admiration for Van Gaal's style of play, emphasising that the Dutchman insists on '*mucha, mucha, mucha posesión*'. Eighteen months on, he remains complimentary but explains why he found the tactical transition under Van Gaal particularly difficult.

'At Bilbao, I had played under Marcelo Bielsa. He is a *bueno loco*, a great crazy guy. He should never stop coaching. He is a positive influence on football. So many coaches these days will think, "Let's look at how they are going to play, and then, depending on how they play, we will set up in a certain way." Bielsa is the stark opposite. He doesn't give a shit how the opposition plays. He has his beliefs, his methodologies, and he sets out to dictate the terms of play. Whether it's Athletic Bilbao against Real Madrid and Barcelona or Athletic Bilbao against Levante, it's the same. He's very good for football. He is the most unique coach I have had.

'Sometimes, it was very tough to work with him. The training could be very long. Training would last as long as was necessary for him to be happy. It could be two hours rehearsing and repeating the same thing, but when you go out onto the field and it translates into a show-stopping performance, it is vindicated. He will take notes from every football game he watches. So, for example, he is watching United and Wayne Rooney and Anthony Martial dovetail in a certain way ... Bielsa will take this clip and simulate and apply it into his system. You will practise it time and time again and, during training, you're thinking, "The same again, the same again", but during the game, you know what your team will do.

'Football needs him. Van Gaal and Bielsa are totally different managers. What I will say is that they are both offensive managers. They both want to win through the ball. That is good for me; but they are different in how they go about it. Bielsa believes you have to move to find the ball. Van Gaal believes the ball has to find you. So with Van Gaal, you are far more rigid and fixed to your positions. Bielsa wants you to be fluid, to show and ask for the ball, to be on the move, taking a risk in your play. He doesn't want to wait for the ball; he wants you to be the protagonist. It was a completely different mentality for me. I have spoken with Van Gaal about this several times.'

Under Van Gaal, Herrera played as part of a three-man midfield and occasionally as a creative player behind the forward. Jose Mourinho has reinvented the Spaniard, employing him as a deep-lying midfielder whose job is to break up the play, recoup possession at speed and set United onto the front foot. Herrera's form impressed to the extent that he won his first senior Spain cap at the age of 26. He told the esteemed Spanish journalist Rodrigo Errasti: 'Mourinho's day-to-day work has impressed me. I am enjoying it hugely. Along with Ernesto Valverde and Luis Milla, he is probably the coach whose way of working I subscribe to most clearly. Mourinho puts on very dynamic training sessions; they vary hugely between the tactical, technical and competitive. This means you don't have very long exercises where you might lose concentration. He keeps us on our toes.'

Herrera became Mourinho's on-field general. Towards the end of the 2016-17 season, Mourinho asked Herrera to fulfil a specific man-marking job on Chelsea's Eden Hazard when Antonio Conte's team visited Old Trafford. Herrera covered every blade of grass in pursuit of the Belgian, nullifying the threat and also producing an assist for Marcus Rashford and scoring himself in a 2-0 victory.

As a youngster at Zaragoza, opinions were split over his best position. His former manager Jose Aurelio Gay said he could be the next Xavi Hernandez. Gay's assistant, the former Tottenham midfielder Nayim, still believes that Herrera could flourish in a more progressive role. 'I knew him as a boy because his dad was the sporting director of Zaragoza. I remember having a chat with Pep Guardiola after a game against Barcelona and he could not stop talking about Ander. He loved him and might have signed him had he stayed there. He said, "This boy has everything I look for in a Barcelona player; he uses his head when he has the ball, he makes the right decisions, he anticipates play and thinks ahead." He played so well in Bilbao. As a person, too, he is unbelievable. I think he's a ten. He maybe lacks the physique for number four, to compete for every ball. As a ten, he is one of the best in the world. His final ball is excellent; he can shoot with both feet.'

Herrera's midfield influences can be traced to a childhood watching his team Zaragoza from the terraces. 'Gus Poyet – he was not brilliant at creating chances but he knew where to be in the right moment; he had great timing and he was a great header of the ball. Paul Scholes is, for me, the one to whom we aspire – the very highest level. He knew how to score goals from midfield; his timing was excellent, how to pass short, how to pass long – Scholes is maybe the best in United's history. I also loved Pablo Aimar, he was a fantastic player. Unfortunately, he came to Zaragoza and suffered injuries so he couldn't reach his Valencia levels.'

At United, Herrera has confounded early critics, so much so that supporters began championing the Spaniard to be the club's next captain by the end of Jose Mourinho's debut season in charge. It would have been a remarkable story of improvement, much like his great friend De Gea, although his progress stalled after the arrival of Nemanja Matic in August 2017. 'What can I say about David?' Herrera says, with a shrug. 'With other players, I can say they are grafters, they stay after training, they are hard workers. With David, he just has something special. He was born with a gift. Of course, he trains well but he has a special talent. There are times in training when I'll shoot and in my head I'm saying, "*Gol, gol, gol, gol!*" like the Spanish commentators, and then this cat-like hand emerges from nowhere and claws it away. I just shake my head, laugh and enjoy him.

'He's made saves during games where I've stopped in my tracks and just said to myself, "Fuck! How good is this guy?" What is amazing is he will make a save and everyone's singing his name, the TV's showing six replays from different angles, Twitter's going mad ... and he just gets up as though it is the easiest and most natural thing in the world. It's just his work. Before games in the dressing room, I am a bit crazy. I get very tense and nervous. I have to shake about, dance, and constantly move before playing. David pats me on the back, shrugs and says: "No, Ander, stand still, don't worry, it can't go wrong. If they shoot, they cannot score because I'm in goal."

'He's extremely calm. It's like nothing has happened. In the FA Cup semi-final against Everton in 2016, he saved a penalty and after the game he's just like, "OK. That happened. What do you want to do tomorrow afternoon?" It's like a student handing in an assignment and moving on to the next one. This is greatness. For me, he is the best.'

CHAPTER 12

The Modern Mister

In a dimly lit meeting room, illuminated only by the glare of a hi-tech whiteboard, Aitor Karanka is extolling the pain and pleasure of football management. Juanjo Vila, the team's head analyst who joined upon Middlesbrough's promotion from the Championship, stares into a laptop alongside Karanka. At Bolton, Sam Allardyce used to call his equivalent war room the 'Oxford University of Football'. Karanka's operation is similarly forensic.

We meet in late February 2017, when the early thrill and excitement of promotion have given way to a sense of trepidation as fears grow of an immediate return to the Championship. Boro are eight Premier League games without a win and have scored in only three games during that run. Supporters are becoming frustrated by the team's blunt edge in front of goal. The January transfer window was a calamity, as a luxury wishlist that featured Bojan Krkic, Robert Snodgrass, Gerard Deulofeu and Jese Rodriguez instead produced underwhelming signings such as Rudy Gestede from Aston Villa and Patrick Bamford from Chelsea.

As the transfer window edged towards its denouement, Karanka did not hold back: 'We need to improve the team, and the club knew a month and a half ago the players that I wanted.

I always said the aim in the transfer window was to improve the squad. At the moment, we haven't done that. We will be disappointed if nobody else comes in, but I have tried my best. Teams in our position are signing players for £14 million – we are signing players that didn't play in the Championship [Gestede]. Patrick didn't play for almost 18 months, so I don't think it is an amazing improvement.'

He later added: 'I didn't criticise the board or the club, it was just showing my frustration. I can't come here to say I'm really pleased when I had three targets [Snodgrass, Rodriguez and Bojan] and lost three targets. I'm not that kind of person. If I have frustrations then I can't hide them.'

This is the third occasion I've spent extended time in Karanka's company this season and I am pleasantly surprised to find his mood remains chirpy. He asks me to arrive at the club's Rockliffe training ground for 7.15am. I arrive in the leafy Darlington countryside to find he was in situ 15 minutes earlier. Sunrise is still half an hour away and training does not start until 10.30am but Karanka has his head in the computer. He walks past the dressing rooms. A quote by the American motivational speaker Robert H. Schuller is emblazoned on the wall: 'Tough situations don't last. Tough people do.'

Karanka is usually the first in, along with Avril Chilton, the 69-year-old cleaning supervisor. The first two to arrive every day, they have struck up a unique bond. She pops by the office to say hello and is greeted by a smile and a hug from the manager. Karanka is still enjoying Premier League life. He insists it is a misconception that he is feeling the pressure, reminding me that, as assistant manager to Jose Mourinho at Real Madrid, he often took the press conferences once the Portuguese had fractured relations with the Spanish media. He feels reassured after chairman Steve Gibson took the rare step of joining players and staff for lunch a few weeks earlier. It was taken as a show of unity.

On a stool in his managerial office, he has every match-day programme from the season. On his desk stand birthday cards from his children and their annual school photographs. During the school holidays, his teenage son comes along to the training ground, acting as a runner for Dad from the touchline. Photo frames adorn the walls behind Karanka's desk. There is a caricature portrait of the former Real Madrid defender, a present from some of his closest friends for his 40th birthday. He has a Jose Mourinho calendar, which was a present from his mentor during the pair's time together at Real Madrid. Mourinho recruited Karanka as his assistant manager. The Spaniard kept the calendar because it included Mourinho's quote: 'A coach can lose a lot of games but he should never lose his dignity.'

Inside another frame sits a reminder of where it all started. He runs his hand over the teamsheet, programme and ticket from his first Middlesbrough home game in the Championship. The team won 1-0 against Bolton Wanderers. Most poignantly, to the right of a mini-whiteboard stands a photograph of Karanka with Alastair Brownlee, the local BBC Teesside commentator who died in February 2016 after a battle with cancer.

Karanka's character was formed in the Basque country, where he emerged at Athletic Bilbao, before joining Real Madrid, where he won three Champions League titles. He explains: 'To be a Basque person brings many connotations. To be noble, hard-working, dedicated and a fighter. There is a mythical image of a Basque, but I like it. My mother is from Valencia. My dad is Basque. From being a little boy, it was drummed into me what it meant to be Basque. I feel similarities between the region and Teesside. I realised this very quickly. The people work hard, support their team, they have regional pride. For Middlesbrough, this was more than a promotion. The region needed it. The fans at Athletic have a sense of ownership about their team and it's the same here; they feel they have a stake and we can never lose that.

'The chairman Steve Gibson is long-serving and a local. It's not about winning or losing; it's the sense that the club belongs to the fans. I saw that as soon as I signed here, and two and a half years on, the feeling is even stronger. When we won at Manchester United in the EFL Cup last season, the supporters all lit up their mobile phones at the same time. It was a show of support for the steelworks industry, which has been decimated up here. We have a societal responsibility. This region is suffering. Jobs have been lost and we are their outlet to switch off for 90 minutes on a Saturday. It provides more motivation. We lost a journalist here, Ali [Brownlee], who was hugely respected. The club had a long-standing relationship with him; I became close to him. As soon as I arrived here, he took me under his wing. He loved the club and I enjoyed spending time with him. You knew he cared. His spirit pushed me on and the fans sang his name.'

During Karanka's first press conference at the club, he declared his ambition to be promoted to the Premier League. He had been a surprise appointment. Karanka's previous coaching work had been in the Spanish national team youth set-up, helping the development of players such as David De Gea, Bojan Krkic, Alvaro Morata and Thiago Alcantara, and then as an assistant for three years under Mourinho. Never before had Middlesbrough appointed a foreign manager, a tradition that extended back to Jack Robson in 1899.

In winter 2013, the club were languishing in the lower reaches of the Championship and required radical change. Chairman Steve Gibson told the *Independent*: 'I spoke to Peter Kenyon, a former Manchester United and Chelsea executive, who's a close friend of mine over many years. Pete has these unbelievable contacts. I said: "Help me. This has to be right this time." We drew up a shortlist and one name stood out: Aitor's. I said: "Let's meet him, let's go to Madrid to see him." Pete said: "Wait a minute, I'll call him." Pete came back into the room and said: "He'll be here tomorrow." Aitor came over. It was like we'd known each other for years. Youth development, ethics, a lot of people pay lip service to all this, but, without being asked,

Aitor made a presentation to us. After it I said: "I've no questions because you've just answered them all." He lit all the fuses.'

When we met in August 2016, Karanka was similarly effu-
sive about his chairman. Upon learning of Boro's interest,
he had spoken to Mourinho, who had consulted the former
Middlesbrough goalkeeper Mark Schwarzer to gather some
more background about the club. 'He is the best chairman
I could wish for. It was the right place, the right project, he
convinced me totally. We didn't talk about money even once in
the interview. It didn't interest me. Money was not a big thing
in my career. It's the last thing on my mind, the last question.
First, the chairman; second, the club; then whether my family
are happy; then making sure my backroom staff have the right
contracts. Then my money.'

Boro were in peril when Karanka arrived and for a few
weeks, he wondered whether he had erred. His team lost 1-0
at home to Brighton in December 2013, on a freezing night at
the Riverside in front of only 13,635 spectators. In May 2016,
33,806 supporters came through the turnstiles for the draw
with Brighton that sealed promotion. 'I had never managed a
club and I had never worked abroad from Spain. So it was a
totally different culture, language. I wasn't going to be working with Spanish kids this time. I tried to observe what things
were like and what needed to change. They'd never had a non-
British coach.

'The crucial moment for me was a conversation with Roberto
Martinez. He called me after the first games didn't go well. I was
panicking. I didn't know the culture, the club, the language and
I was a bit worried. That conversation gave me big confidence.
Fear is a strong word. It was a feeling of uncertainty, insecurity
of the unknown. We won one in five and the language was an
issue also at the start. I wasn't sure if I was successfully transmitting the ideas. You always have that insecurity.

'Steve Gibson was spectacular. After five games without a win
in Spain, the chairman's packing your suitcase and waving you

off at your doorstep. Steve was the opposite. Amazing man. The team was improving, it was a long-term project; the club was evolving. The chairman gave me huge confidence. I realised I had to blend my principles from Spain into the ideology and philosophy of English players. I couldn't change it all overnight.'

Martinez has become a mentor for Spanish coaches landing in England. He is, by common consent, more approachable than Rafa Benitez. 'It is not an obligation,' Martinez explains. 'I understand that when you arrive into British football, it's like a ten-year education overnight. Without having someone to lean on, it can be really hard. Even at the start, you will have three or four moments each day where you have to take a decision that can shape your reign. The margin between those decisions is minimal but the consequences can be grave.

'If I can help someone from my country and help them understand the culture, why not? It's not that I know everything but it's that I've made errors myself and can stop others doing the same. It was a brave decision for him to leave Spain for Middlesbrough; he took a decision he didn't need to do. I only recently learned the phrase in English "learning on your feet". It sums it up; an instinct that you have to have. You are learning a language, culture and taking off the comfort blanket.'

Initially, Karanka came here alone as he searched for schools for his children and a home for his family. He spent three hours a day improving his English. The team picked up form, ending the campaign with six victories in eight games and providing a platform for the new season. In 2014-15, the team finished fourth, and only four points behind the automatic promotion places. They entered the play-offs and a final against Norwich City beckoned. One month earlier, they had defeated Norwich 1-0 away from home in the league. At Wembley, however, hearts were broken. He shakes his head. 'I have a whiteboard here in my office where I stick on Post-it Notes for each fixture. The summer after that Wembley defeat, I probably had my lowest moment as Middlesbrough manager. I came into this office at the start of pre-season and had to stick up another 46 Championship fixtures. It was a terrible feeling. I don't mean that disrespectfully to the Championship but we want to be in the Premier League. It made me more determined than ever.'

Middlesbrough channelled the despair of defeat and achieved promotion in the 2015–16 season. There were complications. In March, Karanka was absent from the touchline for a 2–0 defeat away at Charlton. It had followed an alarming slump in form that had seen Boro win only three of their previous ten games. There was talk of a row between players and staff in a pre-match meeting. On the Monday, Karanka was back at work. It was certainly one of the more peculiar episodes in English football. 'The press and social networks went mad,' he says. 'I had talks with the chairman. I never wanted to leave. There was talk about my relationship with the players, but we went the last ten games unbeaten after that and got promoted. That's some manager who has no relationship with his players but can do that! It was never my idea to leave. I can understand the reaction, of course. The relation that I have with Steve is different and the most important thing is that everything was clear. It was fine in the end. I watched the game with my family at home.'

Promotion was confirmed on the final day of the season with the 1–1 draw at home to Brighton. Karanka said post-match that he 'just wanted to go to bed and cry'. He lets out a rueful smile. 'I couldn't go to bed and cry because we had to celebrate. It's true, though. I was emotional. My children, my wife and my parents were there. It was a big thing for me. It was my first job in management and I took a team from fighting relegation to the Premier League. The year before, we'd had 46 games and lost the final – gutting. It was emotion for the players, for Ali Brownlee. The players were thinking about the meal and the celebration. For me, it was about achieving our aim. I'd said in my first press conference I would achieve it and people nearly fell off their chair.

'Management is a really lonely job. Really, it's hard to imagine how lonely it can be. I learned this with Jose. When you win, everyone takes credit and you have lots of friends. The striker who's scored the goal, the defence keeping the clean sheet, everyone wants a piece of it. When you lose, there's one man to blame. When things go wrong, it's the manager who takes the flak. I was pleased for my family too, they had made such sacrifices. I try and switch off at home but my wife will tell you something else. It can be hard on the family. Football is a 24-hour life. I am trying to improve it but I need to be better.'

Mourinho called to congratulate his friend. 'I learned a lot from him. I was maybe unsure as to how is best to man-manage people. Jose taught me that you have to be honest with people. He will tell people totally honestly, to their face, what he thinks and why he has dropped them. It's not something people want to hear. You have to be able to show them exactly and look them in the eye. He also taught me that no player is bigger than the team. OK, there's Lionel Messi and Cristiano Ronaldo, but I don't have a 70-goal-a-season striker here and with a side like ours the team has to come first and the players must understand that.

'Jupp Heynckes was vital for me, too. He brought me through at Athletic Bilbao, he signed me when I was 23 for Real Madrid and then took me back to Bilbao later on. I'm proud to play for a coach like him and work for him. His methods remain relevant, 16 years on from when I played under him. Training sessions have of course moved on, but Mourinho used the same disci-pline and organisation as Jupp. The principles of punctuality, respect and mealtimes do not change.

'There is this wonderful respect between coaches in England. We played against Hull in the FA Cup in the 2013–14 season and Steve Bruce invited me into his office. It surprised me and he spoke to me as an equal. He was a player I admired a lot. Arsene Wenger let us use Arsenal's training ground before a Wembley game and answered the phone to me. Brendan Rodgers was in touch at Liverpool. Roberto Martinez at Everton was a crucial comfort to me. In Spain, this culture doesn't exist. That glass of wine after a game is hard when you lose. You sometimes just want to get on the bus and avoid everything. You can dodge talking about the game but, for me, it's amazing to listen to these guys and learn from them.'

In Premier League company, Karanka made a bright start. His team had defeated Manchester City and Manchester United in cup competitions while in the Championship and they continued to trouble the elite upon promotion. Boro secured draws against Pep Guardiola's City and Wenger's Arsenal away from home. It is hard to fault their level of preparation. Middlesbrough use software called *3D Fútbol Táctico Coach*. Vila created the application in late 2014 and it has subsequently been used by Pep Guardiola at Bayern Munich, Vicente del Bosque as Spain manager, the Spanish Football Federation in the youth age groups and Jose Antonio Camacho as manager of Gabon. Before every game, Karanka receives an 80-page dossier from Vila and his three understudies. The same depth of work went into Accrington Stanley and Oxford United at home in the FA Cup as it does for a Premier League game.

Vila's team watch up to seven of their opponents' previous games, from three different angles: the TV camera, the tactical camera and from behind the goal. They then package the information into the dossier. It contains the previous four formations used by opponents, how to exploit deficiencies and how to stifle rivals. It includes every set-piece movement the opponents have used and an individual analysis of every player in the opposition squad. It extends to the personality of individual opponents, including their character strengths and flaws. It details whether they can be wound up and gives examples of tactics previously used to trouble them.

After Karanka reviews the dossier, it is packaged into a 14-minute video presentation to the team. On Thursday and

Friday, every individual player spends 12 minutes with the analysis team to prepare for their direct opponent. Striker Alvaro Negredo, for example, would watch specific clips on the opposition goalkeeper, knowing how to address one-on-one situations. Goalkeeper Victor Valdes would receive the likely penalty-taker's last five years' worth of spot kicks. The graphics are even broken down into whether the penalty was taken when a team is winning, drawing or losing.

'There is a clear trend with this,' Vila explains. 'Players revert to type when more pressure is on. What we don't want, though, is players driving themselves mad about it at home. Some players ask for too much information. George Friend could be like that, sometimes too much for his own good. He's a perfectionist. A team can make a sub and he'll be agonising over whether the player coming on is left- or right-footed.'

Karanka smiles: 'When I was a player, we had a VHS tape and we'd watch the opponents' last game. This isn't too much. It's the application of the information that matters. We don't just give them the situation. We give them the solutions.'

Some players require extra guidance from Karanka. He signed the young Spanish winger Adama Traore from Aston Villa as a wildcard option in the summer of 2016. Traore has blistering pace but, surprisingly, lacks tactical nous. It is particularly curious considering the player was schooled at Barcelona's La Masia. 'Adama and I have individual video sessions in my office,' Karanka says. 'He says he's not had proper tactical guidance previously at Aston Villa or Barcelona. But I still only let him play on the wing near my dugout so I can guide him. The fans love him and he commits defenders. The problem is he has not scored a goal or made an assist! Christian Stuani, who is less popular with fans, comes in and grabs a goal. I show Adama videos. Sometimes, we attack and he's not in the box. I say, "Adama, if you're 30 yards away from the box, you might as well be in the stand with a hot dog and a beer." He laughs and he knows where he needs to be. He is getting there but there are still issues. In the FA Cup last week, we played against Oxford. We were 2–0 up and he totally switched off. I had to take him off to save the team. It went to 2–2 and then we got a late winner.'

As he reflects on the season, he can clearly pinpoint the days the preparation worked. He picks up his smartpen and explains the game plan that earned a draw at Arsenal. The clip shows Boro with most players behind the ball as Arsenal control possession. 'So what happens when we are in shape and Arsenal lose the ball?' He draws shadows over Hector Bellerin and Nacho Monreal, high up the pitch and with large swathes of space in behind them. 'We took advantage and trained all week to prepare a way to defend that would allow Traore to neglect his defensive duties and stay high on the wing. It gave us a clear outlet with pace in space on the counterattack. His pace caused Arsenal nightmares and, really, we deserved to win. The key to hurting Arsenal is the first pass on the counter. If you get that right, you're at the heart of their defence in a split-second.'

For every success, there is frustration. Planning and preparation have no guarantees. Against Tottenham at home, for instance, Karanka spent the week demonstrating how to prevent Pochettino's side playing out from goalkeeper Hugo Lloris. The players watched the videos and recreated Tottenham's build in 11-v-11 training drills. To prove the point, Karanka shows me the session where he walked, talked and manhandled his players into position. After promotion, he began filming every session as the club upgraded their infrastructure. Within 80 seconds of the game starting, Boro concede a clear sight of goal from the very situation they worked all week to combat. After seven minutes, the same has happened and they are 1–0 down.

'I go into the changing room at half-time and say, "Are you going to explain this to me?" As a manager, you've done all you can. It's like, "Hello?" You can't account for that. A lot of it is about concentration and belief. In that situation, you just shake

your head and laugh as a manager. When you do all that and
then players do something else. At half-time, I wasn't going to
go in and rip up that plan. I just told them to follow the plan! I
didn't say a word about tactical changes. The same against Man
City. We'd planned to press them high. The game starts and the
players showed too much respect. We spoke at half-time and
reminded them of how to press a Guardiola side.'

He shows two more clips, from the 46th minute and 62nd
minute, and the improvement is clear. Middlesbrough earned a
point through a late Marten de Roon header. Video helps management. 'If a player knocks on my door, and it's always
open, they ask why they are not starting. I have a thousand
videos to show why. It shocks the players. They never imagine
that you have so much information and justification. It's not
opinion – it's clear evidence.'

We head onto the grass for training. Karanka delegates, as
Englishman Adam Kerr puts the team through their fitness
drills. Karanka has sought to retain local influences, including
the club's former academy coach Steve Agnew as an assistant.
The club's medical and fitness department is infused with
Spanish influence but overseen by British staff. Boro's ten-strong
team – eight British, two Spaniards – won the Football Medical
Association Championship Medical and Science Team of the
Year in 2016, as the club had the best injury record in the league.

In the canteen, he greets the club's British chef, Howard
Archer. The breakfast buffet is a selection of scrambled eggs,
toast (white or brown), granola, yoghurt, fresh fruit and coffee
from the machine that Karanka hand-picked himself. Fresh
fruit smoothies are made to order. Lunch is grilled sea bream,
lamb tagine, grilled chicken and a selection of salads. Archer
is given nutritional guidelines but there is room for creativity.
He is attentive to Antonio Barragan's nut allergy and provides
halal meat for three Muslim players in the Boro squad. He has
been experimenting with Spanish dishes, introducing a paella
at lunch, and uses a Spanish food supplier for Iberian meats.

Karanka has not imposed strict rules about players eating breakfast or lunch together. Club staff, the first team and youth team all eat in the same canteen. Nobody is deemed superior. Mauricio Pochettino adopts the same approach. The two took their coaching badges together, on the same course as Karanka's former Real Madrid teammate Fernando Hierro. Former West Bromwich manager Pepe Mel was one of the mentors in the classes. In the canteen, tomato ketchup, mayonnaise and brown sauce are readily available. Karanka does not believe in threats. 'They are grown-ups. If you say, "No, no, no", you're treating them like children. Don't have coffee! Don't have ketchup! A few bad results and they'd resent it, go home and be squirting ketchup all over their food. We had Lee Tomlin here. He lost nine kilos playing under me. I didn't ban anything.

'It's very straightforward. Players want to play. If you want to play, you have to train properly. To train properly, you have to be in shape. It's like the dressing room on match day. When I was playing, it was like church before a game. Focused silence. Now some send text messages, music's blaring out like a disco. People say, "You're crazy, they have their head elsewhere." I don't mind. If they are taking daft pictures and putting them on social media before a game, I'm annoyed. They don't do that. If your daughter's calling you for five minutes and a player wants to hear "Good luck, Daddy", why stop that?'

Yet the Hispanicisation of the club cannot be missed. There are eight Spanish or Spanish-speaking South American players in the squad: Spaniards Victor Valdes, Antonio Barragan, Dani Ayala, Adama Traore and Alvaro Negredo, Colombian Bernardo Espinosa and Uruguayan pair Gaston Ramirez and Christhian Stuani. As the players eat breakfast and lunch together, the Spanish-speaking contingent are clearly close. On the training ground, Karanka uses Spanish words such as *bueno* (good), *eso es* (that's the one!), *vamos* (come on). It has clearly become part of the team's vernacular. Several languages are heard in the canteen.

On the ground floor of the training base, another Spaniard has been appointed to oversee the club's recruitment. Victor Orta arrived at the club in December 2015 with the aim of expanding Boro's international expertise. He had previously worked in the recruitment departments of Sevilla, Valladolid and Elche in Spain, while his most recent position had been at Zenit St Petersburg. Orta is a sparkly and zestful character. He is, in the nicest possible way, the geek to end all football geeks. His office is littered with thoughts, scribbles and, above all, newspapers and magazines.

'I probably have over 5,000 at home. I keep everything, I'm a proper hoarder. I have every *Don Balón* from Spain. I have every *El Gráfico* from Argentina, almost every *Placar* from Brazil, every *FourFourTwo* magazine from the United Kingdom. I studied chemistry. I was nuts about football and a real *madridista*. I was a little boy in love with football. Every day, I'd buy every *Marca* and every *AS* newspaper. It must have been really weird to see a nine-year-old in school with a stack of papers. I read everything before the 1986 World Cup. I had two older brothers, my parents were working all the time and they'd bring me home stickers for those pre-tournament collections. I could name and memorise every player from every nation in every position. I read and listened to everything by the commentator Julio Maldonado on Canal+.

'I remember buying the first *Championship Manager* and becoming engrossed with this crazy thirst for knowledge. In Valencia, I started contributing to a radio programme. I was working as a waiter and studying at university and, three months later, I had a radio programme during the World Cup in 2002. People loved it. We had a huge audience and all the students were listening to it. Then *Marca* took me on. It was hard work. I worked with the excellent journalist Nacho Silvan, who now manages the PR for David De Gea, Juan Mata and Cesar Azpilicueta. When you join a newspaper, it's hard to earn acceptance from the old guard. They don't always treat you well.

People think you will tread on their toes or that you're trying to oust them. There's a lot of office politics. It wasn't easy. Nacho was in Malaga and then Madrid and from the first moment he helped me out a lot. He told me I was good, that I am young; it's difficult but bear it out, and you will do well. My name began to be recognised.'

He then made the move into scouting. 'I started working with an agency, with basketball players and then footballers. When I was 26, the president of Valladolid got in touch and offered me a role in the second division. It went well and in 2006 Monchi at Sevilla approached me. Juande Ramos was the manager at the time. They'd just won the UEFA Cup. It was a far bigger club and there was more pressure to get things right. Monchi was one of my best mentors. He was the genesis of the sporting director position. For over a decade at Sevilla, he has remained the constant as head coaches come and go. The club have won five UEFA Cup/Europa League titles under his guidance.

'When I was there, our biggest signing was Ivan Rakitic. Monchi had all that knowledge and an amazing contacts book. We made more trips and spent more hours on it than anyone. We signed Rakitic in the winter market. We signed him for just over £1m and actually his form just before that winter window was not great under Felix Magath at Schalke in Germany. We had followed him for three years, though, so we could explain that aberration. He wasn't motivated, his contract was short but we had seen him for over two years and could look beyond short form. He did brilliantly and joined Barcelona for a fortune. That example was the embodiment of the club's strategy.

'Another hero of mine is Ramon Martinez, who worked at Real Valladolid, Barcelona and Real Madrid, and he was the first person who had brought the video analysis in, who started travelling to South America in the 1980s. He was an idol to me.'

At Middlesbrough, Orta has overseen an internationalisation of Boro's recruitment apparatus. 'We have Gary Gill, who is the head of English scouting, and there is a team of four alongside me in here. We have an international chief scout, David Ruiz, who is a journalist who has worked for Canal+. He is Brussels-based and we have two scouts in Spain. They do a dual job – video work, watching three or four games a day, and then travel to games at the weekend. There are only 12 or 13 in our team. Man United or Man City have 50 or more!

'One of the things I'm focusing on is to nurture my mind so I can understand clearly what makes a good player for the Premier League. We did a report last year on the top 20 successful players in the Premier League. We included clear characteristics: height, how many years they'd spent in the Premier League, where they had been schooled as a kid. We want a model of footballer that is likely to enjoy Premier League success. It's not quite mathematics but it's not far off. Maybe it's my chemistry mind. Many of my friends say to me, "Don't you get tired of all this football?" I will go to an Under-20 competition in Venezuela and watch three games back to back. I still have that passion of a fan. With the passing of time, most people lose that enthusiasm for the game itself. I have my wife, my parents, my kids . . . but I consider everything in relation to football.'

Boro's best signing ahead of their Premier League campaign was Marten de Roon, a £12m midfielder from Atalanta. 'We had watched him for over a year. He had showed some qualities in Holland but, from the point of view of an immediate trans-fer, he wasn't right. However, he took his technical and tactical qualities and harnessed them with the competitive spirit of Italy in a very short space of time. It made us sit up and go, "Fuck! We need to get this guy." We tried to get him in January and eventually got him in July.

'There were two lines in our thoughts in January 2016. If we stay in the Championship, we'll want fewer foreigners and more who know the division inside out. If we go up, then De Roon is a goer. From February, we watched every one of his games live at the stadium. We all agreed it was right. I need to be very sure that he is right before taking the name to the manager. I can't go with 20 names. It's three or four and I will state my preference. Then you begin the process of investigating possibilities. I knew the agent of Maxi Moralez, a former Atalanta player, so I could ask Maxi what this boy is like in the dressing room and off the pitch. I was told he was a leader. I read every interview he ever gave, all his social media posts. How many yellow and red cards? He has to be the right character.'

Some signings depend less on research and more on the manager's credentials. 'We signed Victor Valdes on a free and Alvaro Negredo on loan. The players simply wanted to play for Aitor. Valdes had endured a terrible time in his career at Manchester United and Negredo needed a change. He had been criticised a lot in Valencia and a change of scenery was needed. Valencia is a hard club to play at, with all their flux and media pressure.'

Valdes produced a handful of magnificent displays, particularly away at Manchester City, but he was hard work in the dressing room. On one occasion after a defeat, he reminded team-mates of his pedigree as a Champions League winner at Barcelona. More than once, coaching staff were forced to intervene to prevent a physical confrontation with Valdes.

The week we meet is the eve of a crucial relegation six-pointer against Crystal Palace. Boro went on to lose the game 1-0. Then Karanka's side surrendered meekly at Stoke. It would be his last Premier League game. Stories emerged of training-ground quarrels with long-serving Boro winger Stewart Downing. The former Liverpool player had been omitted from the squad against Stoke and taken umbrage at the decision. Relations between Karanka and Downing had been frosty for a long while. Karanka had been open to selling the player upon gaining promotion and might have allowed him to leave in January too. In the weeks preceding his departure, Karanka had made attempts at uniting the squad.

'Before the Everton game in February, we had a big chat. We went to Benidorm, cleared our heads a bit. I said we have to play more, get more bodies into the penalty area, that we are playing at home and need to do more. We had drawn against West Brom and lost to Spurs. They were giving everything. It was annoying me that we needed to go behind to get going. Against West Ham, we scored a brilliant equaliser, flowing football. Against Man City, the same. Why do you have to let a goal in to get going? You can think, "What more can we do? What more can they give?"'

Middlesbrough's biggest problem was at the Riverside, where they had won only three of 13 home games and scored only 11 goals. An early warning sign came with a 1-0 defeat by Watford in October. 'It affected me, of course. After that game, I went to the manager's room in the stadium. I felt sick; I knew it was a bad one. But you can't show that in front of the players as a leader. If you do, you are fucked. The following morning, I came into my office after training and started looking at how to get Adama Traore into our team for the Arsenal game.

'When we've finished games, so many managers have come up to me, blown their cheeks out and said, "What a team, we can see your preparation." Ronald Koeman was glowing. After the defeat at Manchester United, Mourinho's assistant Rui Faria was going mad with me, *"Pesados, pesados"*. This organisation frustrates teams but they respect it. They know they are in a game. Antonio Conte beat us 1-0 with Chelsea and said the same. I understand the frustration because I would also like to win every game 5-0. If I was coaching Cristiano Ronaldo, Lionel Messi and Dele Alli, maybe we'd do that. We work to the strengths of the squad we have.'

Ultimately, it became clear that the players were no longer responding. It is rare these days for a manager to survive over three years at an English club. Karanka had been well aware of his side's deficiencies. It was why he pursued creative midfielders so vigorously in the January. He'd also wanted an experienced centre back to play alongside young English defender Ben Gibson. He said of Gibson: 'This boy has got personality, class on the ball. He'd be perfect with someone a bit older next to him. When I was first playing at Real Madrid, I was running all over because Roberto Carlos was raiding up the wing and Fernando Hierro would go mad, saying, "Stay here, stay in your position." I remember an episode at the Under-17 World Cup in Nigeria. I was coaching the Swansea defender Jordi Amat in a five-a-side game and played alongside him. I said, "You aren't going to move unless I tell you because I'm 37 and can't move a muscle." We won the game without conceding a goal.'

In the training session I observe, he has designed a counter-attacking drill that is aimed at making Middlesbrough more ruthless on the transition. The session involves a congested midfield battle and then three-v-three situations as the ball breaks from midfield. When Gaston Ramirez misses a chance, Karanka blows his whistle. 'We need to score. When we get an opportunity we need to score – come on! We have to take our chances.'

He was considering new motivational techniques but he concedes the modern player can be hard to control. At Real Madrid, Karanka had seen excesses. He told the *Daily Mail* in an interview in 2014: 'I had a Jeep Cherokee. My kids sometimes say to me, "Dad, why didn't you have a Ferrari as well?" But that was never me. I would rather put that kind of money into an apartment. Arriving there, it was a curious time for me. I was from Vitoria. A Basque. I preferred to stay in the background. It was very different, to walk into that changing room with Roberto Carlos, Hierro, Raul, Morientes. Very good players. But I was struck by the humility of the players. Yes, there were Ferraris outside and lots of Versace and Armani inside. But these guys always supported me and we became great friends. When I met Jose he said, "You have very good friends." I asked him why. He said he had asked Mijatovic, Figo and Seedorf, and all of them had spoken very highly of me. That was why he chose me.'

Karanka then tells me: 'The problem these days is how many people surround players. Agent, social media, marketing, the agent's assistant, the brother's an agent, their dad's the agent, the stepdad's the agent, their girlfriend … it makes life difficult. I can explain and justify my decisions to a player. They can be fine. Then they go home, and Dad's saying, "You are the best in the team!" The agent's saying, "I'll get your money and find a team."

'The boys themselves are fine. You need them to believe in the project. Most motivational stuff is awkward. I know Pep Guardiola showed a video of Barcelona players mocked up as gladiators before one Champions League final. Before the game against Norwich in the Championship, which we won 1-0, I asked our media team to do up a video for us. I put *Rocky* music and the Foo Fighters as the backing track. It included our best moments of the season, our best goals, best tackles, best saves, so everyone was involved.'

The video included a famous Rocky Balboa monologue. 'You, me or nobody is gonna hit as hard as life. But it ain't about how hard you hit … It's about how hard you can get hit, and keep moving forward … how much you can take, and keep moving forward. That's how winning is done.'

He smiles as he watches back the video. Three weeks later, he was gone. The split was amicable, as the two parties agreed a parting of the ways had been required. Chairman Gibson told *The Times*: 'Aitor is tired, he has worked so hard for our football club over the last three and a half years and the tension surrounding the end of last season would have taken its toll on anyone. Then we had a very busy summer. He was working his socks off trying to bring players in and he hasn't really had a break since the minute he walked through the door. What we concluded – he and I – was that he perhaps wasn't the guy at this point in time to deliver that change. I know people are cynical when you say that a decision was mutual, but he wasn't sacked. He sacrificed himself. He's in a good frame of mind. I think he's relieved. He has been enormous for our club.'

Karanka's mini-regiment of Spanish staff, including Juanjo

Vila, fitness coach Carlos Cachada and goalkeeping coach Marcos Abad also left the club. Karanka's assistant Agnew, a Yorkshireman, took the reins. He brought Jonathan Woodgate and Harry Redknapp's long-serving ally Joe Jordan into his staff. Orta, who some at the club felt became overly involved in first-team affairs, soon followed the exodus, heading to Leeds United where he would do it all over again with the Spanish coach Thomas Christiansen. Boro's Bernabeu experiment was over, but Karanka impressed sufficiently to be granted the chance to breathe life into one of English football's sleeping lions. In January 2018, he returned to management at Nottingham Forest. There will be no repeat of Rocky Balboa-inspired videos, but Karanka may just pick Forest up from the canvas.

CHAPTER 13

Paving Pep's Path

Only seven weeks earlier, Joe Thompson lay horizontal in a secluded room at Manchester's Christie Hospital. For the second time in four years, the Rochdale midfielder faced a battle for life, having first been diagnosed with nodular sclerosing Hodgkin lymphoma in 2013. He fought back once, receiving an all-clear in 2014, but on Christmas Eve 2016 he attended a check-up. The news came back with the force of a sledgehammer: the cancer had returned.

Thompson, however, would not be defeated. He played on for four months, even as the cancer cells were active, spreading from the middle of his chest and across to the lymph nodes in his armpits. He underwent two rounds of five-day chemotherapy sessions, and then came 18 days in isolation for stem-cell treatment. The medical professionals had warned it usually meant a six-week stay in hospital. Thompson was out within less than three weeks, although his weight had plummeted by two stone, and, shortly afterwards, he was invited along to Manchester City's hi-tech training complex.

In earlier, happier times, Thompson had trained with Manchester United. He met Sir Alex Ferguson as a teenager and, following his first diagnosis, United invited him to watch a game from a box at Old Trafford. We should remember, for all the lurid headlines this sport creates, that the great and good of football do have a wonderful capacity for uniting behind their own.

Standing outside Pep Guardiola's office, Thompson recognised the strength of his own story. 'Pep came up to me, saying, "Joe! How are you? Are you on the mend?" He was saying, "You look well!" I knew I didn't really. It was outside his office. I was like a little girl, so excited he was talking to me. All I could think was this man has changed the game, imagine all the people he has come across and now he knows my story.'

In the grand scheme of things, it might be a small gesture but to Thompson it meant the world. Guardiola is football royalty and his work has altered the landscape of a sport. Yet at times during his first season in England, it appeared Guardiola misjudged the English mood towards him. His record at Barcelona, allied with the success of the Spanish national team, provoked introspection and rethinks in English football academies, challenging the cult of gigantism and encouraging the world to hand opportunities to smaller footballers. His success convinced people that there can be another way, that aestheticism can triumph over or, at the very least, blend with athleticism.

He challenged even the most traditional of British clubs. In the corridors of power at Stoke City, directors became aware that the current trend leaned towards the more progressive approach pioneered by Guardiola. Under the Welsh manager Tony Pulis, Stoke earned promotion to the Premier League in 2008 and secured their top-flight survival for five consecutive seasons. Yet Stoke became a crude stereotype and even shorthand for an absence of sophistication. Armed with their 'human sling', as Everton manager David Moyes once disdainfully described Rory Delap, more than half of Stoke's first 13 goals in the Premier League originated from the Irishman's long throw-ins. The freezing Tuesday evening away from home at Stoke became global football code for unpleasantness and intimidation.

Some criticism was harsh. There was often far more talent

in Stoke's ranks than their detractors wished to believe and, often, it was those who came unstuck who had the more negative reflections. Pulis' side chopped the pompous and pretentious down to size, nurturing a street-fighting mentality against clubs such as Arsene Wenger's Arsenal. The same was true of Sam Allardyce's Bolton after their promotion to the top flight in 2001 and Wimbledon's Crazy Gang in the 1980s. Gary Lineker once said the best way to watch Wimbledon was on the old Ceefax. Vinnie Jones responded by branding Lineker's charisma as being as 'wet as a jellyfish' and then suggested the BBC presenter should go down to the training ground to discuss matters further. Perhaps wisely, Lineker did not take up that invitation.

For Stoke, the nadir came in 2010 when Arsenal manager Arsene Wenger compared Pulis' side to a rugby team. Six years later, the insult came full circle when England rugby head coach Eddie Jones felt the need to use the example of Stoke as a contrast to the more freewheeling and sophisticated rugby he planned to introduce. Jones said: 'If you want to play like the old Stoke City then that's the safest way to play, isn't it? Just stick the ball in the air, chase hard and get everyone to clap. We don't want to be reckless. But we don't want to be like an old Stoke City either.'

Stoke supporters made light of the jibes, teasing Wenger with the chant 'Two-nil to the rugby team' during one fixture, and also belting out their own version of 'Swing Low, Sweet Chariot', often sung by supporters of the England rugby union team. Yet for all the progress under Pulis, the club did not finish in the top half of the Premier League and, in the boardroom, a consensus developed. Direct and aggressive football has a shelf life and Stoke began to feel the team lacked sufficient wit to continue the club's forward direction. The club required a change in style to elevate itself to the next rung of top-flight football.

Sitting behind a meeting table in his office at the club's stadium, the chief executive Tony Scholes explains: 'Tony had his own style. Our highest-placed finish was 11th but, to develop further, we felt we had to change the way we play. We felt Mark Hughes could bring a more expansive style and he wanted to change some of the personnel to play in the way he wanted.'

Hughes had played in Barcelona during his own playing career but it was mostly an unhappy experience. Yet he had maintained some contacts in Spain and he also had vast Premier League experience as a manager and an impressive track record at Blackburn Rovers, Manchester City and Fulham. His most recent job, however, had been a disastrous spell at Queens Park Rangers. The London club spent huge sums erratically and then failed to win any of their first 12 Premier League fixtures of the season. So when, at the end of the 2012–13 campaign, Pulis' reign came to an end, a dose of scepticism accompanied Hughes' arrival.

'Yes, yes,' Scholes frowns. 'But if you look at his record, what he had achieved, he had been very successful with the resources available at most of his clubs. The common misconception we saw was people viewing Mark on 12 games at QPR when he got sacked. I had all the numbers from his career. He managed over 250 games before that and we formed a proper, mature opinion based on that.'

Scholes repeatedly highlights Hughes' ability to extract the most from what is available. Stoke wanted to alter their playing style but, to achieve aesthetic change, the personnel needed to change. Yet Stoke's annual salary spend is regularly among the lowest in the division and players need some persuasion to uproot to one of England's less fashionable regions. Throughout his managerial career, Hughes has demonstrated an ability to bring improvements from players previously typecast as troublesome characters. At Blackburn, he brought the best out of David Bentley, who would go on to flop at Tottenham and retire from the sport at the age of 29. At Manchester City, he coaxed outstanding form out of Stephen Ireland and Craig Bellamy. He had the pedigree of managing Champions League winners Roque Santa Cruz and Benni McCarthy at Blackburn. Many of his signings at Stoke fitted into a similar mould – players who, for one reason or another, had at one time been noted as extraordinarily gifted but rarely fulfilled their vast potential.

Scholes continues: 'One of our first signings was Marko Arnautovic, an Austrian with a pedigree for flair.' Arnautovic had exasperated Steve McClaren at Twente and Jose Mourinho at Inter Milan, where he became bosom buddies with Mario Balotelli. One one occasion, he even contrived to be late for Mourinho meetings three times in a single day. Before signing Arnautovic, Hughes had been alerted to a video of the winger fighting with his own captain while playing in Germany. Yet at £2m, Hughes saw enough potential to take a punt. He was handsomely rewarded, with four seasons of impressive showings.

Arnautovic, in his strut and bravado a doppelgänger of Zlatan Ibrahimovic, could exasperate at times but he also knuckled down. One member of Stoke's coaching staff explained to me at a dinner function how his ambitions to become a perfection-ist extended to regular demands for extra video analysis clips. During evenings after a match, he would even call repeatedly to discuss the day's game. He could amuse, too: he once called the club's player liaison officer late in the night with a special request for Rentokil, as a spider had appeared in his bathtub and this arachnophobe had little intention of resolving the issue for himself.

Stoke cashed in on the Austrian in a £20m deal in the summer of 2017, as Arnautovic departed for West Ham. It is a model that represented a change in tack for Stoke. Under Pulis, the club had a net spend of £80m over five seasons. In the Premier League, only Manchester City and Chelsea had a more lavish return during the same period. 'We have always insisted on value,' Scholes says. 'But I think over time you look at the squad and perhaps we have recently been looking more at the resale value of players as well as bringing them in. Our priority had been to retain our Premier League status. We had to sign a couple of players on big deals with limited resale value for what they could bring at a certain time to us. It ensured we stayed in the league. It remains our priority but we want to do it in a sustainable way. What we spend in one hand we must now bring in with the other as well. The cost and potential resale value of the player has been a bigger concern.'

As Stoke broadened their horizons, they began to fix their gaze on Catalonia. 'The first one we signed was Marc Muniesa, within five weeks of Mark Hughes joining the club. He was a Spanish Champions League winner with Barcelona in 2011. He typified the change we were looking to make. He was not just a centre half, he was a centre back, left-back and holding midfielder rolled into one. He was different to the six-foot-three or six-foot-four defenders we'd got in previously. They were physically stronger, while Marc was much more cultured. He was the first one we brought in from Barcelona.'

Hughes recognised the perils of revolution and promoted gradual change. It is a basic for most Premier League teams but the manager had to spend the first months drilling his side intensively on the training ground to split the centre halves and offer their services when the goalkeeper has possession. After 23 games, Stoke were 16th in the Premier League table and only three points clear of the drop zone. However, a run of only three defeats in the final 15 matches saw Stoke click into gear and end the season in ninth place.

The statistics told a story of Hughes' work. In Stoke's first five seasons in the Premier League under Tony Pulis, the club's average possession stood at 39.4 per cent, they averaged 280 passes a game and Pulis' side had more possession than the opposition in only 12 of their 190 Premier League matches. In Hughes' first four seasons, the average Premier League possession rose to 48.2 per cent, Stoke averaged 405 passes a game and they had more ball than their opponents in 69 matches. The club's final league position reflected their improvement as the club achieved three consecutive ninth-place finishes.

Within three years, Stoke reached the remarkable point

where their squad contained more Champions League winners than any other Premier League team, as Muniesa was joined by fellow Barcelona medallists Bojan Krkic and Ibrahim Afellay. Arnautovic also claimed the medal at Inter Milan, while Xherdan Shaqiri won the trophy at Bayern Munich. Stoke's reinvented *Galáctico* status was affirmed when the former Barcelona defender Carles Puyol arrived at the club's modest training complex as an agent to agree terms on a new five-year contract for Krkic.

When I meet Scholes in December 2016, there is a batch of recruits from Spain on Stoke's books. Striker Joselu, who partnered Alvaro Morata in the Real Madrid B team and received a first-team debut from Jose Mourinho, followed Muniesa and Krkic. There are also two young prospects on board in the form of Sergio Molina, a Real Madrid academy graduate, and Moroccan forward Moha El Ouriachi, signed from Barcelona. Real Madrid's former striker Jese Rodriguez signed on loan in a high-profile move in 2017.

The transformation in Stoke's personnel was quite remarkable. Pulis' starting XI for the FA Cup final defeat against Manchester City in 2011 featured eight players from the UK or the Republic of Ireland. As for the other three, Danish goalkeeper Thomas Sorensen spent the 13 previous years in England, German defender Robert Huth played out his entire senior career in English football, and Trinidad and Tobago striker Kenwyne Jones left behind his native country in 2004. Two and a half years into his time with the club, in December 2015, Hughes' Stoke demolished City 2–0 and seven of his starting players were from overseas, including a marauding Dutch left-back in Erik Pieters and all the creative talents of Afellay, Krkic, Arnautovic and Shaqiri. The BBC described the Swiss star Shaqiri that day as Stoke's 'alpine Messi'.

Krkic's arrival is reflected upon as the major trigger for the change. Krkic was a boy wonder in Barcelona's academy. In his first season, he scored 126 goals. He became the greatest marksman La Masia has produced, scoring nearly 900 goals. He was

Spain's leading forward at youth tournaments, hitting five in the Under-17 World Cup in South Korea in 2007. Manchester United pursued him vigorously at the age of 16. A year later, Chelsea's sporting director Frank Arnesen flew out to Barcelona to hold talks over a transfer. Hughes himself had previously tried to sign the player twice, first at Manchester City and then at Fulham.

Yet Bojan, in truth, should not have ended up at Stoke. In an era when talents such as Thierry Henry, Ronaldinho, Lionel Messi, David Villa and Zlatan Ibrahimovic graced the Nou Camp, Bojan struck 41 senior goals before he was 21. Yet after falling out of favour under Guardiola, loan spells at Milan, Roma and Ajax saw Krkic lose his way. He arrived at Stoke in a scarcely believable £800,000 transfer. Memories of glorious times remain. At his Catalonia home, Krkic retains thick scrap-books filled with every clipping from the Spanish sports pages. In a downstairs room, he houses his two Champions League medals and three La Liga medals. Bojan keeps the white Nike boots with which he scored his first Barça goals and has the match ball from the night he scored the winner in a Champions League quarter-final against Schalke.

More than 50 jerseys are lined up. Iniesta's shirt, swapped after a game between AC Milan and Barcelona, is the centrepiece and he keeps the playmaker's autobiography by his bed. Cristiano Ronaldo's Manchester United shirt from the 2008 Champions League semi-final at Old Trafford is near the front. At Stoke, he could not trade on past glories and the club's conditioning trainer Andy Davies worked on his upper body strength. In the space of five months, Krkic gained over three kilos of muscle. He was by now equipped for the Premier League and attracted headlines with marvellous goals in victories at Tottenham and at home to Arsenal.

Scholes smiles: 'He played a half against Arsenal in the back end of 2014 that was probably one of the finest individual per-formances we have ever seen here. We were 3–0 up and Bojan was running the show. He played the Arsenal midfield on his own, he then scored a magnificent goal to go 4-0 up but the referee wrongly gave offside. Had we gone 4-0 up, and the way he was playing, it could have been anything. It eventually came back to 3-2 but he was mesmerising.

'The big deal was Muniesa. Bojan could see from the outside how we were trying to develop as a club and he was very close to Muniesa. He explained to Bojan how we train and look after players. We absolutely asked him to help. If you are proud of what you have got, you want the players here to talk you up. With new signings, we always say they should speak to players who are already here and get a feel for the place. They will tell you honestly how it is. When Shaqiri signed, he actually said he'd watched our games with Bojan and could see what we were doing.'

Stoke became accustomed to sitting across the negotiating table from Barcelona representatives. Was the first meeting daunting? 'There is no question it is hard to deal with new people. It was harder dealing with Barcelona the first time than an English club down the road. That said, the people at Barcelona were excellent with us and we have a very good working relationship. Once we did Muniesa, it was so much easier to do Bojan and Moha. Then it becomes a deal with people you know. We do not have permanent scouts in Spain. We have a team of scouts here who monitor the games and we rely on local knowledge to a degree. We get the feeds of every game here and can watch any game across Europe. A new thing in the past three or four years for us has been watching and scouting every single Barcelona B game. We do the same with Real Madrid and several other Spanish clubs. Our scouts will go out to watch individuals.'

Stoke's scouting team is comprised of Mark Cartwright and technical director Kevin Cruickshank. They regularly fly out to Barcelona B matches, sometimes providing in excess of a dozen reports on a single player. Besides the tactical innovations, there were also financial benefits for English clubs shopping in Europe, partly due to the weakness of the euro and strength of the pound during Britain's pre-Brexit recovery. 'Europe has been a good market for English clubs,' Scholes explains. 'The Premier League has been extremely successful and our buying power increases. Sterling has been strong against the euro, prior to Brexit at least. If you were buying in euros, you received a better value.'

Scholes was speaking in late 2016 and by August of the following year, the euro had become 13-14 per cent higher against the pound, meaning that clubs in the 2017 transfer window were having to pay more for their purchases from European clubs. A report by Sky News business correspondent Ian King stated that in August 2017, 'A player on £100,000 a week, prior to the referendum and the drop in the pound, that would have been worth something like €130,000 to a European player. Now, that only buys them €110,000, so they will clearly be looking to defend their salaries.' However, many Premier League sponsors come from outside the eurozone and overseas television rights deals remain extortionate, so most top-flight English clubs will sleep soundly for the short-to-medium term.

The peak of Stoke's upturn appeared to come in the 2015-16 season. As Shaqiri, Arnautovic and Krkic dovetailed to beautiful effect, Stoke went on a run of nine wins in 15 matches, including 2-0 victories over both Manchester clubs and a splendid performance in their 4-3 win at Everton. Stoke played with such enterprise that Chelsea even considered Hughes among the contenders to replace Jose Mourinho when the Portuguese coach left the club in 2015. The club reached the semi-final of the EFL cup where a 1-0 home defeat by Liverpool was followed by an outstanding 1-0 victory at Anfield to take the tie to penalties. Peter Coates, the club's 78-year-old chairman, went as far as to say on the eve of the game that this was the best Stoke side he has ever seen, eclipsing the Stoke team featuring Gordon Banks and Jimmy Greenhoff that won the League Cup in 1972. They deserved to reach the final, outplaying Liverpool over 120 minutes at Anfield, but lost on penalty kicks.

As the 2016–17 season began, Stoke's evolution seemed to stutter. This may have been partly influenced by a desire to survive, as well as a response to another trend in English football, with powerful and athletic counterattacking play setting the agenda once more as Leicester City and then Antonio Conte's Chelsea won the Premier League title. At the start of the 2017–18 season, only Arsenal's Arsene Wenger, Burnley's Sean Dyche and Bournemouth's Eddie Howe had spent longer in situ at the same club than Hughes at Stoke. In total, only nine managers in the top four divisions of English football had managed a longer stint.

There is a perception, these days, that three years is the most that managers can hope for at an elite club. It is backed up by the experiences of Mourinho, who has encountered third-season discontent at Real Madrid and Chelsea, while Pep Guardiola ran out of steam in his fourth season at Barcelona and subsequently spent only three years at Bayern Munich. His first contract at Manchester City was a three-year deal, the same as Conte and Mourinho at Chelsea and Manchester United. In the same way that Stoke supporters began to tire of Pulis they also wearied of Hughes. After three top-ten finishes, Stoke ended the 2016–17 season in 13th position, although they were just two points behind eighth-place Southampton. Compared with the previous campaign, Stoke's possession figures dropped from 49.73 to 46.07 per cent and the average passes per game diminished from 430.05 to 383.11. Against the established top six, Stoke slumped from a 12-point return and to just three points and no victories.

Muniesa and Krkic left the club on loan in the summer of 2017, as Hughes reverted to a more pragmatic approach. The question now is how to make that jump, from the purgatory of ninth place to the top six and beyond. Leicester achieved the feat in improbable fashion. Stoke, however, hit a ceiling. In the 2017–18 season, Hughes was unable to reverse the trend of poor results and he was sacked in early January with the team languishing in the relegation zone. Stoke's progressive project had stalled and the club's immediate future was placed into peril. There is, now, an increasingly large batch of mid-table Premier League teams who have been cast adrift from meaningful progress in the top flight. Instead of looking up and threatening the top places, their eyes are now fixed almost permanently over their shoulders. Leicester's triumph was supposed to invigorate clubs who had accepted their fate in the middle echelons of the Premier League, but it has had the reverse effect, nudging the established leading pack to spend more and reinforce their superiority, while lower sides are engaged in a perennial relegation battle.

Scholes explains the real-politik that drives most Premier League clubs: 'It was a magnificent thing to happen to the Premier League and football. We'd all started to assume those unbelievable dreams cannot happen anymore. The dominance meant it cannot happen. Leicester proved you can. Do I think it is an anomaly? Yes, I do. There were factors at play. The bigger teams underperformed. They would admit that and it gave Leicester the opportunity, which they took of course. Normal service has been resumed.

'For a club like us, it means you are entitled to dream and you must put structures, processes and people in place who enable us to perform at the best possible level. Who knows what can happen? If you get a season where one or two of those top six clubs don't reach a certain level, we can reach a level beyond expectations. But this is an incredibly tough league. It's the best and toughest. It means that at the start of the season the priority is to make sure you are there at the start of the following season. It doesn't matter who you are. The top six aside, the priority is not to take your eye off the ball. We can't have a "We've cracked it here" mentality.

'The priority is to stay in the league because you can bet your life the other 13 teams will be doing that. Every year is zero again and it's hard work just to retain your status. Then you look and see how far you go. To finish ninth is a good achievement. We are doing extremely well to maintain that. But then we sit back and say, "How do we get to eighth or seventh?" You absolutely have to improve every year to stand still. The greediness comes in when you try to be something that you are not. Then you overstretch. Don't structure yourself to do too much because it would be folly.'

Guardiola's influence extends far and wide. His appointment as Manchester City manager was a landmark moment for English football. Everybody was excited. This, after all, was the manager whose entire playing squad turned out to sit in on the press conference where he announced he would leave Barcelona. Xavi Hernandez says he almost has a 'sickness for football'. Xabi Alonso described the experience of playing under him as a 'master's degree in football'. Every major club in the world would take Guardiola in a heartbeat. Chelsea's Roman Abramovich has long held designs, AC Milan's Silvio Berlusconi made overtures and Sir Alex Ferguson took him for lunch in New York. He is the master of his art, a manager who not only wins but dazzles the world in doing so.

City's Abu Dhabi owner, Sheikh Mansour bin Zayed Al Nahyan, had craved Guardiola's signature since buying the club in the summer of 2008. The initial suspicion was that Abu Dhabi sought to buy global influence through incursions into the sporting world. If your wish is to charm the world, then who better than Guardiola, the most aesthetically pleasing incarnation of the planet's most popular cultural pursuit? A Human Rights Watch report in 2013 summed up the cynical view of Sheikh Mansour's investment programme. The organisation argued that Abu Dhabi ownership of the Premier League's richest club allowed the state to 'construct a public relations image of a progressive, dynamic Gulf State, which deflects attention from what is really going on in the country'. Certainly, it is true that Abu Dhabi has long been driven by an aspiration to go one better than its Gulf rivals Dubai in its desire to win the admiration of the world.

James Montague wrote in the *Guardian*: 'When Dubai built its own seven-star hotel, the Burj Al Arab, Abu Dhabi responded with its own, the Emirates Palace. When Dubai embarked on huge, glamorous construction projects that stole headlines across the world, Abu Dhabi followed suit with plans to build a Guggenheim and a Louvre. Even sporting events have witnessed this economic one-upmanship, with Abu Dhabi setting up a rival to Dubai's PGA tour golf event and tennis tournament.'

Yet the further along we go, the more it appears that the owners have a credible global business model. This is not a case of national pride before profit. It has become abundantly clear that the City owners are here for the long haul. Sheikh Mansour's chase for Guardiola began when he appointed Ferran Soriano and Txiki Begiristain to the club in 2011. The two men, who had worked with Guardiola previously at Barcelona, held the key to the new manager, but Soriano also understood the mechanism behind a global football enterprise. City have now bought five football clubs on five continents, where they exchange scouting and conditioning information, while tie-ups are also in place with Dutch team NAC Breda and Spanish club Girona. In his time at Barcelona, Soriano exploited growing commercial and digital markets.

In his book, *Goal: The Ball Doesn't Go In By Chance*, Soriano said: 'It's about reaching a point where a club no longer seems purely local and instead appears a global phenomenon, like Walt Disney or Warner Bros. Disney uses its characters (Mickey Mouse, for example) to produce audiovisual content, sell t-shirts, hats or theme parks. Manchester United did not rely on Mickey Mouse but instead David Beckham, thanks to whom they increased TV sales and shirt sales, and they in essence converted Old Trafford into a lucrative theme park.'

Make no mistake, United were the model that inspired Soriano at Barcelona. In the 1995-96 season, Barcelona had an income of £58m compared to United's £62m. Seven years later, in the 2002–03 season, United's had risen to £251m, as Barcelona lagged behind on £123m. By the 2011–12 season, United rose to £396m but Barcelona overtook them to rake in £483m. Having overseen Barcelona's commercial rise, Soriano is now doing the same at City. The New York City MLS franchise offers a stake in the growing US market. The Latin American market has been tapped into with the purchase of Uruguayan outfit Club Atletico Torque. City Football Group also have a stake in Japanese club Yokohama F. Marinos in conjunction with City sponsors Nissan, while City expanded into Australia, where they purchased Melbourne Heart.

Curiously, research in 2016 found that more Australians were signed up to play for a local football club than any other sport. Over a million were members of a football club, compared with under 600,000 in the case of tennis and cricket. City then saw off competition throughout Europe when the Chinese state-backed investment firm China Media Capital (CMC) took a 13 per cent stake in City Football Group for a price of £265m. It followed a visit to Manchester by Chinese President Xi Jinping, a sports fanatic who has outlined a 50-point plan to transform China into a football powerhouse. On the same day, the former City defender Sun Jihai, a club ambassador for China, was bizarrely enrolled into Manchester's National Football Museum hall of fame. According to the *Financial Times*, 'the City operations will expect to contribute substantially to the requirements for more coaches, academies and building a football infrastructure in China.'

In January 2017, the Deloitte Football Money League placed City in fifth place, their highest ever position, following revenue of £524.9m. The aim had always been to record a profit within a decade and this has been achieved. These statistics do not count as silverware, but City's marketing team believe the operation to be the fastest-growing at any major club since 2011. Over the past few years, City Football Group has expanded to 11 offices across the world. Manchester City now have the Premier League's most popular YouTube channel, while they have recorded a 1,239 per cent growth in Facebook likes and a 238 per cent rise in their fanbase.

Yet City have been cute in their approach. They have gone global *and* local. Mansour has invested hugely in the Ancoats area of east Manchester and his Abu Dhabi United Group agreed in 2014 to contribute to the building of 830 new homes. City have also constructed the £150m Etihad Campus, which was opened in December 2014, within a ten-minute walk of the club's stadium. The construction of the mini Etihad, a 7,000-seater stadium, drew comparisons with the Barcelona Mini Estadi, and the Catalan presence in Manchester might be tempted to cry copy-cat.

However, Brian Marwood, the former sporting director and now managing director of City Football Services, took a long-lens snapshot of global sport. In total, he visited 30 sporting facilities in nine countries on four continents, including his former club Arsenal, Ajax, the New York Knicks, the LA Lakers, the Australian Institute of Sport and the Aspire Centre in Qatar. There was, of course, also a trip to see Barcelona, and the desire to implement the same style of play from the youngest age group to the senior team is clearly inspired by the Catalan club. The same can be said of the proximity of the academy stadium, which, like the Mini Estadi, is within a stone's throw of the club's main stadium.

City clearly went to remarkable lengths to perfect every last detail. Thousands of trees were planted to protect the training pitches against Manchester's biting wind. Louis van Gaal subsequently looked to do the same at Manchester United's Carrington base. In the bedrooms reserved for players, sleep specialists were consulted before the club decided on a circular wallpaper design to ensure the best night's kip. The City academy has produced outstanding youth results for several years now. A presentation was made to the club's decision-makers in 2010, which also included a video segment that featured a goal by a ten-year-old Phil Foden, who in 2017 joined Pep Guardiola's squad on a tour of the USA and then emerged as the headline act of England's Under-17 World Cup triumph.

On 30 October 2017, meanwhile, Manchester United celebrated a run of 3,883 consecutive games over an 80-year period in which the team has featured an academy graduate. City have yet to truly bring on a player from their academy in the Mansour era and, for all the investment in infrastructure, we are yet to witness any of City's own take the world by storm. Highly rated teenage midfielder Jadon Sancho left the club in 2017, privately fearing a development pathway at City was blocked off by the club's dependence on expensive attacking recruits.

Yet Manchester City are a club founded in 1880, not 2008, and the regular meetings their operations teams hold to discuss how the club can expand their fanbase without alienating traditional supporters underline some of the anxieties and contradictions at the heart of their project. On the day the club presented Guardiola as manager, the accompanying hashtag read #ItBegins. This perhaps did a disservice to Manchester City's own proud history, to Malcolm Allison and Joe Mercer, but it captured the feeling that City were entering their nirvana.

City's rise remains remarkable. Eighteen years before Guardiola arrived, City began the 1998-99 season in the third tier of English football. These were the days when City were known less for their football and more for celebrity supporters, such as rock band Oasis, comedian Bernard Manning, and Kevin Kennedy, the actor who played Curly Watts in *Coronation Street*. The club was in thrall to their more illustrious neighbours, United. There was a time City even refused to serve tomato ketchup in their hospitality suites, with head chef John Benson-Smith preparing a blue-coloured equivalent for 3,500 corporate guests at a Manchester derby in 2006. Only in 2010, some City fans admitted to voting for the Conservative Party because they could not bear to be associated with anything red.

City supporter Mark Hodkinson wrote a diary of the club's 1998-99 season and it brims with nostalgic anecdotes. Back in 1998, the official club shop sold shirts that labelled their dashing blond goalkeeper Nicky Weaver as 'City's David Beckham'. City fans even wrote to Buckingham Palace to complain that the Queen and the Duke of Edinburgh had signed a Manchester United shirt on a visit to Malaysia in September 1998 in the presence of Sir Bobby Charlton. The Palace did reply, insisting: 'Her Majesty is well aware that there is more than one football club in Manchester.' Yet that season, it may have felt otherwise. A Manchester derby felt a lifetime away and when the two clubs' reserve teams met in the Manchester Senior Cup, it became a fully policed all-ticket affair at non-league Hyde United's stadium. City privately discussed the possibility of fielding some first-team players, if only to land a blow on United, who enjoyed the club's greatest season by lifting the Premier League, FA Cup and Champions League under Alex Ferguson.

City became a national laughing stock. On the BBC's satirical panel show *Have I Got News for You*, comedian Paul Merton remarked on the news that Manchester-born painter Chris Ofili had won the £20,000 Turner Prize after wowing the judges with glow-in-the-dark art that featured resin-coated elephant dung. 'There isn't much elephant shit to be found in Manchester,' a guest interjected. Merton responded: 'Haven't you seen Manchester City lately?' Three days later, on 8 December 1998, City lost 2-1 at home to Mansfield Town in the Auto Windscreens Shield and, at 3,007, the club recorded the lowest attendance in their history.

Yet City's fanbase mostly remained strong. In August, City drew 0-0 at home to Wrexham. The attendance, 27,677, was the fifth highest of the day and larger than the crowd at Upton Park where Manchester United were the visitors to West Ham. The season ended in promotion and an upwards curve began once more, but nobody could have dreamed that less than two decades letter, the world's most coveted manager would rule the City roost. It is certainly a long way away from the scenes in the 2010 feature-length production *Blue Moon Rising* by *Big Brother* creators Endemol. It followed City's 2009-10 campaign and one memorable clip included the club's former secretary Bernard Halford scouring City's trophy haul – one of which included a small porcelain cow.

Yet Guardiola was not an instant success. His first season at City was, by his own measure, a failure. Before arriving in England, Guardiola had won 21 trophies in his decade as a manager, yet City found themselves 15 points behind table-topping Chelsea by the beginning of April. He even reverted to the Arsene Wenger view that qualifying for the Champions League equated to winning a trophy. 'Here, yes. Definitely. It's like winning titles, definitely, because there are so many strong teams.' He went further: 'In my situation, at a big club, I'm sacked. I'm out. Sure. Definitely. At Barcelona or Bayern Munich, if in six months you don't win [anything], you are really out. They don't give you a second chance.' City had started like a steam train with six consecutive Premier League wins but the momentum fizzled out as his team then won just three of their next nine league games. In his book *Pep Guardiola: The Evolution*, Guardiola's confidant Marti Perarnau wrote: 'Guardiola will always be subjected to the scrutiny of conventional, pedestrian minds and those who don't understand his ideas will resort to dismissing or even ridiculing them.'

Now, time is a necessity but this is the fast-paced Premier League and question marks were legitimate. We should remember that Manuel Pellegrini, his predecessor at Manchester City, along with Jose Mourinho and Carlo Ancelotti, the former Chelsea managers, all won a Premier League and domestic cup double in their debut seasons. Rafa Benitez won the Champions League in his debut campaign with Liverpool. Antonio Conte took a team from tenth in the Premier League to the title and the FA Cup final. City had flaws in their squad, most notably in the fullback positions where Bacary Sagna, Pablo Zabaleta, Aleksandar Kolarov and Gael Clichy were past their best and struggled with the intense demands of Guardiola's system. But the manager spent just short of £200m in his first summer and it was a surprise to see City fail to win 15 of their 38 Premier League games and finish only three points clear of Arsenal in fifth place.

Signs of strain became apparent. City received seven red cards by New Year's Day. Fernandinho, the overstretched holding midfielder, was sent off on three occasions in the first half of the season. Guardiola began to study the tendencies of English referees, learning swiftly the advantages his side could seek and where he might need to adapt. He did note, for example, that officiating leniency meant that City could commit more tactical fouls without too much fear of retribution.

Guardiola appeared extremely stubborn, to the detriment of his own side. After a 4–2 defeat at Leicester City, the former Manchester United and City goalkeeper Peter Schmeichel argued that Guardiola's reluctance to alter his tactics to stifle the direct threat of Claudio Ranieri's side made the manager appear a 'very arrogant man'. He attracted further criticism after the Leicester game when he declared: 'I am not a coach for the tackles, so I do not train them.' Fernando Hierro, the former Real Madrid captain who ended his career at Bolton, was bemused that winning a challenge or a second ball could elicit standing applause from British football supporters. But Hierro adapted and embraced the idiosyncrasies.

The suggestion arose that Guardiola became more irked than invigorated to be moved from his comfort zone. The early quirks of English football had entertained him. The club's communication department made an early presentation to Guardiola, introducing the Catalan to the demands of the English media. The club's head of communications outlined the top ten most-read stories in the Spanish, German and British media during the previous campaign. While Spain's most

popular articles focused on match action (with the exception
of Lionel Messi's tax-planning scandal), the top ten in England
were mostly made up of tabloid sex scandals and training ground
brawls. Guardiola found the discrepancy curious but embraced
elements of English football culture. In his first press conference,
he referred to Sam Allardyce as 'the Big Sam'. His first major
interview came with Oasis rock star Noel Gallagher. He saw his
team win 3-0 at Hull City on Boxing Day and then wandered
into the press room and munched on a mince pie. Yet after a
defeat at Liverpool a few days later, he said: 'The kind of football here, it's like this – no time to think, so aggressive, up and
down, up and down, second ball, second ball . . .'

While Guardiola appeared dismissive of British blood and
thunder, training-ground sources revealed that he did subsequently place a greater emphasis on winning the second ball in
defensive situations. Greater attention was paid to combating the
strengths of opponents. In a BBC interview with Gary Lineker
in autumn 2017, Guardiola said: 'If they play long balls, I have to
adapt. In Barcelona, it was never a focus the long balls or second
balls. I could never imagine having to make training sessions or
reviews on long balls, deciding whether we have defended that
kind of situation in the right way. It's boring to train it. I like
to train the things I enjoy.'

Guardiola felt the English football calendar, without a winter
break, was unhelpful. Mikel Arteta, a member of his coaching
staff, spoke to me primarily about life as a player but he did hint
at Guardiola's exasperation with the logjam of fixtures. 'I would
change the football calendar in an instant,' Arteta said, a couple
of months into Guardiola's tenure. 'English football doesn't help
its clubs. If you're in Europe, it's every three days without a
break. It's counter-productive for the sport in this country. We
have played three weeks in a row with three games a week and
then tomorrow night, it's Manchester United away in the EFL
Cup. Why? What are we meant to do in that? We are thinking about how to tackle that game but then it's Barcelona next

week. Then they go to the international break and one's off to Chile, one's off to Paraguay … it's not frustrating … it's our profession, but we can't have it this way and then expect players to maintain their optimum level. They don't get a rest. This is a sport that is physically more demanding than ever, every season is a marathon.'

There were further teething problems and none more so than the calamitous situation in the City goal. Joe Hart was a popular figure among supporters and had been a mainstay of two title-winning teams, England's number one and the club's first-choice goalkeeper since ousting Shay Given in 2010. Yet in Barcelona, even in the couple of years that preceded Guardiola's City arrival, it had been an open secret that Txiki Begiristain had designs on moving him on. Pepe Mel recalls: 'In Spain, absolutely everyone knew Joe Hart would be off. It was very strange to see everyone go crazy.'

The reason for Hart's exit has several layers. First and foremost, Guardiola did not believe Hart to be capable of adapting to his vision for goalkeepers. Guardiola is a disciple of Johan Cruyff, who once said: 'In my teams, the goalkeeper is the first attacker.' In Spain, first-team goalkeeping coaches often design the training schedule for goalkeepers at every age group, ensuring a pathway and consistency of style. In the 1990s at Barcelona, for example, first-team goalkeeping coach Frans Hoek regularly ran sessions for teenagers such as Pepe Reina and Victor Valdes. Claudio Bravo, a Chilean Champions League winner with Barcelona, was identified as the ideal replacement for Hart. Xabier Mancisidor, the goalkeeping coach Guardiola inherited from Pellegrini, had previously worked with Bravo at Real Sociedad. Bravo played as a striker until the age of 11 and even scored a free kick for Real Sociedad against Numancia.

Statistical analysis backed up Guardiola's view that Bravo fitted his approach. In the 2015–16 season, Hart made 721 passes in the Premier League and only 52.57 per cent of those were successful. In La Liga, Bravo made 854 passes with an accuracy of 84.31 per cent. In South America and Spain, futsal and small-sided indoor versions of football are crucial to the development of technically assured players. I met David De Gea shortly after Hart was jettisoned, and although he was reluctant to be drawn into the politics of the decision, he did underline the importance the Spanish place on a goalkeeper's technical proficiency: 'As a kid in Spain, I learned my craft through indoor seven-a-side football in small spaces and it is really drummed into you. Under Sir Alex Ferguson, his focus was first of all making sure I was keeping the ball out of the goal but that was also because of my early difficulties. It was about establishing the basics first. Under Louis van Gaal and his goalkeeping coach Frans Hoek, there were more sweeper-keeper demands.

'Above all, though, the biggest test for me is when I am in goal for the Spanish national team. It is extraordinarily demanding; sometimes there will be myself and two defenders and you are playing it across your own box with strikers pressing you. You are receiving the ball under pressure, thinking quickly, reacting and playing the right pass at high speed. It's hard to train this for a match situation because the pressure in front of thousands of people is different. You have training sessions with the team and the rondos are hugely important too. It's a circle where you play one-touch or two-touch, piggy in the middle. I am lucky I grew up with this in the national team age groups.'

His teammate Ander Herrera insists De Gea's calmness is the key and the goalkeeper agrees. 'Really, I can't imagine anything worse for a defence than playing in front of someone who is edgy. One of my jobs is to transmit calmness to the team. It's a non-negotiable quality for the whole team. As a kid, I was maybe a bit more daring or anxious but, with age, I have become calmer and calmer, both on and off the pitch.'

The concept of a ball-playing goalkeeper, however, is not a new one. Xavi Valero acted as Rafa Benitez's goalkeeping coach at both Liverpool and Real Madrid. He says: 'Hoek was very influential. He went into Barcelona and evolved the art of goalkeeping. He introduced a different way of thinking about the sport. I identify myself with that kind of understanding of coaching goalkeepers. It's based on the idea that everything comes from there, you cannot split the goalkeeper from the team. You cannot have the goalkeeper training separate from the group all the time. For 80 per cent of the time, he should be training with the team.

'In big games, you need the goalkeeper for the defensive and attacking phase. The ball moves at high speed, the players are prepared tactically and the goalie has to be aware of the group's plan. You cannot develop a goalkeeper's decision-making process if you don't place them into a context and situations where they gain that experience and tactical nous and in game situations. The more time you dedicate to that, the better. Manuel Neuer, who Guardiola improved at Bayern Munich, is maybe the extreme version of this goalkeeper. I'd place Pepe Reina, Fabien Barthez and Marc-Andre ter Stegen in the same category.

'But really, not all of this is new. A few years ago, I discovered that Bert Trautmann lived near me in Spain. He was in his late eighties. He's had a very interesting life, a prisoner of war and then a goalkeeper with Manchester City. I remember him explaining how he was forced to deactivate bombs in the Liverpool area. I spoke with him about goalkeeping coaching. He used to laugh when I said we integrate goalkeepers into the team in training. He said that training back in his day was simply to play a game and therefore you were always involving the goalkeeper. Then, at the end, you did some specific things. Bert Trautmann in the fifties was playing outside the box, coming for crosses, looking to cover his defence. He was a modern goalkeeper but there was no TV or Sky Sports to enlighten us. Nothing is really new in football, even this false-nine stuff has happened before. Some teams in Latin America were doing this in the late 1940s!'

Joe Hart was 29 when Guardiola arrived and the manager

clearly decided he could not be reinvented. The case for Hart's exit was emphatic but his replacement failed to shine. Never mind a false nine, City appeared to have a false number one. Bravo kept only five clean sheets in 24 matches and, during one particularly rotten nine-game run over the winter, he managed to concede 16 goals from 24 shots on his goal. Guardiola subsequently dropped him from the side, but he was reinstalled for City's FA Cup replay against Huddersfield, when he was sarcastically cheered by his own support every time he made a save in their 5-1 win.

When he was ousted by Willy Caballero in February, Bravo had the division's highest passing percentages and the lowest save ratio. He saved only 53.1 per cent of the shots he faced in the Premier League in his 23 appearances, the worst of any goalkeeper to have played more than ten games in the division in that season. Bravo's technical capacity remained undiminished but the pressure and physical demands of the division took a toll. When looking back on his own start at Liverpool, goalkeeper Pepe Reina reflected: 'The physical aspect is the biggest; you have to cope with that fundamental change if you want to survive. The football is fast and furious. It wasn't a shock to me. I knew what was coming, I adapted from the first day and De Gea was the same . . . he came as a *niño* and now he is a *porterazo* [a magnificent goalkeeper].'

In the summer of 2017, Guardiola acted swiftly to recruit the £34.9m Brazilian goalkeeper Ederson from Benfica. Ederson immediately appeared an upgrade, blending steel and silk. He took a boot to the face from Liverpool's Sadio Mane and started four days later, away at Feyenoord in the Champions League. Nine games into his first Premier League season, his passing percentage stood at 84.08 per cent, compared with Bravo at 73.09 per cent the year before, and his save percentage at 73.33. Guardiola's model could now be implemented.

There were other reasons Guardiola shifted Hart aside. According to Marti Perarnau, the author who spent a season shadowing Guardiola's work at Bayern, the manager wanted ten new signings in his first summer alone, and he was worried by the age range of a squad that included 17 players over the age of 28. It is curious that City, as a club, seemed prepared for Guardiola's arrival in every way except for the personnel. They had the academy infrastructure, outstanding facilities, the support staff – everything he required save for the players to fulfil his vision. After a 6–0 victory at the start of his second season, he said: 'Day by day I say thank you to Khaldoon [the chairman], Txiki and Ferran for buying these players. Every manager has good ideas but without the players that we have it is much more complicated.'

Pellegrini had previously dropped Hart for an extended period and the goalkeeper was also one of those who irked Roberto Mancini in the Italian's fraught final campaign with the club. Hart was not the only figure to come under pressure. Samir Nasri and Yaya Toure were ordered to train separately after returning to pre-season overweight. It was a similar story in Guardiola's early days at Barcelona. Writing in his book, Soriano recalled: 'In 2008, Pep exercised his decision-making power to cut players adrift and create a more demanding environment. He said very clearly he did not want Ronaldinho, Deco or Eto'o, three key players in the team but also generators of negative dynamics that Guardiola wanted to change. The club found an exit for the the first two but not for Eto'o who stayed an extra year, worked like everyone else and was a fundamental part of the most successful season in the club's history.'

Toure eventually followed Eto'o's model, as he shed eight kilos and became part of the squad once more in November. Captain Vincent Kompany, an outstanding defender but dogged by injuries, also feared for his future. Indeed, one well-placed source in Belgium admits Kompany confided that he suspected his time at City was over midway through Guardiola's first season. He eventually worked his way back into the team.

Guardiola set about establishing greater togetherness. At the club's training base, the players eat breakfast and lunch together every day. Changes were made to the menu. At Bayern, Guardiola immediately banned pastries and recruited dietician Mona Nemmer. At City, he instantly banned fruit juices, and post-match pizza was taken off the menu. Instead, after matches, players are told to snack on nuts to restore energy levels. The saturated fat and salt found in foods such as pizza slow down glycogen recovery, so lean protein or complex carbohydrates are preferred. He appointed the former champion triathlete Silvia Tremoleda to oversee the club's diet and nutrition. She is the wife of former Barcelona club treasurer Xavier Sala-i-Martin, who has also lectured in economics at Columbia, Yale and Harvard in the USA.

Sala-i-Martin remains extremely close to Guardiola. He is a man of principle. Raphael Minder's book on Catalonia reveals that the erstwhile treasurer was one of those who insisted that the club take on Unicef as a shirt sponsor and in turn reject an £85m offer from a gambling firm. The betting company instead turned to Real Madrid, who opened out her arms. He resented the subsequent decision to agree a deal with Qatar Airways as the club's shirt sponsor. 'Barcelona is a club of democrats,' Sala-i-Martin said. 'You cannot have the name of a dictatorship on your shirt.'

Tremoleda cut down the red meat, particularly favoured by Argentine, Uruguayan and Brazilian players, and came up with gluten-free and sugar-free menus. Meals are highly specialised, in both the content and the time of eating. Guardiola takes the same view as Pep Clotet that a player must restore glycogen levels within the metabolic window. It is why he will check in with the nutrition team to see if players attend meals at the correct time both at the training ground and after games, where the squad are also expected to eat together within the timeframe where nutrients can be easily absorbed.

In the summer of 2013, as Lionel Messi became concerned by

injuries, Tremoleda made changes to his diet in tandem with the Italian nutritionist Giuliano Poser, introducing an olive oil-based eating regime with an emphasis on fresh fish. Some City players took it upon themselves to hire a personal chef for their final meal of the day. Kevin De Bruyne, Ilkay Gundogan and Kyle Walker all call upon the services of the Michelin-starred chef Jonny Marsh, who served an apprenticeship under Raymond Blanc at the Frenchman's Oxfordshire restaurant. The left-back Benjamin Mendy recruited Monaco's team chef Simone Bertaggia for his personal services upon leaving the French club.

Guardiola's culture change extends even to administration staff, who are granted free breakfast and lunch at City's training ground. They are encouraged to trial the healthier options and fruit is always freely available, which is the case too at the club's London offices. Staff are also treated to free yoga lessons and bootcamp-style fitness sessions should they wish to take part.

Guardiola made further changes, seeking to guide every facet of a player's life. After noticing a couple of players becoming distracted at the training campus, he ordered Wifi and 3G internet connection to be wiped out to restore focus. The Wifi has gradually been re-established. Guardiola has been known to call players in the evening and discuss tactical plans. Despite the campus boasting luxurious bedrooms, he decided they should stay at home before matches at the Etihad Stadium in order to reduce pre-match tension.

Guardiola wants his coaching staff to be close to his players. Five months into his time at Barcelona, the father of goal-keeping coach Juan Carlos Unzue died suddenly. On the same evening, the team won a La Liga game and Guardiola chartered a flight for the entire squad and staff to be in Pamplona for the funeral the next day.

Upon joining City, Guardiola immediately promoted Rodolfo Borrell to the first team. The Catalan, recruited by Begiristain in 2014, had previously been the technical director of the club's academy. He had spent 14 years as a coach at La

Masia and was responsible for the development of the 1987 generation of talent that included Messi, Cesc Fabregas and Gerard Pique. He was among the first Barcelona coaches to train Messi. Rafa Benitez first brought Borrell to England as Liverpool's Under-18 coach in 2009. Guardiola was a first-team player during Borrell's first stint with Barcelona and the pair have a long-standing friendship.

They tell one particularly heartwarming anecdote of their time in Catalonia. When Cesc Fabregas was a 13-year-old in 2001, the young player was enduring the heartache of his parents' divorce. His mother, Nuria, called Borrell and warned that Fabregas might require emotional support. Borrell became a coach-cum-psychologist, frequently stopping by for motivational chats with Fabregas. He knocked on the door of the first-team dressing room and presented Guardiola with a replica number four shirt and asked for the midfielder's signature. Guardiola went a step further, writing a message: 'Dear Cesc, one day, you will be the person to wear the number four for Barcelona. Best wishes and good luck.'

During a trip to England in the following weeks, Borrell checked in on a fragile Fabregas. 'I called him into my room and explained that I was aware of what was happening in his family,' Borrell told the BBC. 'He started to cry, so I showed him the famous shirt. You can imagine the reaction. His idol has written a message for him on his shirt. It was a fantastic moment.'

Borrell adapts his approach, light or shade, strong or soft. At Liverpool, he took the lead role in the development of Raheem Sterling. As a 15-year-old, Sterling was asked to start a Merseyside derby against Everton in the Under-18 age group in a 4–3 victory. On the touchline, Liverpool legend Kenny Dalglish watched on. On Merseyside, they recall another story when Sterling was included in a Europa League squad with the first team in 2011. He returned to Liverpool's Melwood training ground and Borrell adopted a firm stance with his young talent. He asked Sterling – in front of his teammates – to set up the cones and lay out the bibs for the session. The aim was to keep Sterling grounded, and the player responded by scoring in his next two youth-team matches.

Guardiola wanted Borrell to be part of his first-team set-up not only to act as a bridge to the first team but also to rebuild Sterling's confidence. Guardiola has always admired Sterling and, while at Bayern Munich, he had made discreet enquiries with a view to possibly signing the young player from Liverpool. He also personally made contact with Sterling following England's disastrous European Championships. Guardiola elevated Sterling's game, as the winger demonstrated greater tactical maturity and a clinical edge by scoring 15 goals before Christmas in the manager's second season at the club.

After recruiting goalkeeper Ederson, three fullbacks – Kyle Walker, Benjamin Mendy and Danilo – as well as attacking talents Gabriel Jesus and Bernardo Silva in 2017, the result was explosive. City began the season with 17 victories in their opening 18 Premier League games. They defeated Chelsea and Manchester United away from home and put three, four and five past Arsenal, Tottenham and Liverpool respectively on home turf. Their 29 goals in eight league matches was the highest scoring start since the Victorian era and Everton's 1894-95 team. In the wake of a 6-0 victory at Watford, City's former forward and ex-chairman Francis Lee declared the brand of football the greatest he has ever witnessed from Manchester City.

In Jose Mourinho at Manchester United, he has his ideal sparring partner. Once upon a time, Guardiola sought to learn from Mourinho. During his time as director of the Catalan School of Coaching, Clotet recalls Guardiola making his way into the lecture theatre with a pad and pen tucked under his arm. 'Pep took his badges with the Spanish federation in Madrid. At our school, we made a Master's course for a year with one module a month by specific coaches. He joined us twice. He attended when Mourinho's staff presented a module on periodisation [which in essence refers to how coaches bring players up to their

peak performance level through fitness and recovery planning].
Mourinho is the reference point for that topic, inspired by Vitor
Frade and Julio Garganta. Pep was just starting off and then
Mourinho was at Chelsea at the time. Jose was unable to come
himself that day but he sent all his coaching and technical staff
along. A couple of years later Pep came back to also deliver a
masterclass on how to organise a team offensively.'

The great Italian coach Arrigo Sacchi described having the
two men in Spain as having 'two Picassos in the same period'
and the duo are now repeating the rivalry in Manchester.
Inside his office at Real Madrid's Valdebebas training ground,
Mourinho used to keep a cardboard cutout of the moment
he ran across the turf, finger pointing to the heavens, after
defeating Guardiola's Barça when he was manager of Inter
Milan. As the 2017–18 season got underway, the rivalry began
to intensify. Guardiola's artistry contrasted ever more acutely
with Mourinho's pragmatism. On the day Liverpool hosted
Manchester United, a game Mourinho's tactics reduced to
a goalless bore draw and the last match to be shown on that
evening's *Match of the Day*, Guardiola's City scored seven in an
annihilation of Stoke City.

Guardiola has his talent base and rivalries in place. So Pep's
path finally appeared clear. Yet for how long? Guardiola is a
manager who appears to set limits on his tenures. If his heart
would not allow him more than four years at his beloved
Barcelona, what are the chances of him falling head over heels
for English football? We hope he will be one of those figures
enchanted by the quirks of English life. 'He'll always see his
commitments through but don't expect him to stay a day longer
than promised,' wrote Perarnau. Regardless, his legacy will
endure far longer.

EPILOGUE

It is December 2017 and bookmakers are already paying out on Pep Guardiola's side to lift the Premier League title. The Catalan has elevated Manchester City to record-breaking levels, exasperating his rivals and delighting his many admirers. After chief executive officer Ferran Soriano presented his keynote speech at Manchester City's Christmas party at the city centre bar Menagerie in 2017, joy filled the room. Guardiola led the way on the dance-floor, popular left-back Benjamin Mendy took on City's London-based admin staff in games of beer-pong and cheers went up when the news filtered through that Bristol City had defeated Jose Mourinho's Manchester United in the quarter-final of the Carabao Cup.

The sub-heading of this book states that the Spanish have conquered English football. In light of the myriad traumas and tribulations endured by some of those mentioned in this book, it may appear a hasty conclusion. Yet Guardiola's dominance has been so eye-catching, so compelling, that it became difficult to resist. Consider these statistics. The two most celebrated English sides of recent times are Sir Alex Ferguson's Manchester United 1999 Treble-winners and Arsene Wenger's Arsenal Invincibles. Yet after 18 Premier League games in the 1998-99 season, Ferguson's side had scored 36 goals and accumulated 31 points. Wenger's 2003-04 team had 34 goals and 42 points at the same stage. Under Guardiola, City demolished those records, recording 56 goals and 52 points. The trophy cabinet will ultimately define Guardiola's success, but these are staggering warnings of intent.

After ending Manchester United's 40-match unbeaten run at Old Trafford in a fiery 2-1 victory, it all became too much for Mourinho, who was reduced to his snarling worst as he was caught up in a brawl outside the City dressing room. In six words that cut painfully to Manchester United's core, Guardiola simply said: 'We won because we were better.' Nothing more, nothing less. Forget the sideshows, forget the episode of 'Punch and Jose' that broke out in the Old Trafford tunnel, forget the Manchester United protestations against referees. City were simply better.

Eighty years on from the first patter of Spanish feet into English football, Guardiola has overseen a benign takeover, challenging his footballers to think more deeply and move more swiftly. As City plan to invest more emphatically in the years to come, Guardiola will be offered the opportunity to define a generation in English football. Whether he embraces this possibility is his own prerogative, but we must hope that his colleagues and rivals have been watching closely.

For Guardiola has confronted and countered every convention in English football. The tika-taka approach was supposed to be in retreat. The Barcelona of Xavi Hernandez, Andres Iniesta and Lionel Messi was supposed to be a once-in-a-lifetime thrill. Guardiola was unable to win the Champions League with Bayern Munich. Spain stuttered and stumbled through the 2014 World Cup and 2016 European Championship. The power and pace of Cristiano Ronaldo, Gareth Bale and Karim Benzema spearheaded Real Madrid's back-to-back Champions League triumphs, putting Barcelona's more dainty approach into the shade. In the Premier League, brawny and counter-attacking sides such as Leicester City and Chelsea lifted titles in 2016 and 2017 under Italian coaches Claudio Ranieri and Antonio Conte. At Manchester United, Jose Mourinho reverted to power over panache. Six of his first seven signings as United manager stood between 6ft 1in and 6ft 4in. The CIES Football Observatory records that City's squad, by contrast, was the smallest in the Premier League with an average height of 5ft 10in.

Guardiola demonstrated remarkable self-belief, some might suggest arrogance, to remain faithful to his creed. We should remember that many in Spain think differently. Rafa Benitez and Aitor Karanka share little in common with Guardiola's vision. The most influential Spanish footballers in England have blended fire and ice. David Silva has developed an aggressive streak and is a fierce competitor. The same goes for Cesc Fabregas. They do, as the cliché goes, earn the right to play. And, let us be clear, City are no snowflakes. They refuse to be bullied. They compete. They score a surprisingly high number of goals from set pieces.

Diversity is to be encouraged, yet it has been curious to observe the response of English football in the early months of the 2017-18 season. In some quarters, there has been a tendency to double down on the fundamentally conservative outlook of British football. Since the turn of the millennium, clubs have been braver and bolder in their approach, but as the recompense of Premier League football continues to sky-rocket, many owners are becoming middle-of-the-road and turning to safe and experienced British minds. A theory, perhaps, has developed that Guardiola's expansive style has reached a level of such mighty excellence that it is now an inaccessible ideal to those who do not possess Manchester City's riches. The fear of demotion overwhelms aspirations of challenging norms and adopting a broader outlook. It is why Everton, West Brom and West Ham turned to familiar faces in Sam Allardyce, Alan Pardew and David Moyes when the time came to revive their ailing campaigns last autumn.

It is obvious, therefore, that while English football clearly appreciates and revels in Guardiola's sorcery, there is not, at present, a movement to replicate or imitate his core principles at the highest level. Yet to aspire to Guardiola does not mean that every player must reach the levels of Kevin de Bruyne. It should encourage coaches and players to consider football in a more innovative manner. Guardiola may have spent a fortune, but his triumph has also been one of magnificent coaching, one of the preparedness to listen and solve problems. When left-back Mendy suffered a season-curtaining injury, Fabian Delph was transformed into a competent fullback. John Stones showcased signs of further defensive maturity by taking note and embracing his manager. Raheem Sterling developed a clinical edge. These are three English players who all looked safely at home in a world-class outfit. They did so by opening their minds.

Similar narratives can be found throughout this book and one of the major objectives has been to demonstrate that this has not been a one-way street. Many Spaniards owe England a great deal of gratitude, too. The physical demands of English football provoked David De Gea to transform his build and, harnessed with the technical talents honed in his native Spain, he has become the sport's greatest in his discipline. De Gea, in many ways, embodies the relationship between Spaniards and English football. He describes English football as the 'perfect finishing school'.

At its best, this is a story of give-and-take mutual interests. It is a story that began by British citizens opening their hearts and minds to young and vulnerable Basque children. England reared these talents, returning iconic figures to Barcelona, Real Madrid and Athletic Bilbao. If we are to believe the convincing account of John Aldecoa, his father Emilio, nurtured in Coventry, may even be the man who pioneered Barcelona's extraordinary football factory that has provided so much joy and happiness to the world. Spain's success between 2008 and 2012 was aided by the learning experiences of Cesc Fabregas, Xabi Alonso and Fernando Torres in English football. This summer in Russia, the development of De Gea, David Silva, Alvaro Morata and Diego Costa will do much to enhance Spanish aspirations.

For the English part, the greatest benefits may yet be long term. Many academies now pursue reformed ideals, often inspired by enlightened minds that have been captured by a Spanish vision, and England's recent success at youth level offers hope that a new generation of footballers is beginning to view the sport differently. We hope that Phil Foden, the prodigiously talented star of England's Under-17 World Cup triumph, embraces the Guardiola doctrine and that the Football Association continues to follow in Spanish footsteps by training more elite coaches. Guardiola's stay may only be a fleeting one, but his foundations were laid nearly a century earlier and, in the right hands, they will live on for generations to come.

ACKNOWLEDGEMENTS

The obsession behind this book began in 2015, when I met Amnesty International's researcher Naomi Westland and she introduced me to the extraordinary stories of the Basque refugee children and a short Spanish television documentary entitled *Los Niños del Habana*. At the time, I was a 21-year-old university student, and transforming an idea into a published book remained a pipe dream. Telling the stories of all these Spanish footballers has been an honour. From Stoke to Seville, Milton Keynes to Mallorca, this is a journey that began in a crematorium in Cambridge and culminated in a beach bar in Cataluña. It has been a privilege, but it would not have been feasible without the kindness and support of so many people.

I have dedicated this book to my grandfather, Martin Glyn. My grandpa loved his football, particularly Manchester United, but he also passed down a true love of newspapers and reading. My earliest memory of newspapers is to be sat alongside him at breakfast time, where he would start his day with a boiled egg and then bury his head in the morning reads. He'd often turn straight to the back of the *Daily Mail* to pore over Ian Wooldridge's columns. I hope he would be extremely proud of me for writing this book, and I hope his wife – my grandma Estelle – considers this a fitting tribute. Thank you to my mum, Andrea, and dad, Garry, for your love, which I know is unconditional.

I am grateful to all those who assisted me in this project. I was humbled by the goodwill of many people and gratitude must go to a vast army of fixers and go-betweens that made this possible. My thanks must go to Nacho Silvan and Imago Sport, who understood the value of the project and went above and beyond to convince David De Gea, Juan Mata and Cesar Azpilicueta of its merits. Thank you to Ben Miller, who teed up Ander Herrera. Thank you to Begoña Perez and Marcelo Mendez, who organised interviews with Aitor Karanka, Pako Ayestaran and Pep Clotet, and often put in a positive word behind the scenes. Thanks must also go to Fraser Nicholson at Stoke City, Vicky Kloss, Simon Heggie and Alex Rowen at Manchester City and Max Fitzgerald at West Ham United. I will always be thankful to Xavi Valero, who offered so much of his own time and also vouched for me to both Pepe Reina and Fernando Hierro. Arnau Riera and Marcelino Elena were self-deprecating but searingly honest company. Thank you for your openness.

Barcelona's official historian Manel Tomas Belenguer and Opta answered important queries. Bojan Krkic is one of the warmest characters in football and his father Bojan Sr is the kindest man in the game, with an enviable bank of anecdotes and recollections. Thank you to Roberto Martinez for his generosity of time and spirit, allowing me to disrupt his holiday time. Thank you to Alex Calvo-Garcia and his kind friend Jose, who even provided me with a roof on one summer's night in the Basque country. Thank you to Nayim, Pepe Mel and Juande Ramos for your candour and sincerity. Thank you to Aitor Karanka, Victor Orta and their backroom staff at Middlesbrough, who provided a portal into the realities of life in the Premier League over the course of a season.

I have leaned heavily on the works of the defining chroniclers of Spanish sport and modern history, particularly Jimmy Burns, Sid Lowe, Paul Preston and Javier Tusell. Thank you to Iñigo Gurruchaga for your wisdom and encouragement at a very early stage of this process. Thank you also to the helpful staff at the National Archives and British Library, in addition to the many libraries and town halls that assisted me in Madrid, Barcelona and Bilbao.

I will always be indebted to Ian Marshall of Simon & Schuster for his faith, guidance and patience. Thank you for your encouragement and support. Thanks also to Lorraine Jerram for her sensitive and meticulous editing of the text. Thank you to David Luxton, who took a chance on a pretentious university student and provided me with rock-solid support throughout the process. Lee Clayton is the *Daily Mail*'s Head of Sport and I would not be a journalist without his guidance and trust. Lee took me in on work experience at the age of 16 and I continue to learn from him and his team every day. Thank you to senior colleagues Ian Ladyman and Matt Lawton for always being on the end of the phone and to Jack Gaughan for providing a non-judgemental ear and the right advice. Thank you to my friends, many of whom I deserted for a while as I buried myself away to pursue my hobby.

Above all, thank you to the families of the Basque refugees, to John Aldecoa, Almudena Barinaga, Manuel Perez Lezama and Joan and Paul Gallego. Thank you for welcoming me into your homes and opening up a treasure trove of sepia-tinged keep-sakes and memories. I hope this book is a fitting tribute to the extraordinary lives endured and enjoyed by your husbands and fathers.

BIBLIOGRAPHY

As far as possible, I have sought to attribute the work of other journalists and authors as I have gone along in this book. The following list of books and both online and print sources were particularly useful in bringing together my project. The National Archives in Kew Gardens provided access to important UK government cabinet documents, while a vast number of newspaper archives, some at the British Library and some available online, were essential to my research. I am particularly indebted to the *Daily Mail*, *Times*, *Sunday Times*, *Guardian*, *Daily Mirror* and BBC for their back catalogue of original material. In Spain, *El Mundo Deportivo*, *Marca*, *El Pais* and *El Mundo* all provided important insight.

Books

Allardyce, Sam, *Big Sam: My Autobiography* (Headline Publishing, 2015)

Attenborough, Richard, *Entirely Up to You Darling* (Hutchinson, 2008)

Balague, Guillem, *A Season on the Brink* (Orion, 2006)

Benitez, Rafa, *Champions League Dreams* (Headline Publishing, 2012)

Bradford, Tim, *When Saturday Comes: The Half Decent Football Book* (Penguin, 2005)

Brooking, Trevor, *My Life in Football* (Simon & Schuster, 2015)

Burns, Jimmy, *Barça: A People's Passion* (Bloomsbury, 2009)

Burns, Jimmy, *La Roja: A Journey Through Spanish Football* (Simon & Schuster, 2012)

Calvin, Michael, *Living on the Volcano* (Century, 2015)

Clough, Brian, *The Autobiography* (Transworld, 1995)

Cruyff, Johan, *My Turn: The Autobiography* (Macmillan, 2016)

Douglas, Mark, *Inside the Rafalution* (Trinity Mirror Sport Media, 2017)

Ferguson, Sir Alex, *My Autobiography* (Hodder & Stoughton, 2014)

Gerrard, Steven, *My Story* (Penguin, 2015)

Grant, Michael, *Fergie Rises* (Aurum Press, 2014)

Guillen, Fran, *Diego Costa: The Art of War* (Arena Sport, 2015)

Gurruchaga, Iñigo, *Scunthorpe Hasta La Muerte* (deCoubertin Books, 2016)

Hardy, Martin, *Rafa's Way* (deCoubertin Books, 2017)

Harrison, Paul; *Keep Fighting: The Billy Bremner Story* (Black and White Publishing, 2010)

Hawkey, Ian, *Feet of the Chameleon: The Story of African Football* (Portico, 2010)

Hodkinson, Mark, *Blue Moon* (Mainstream Publishing, 1999)

Hughes, Mark, *Sparky: Barcelona, Bayern and Back* (Hutchinson Radius, 1989)

Hughes, Simon, *On the Brink* (deCoubertin Books Ltd, 2017)

Hughes, Simon, *Ring of Fire* (Bantam Press, 2016)

Hunter, Graham, *Barça* (BackPage Press, 2012)

Lowe Sid, *Fear and Loathing in La Liga: Barcelona vs Real Madrid* (Yellow Jersey Press, 2013)

Maier, Klaus, *Guernica 26.4.1937: La Intervención alemana en España y el Caso Guernica* (Sedmay Ediciones, 1976)

Martinez, Roberto, *Kicking Every Ball* (Y Lolfa, 2008)

Minder, Raphael, *The Struggle for Catalonia* (C. Hurst & Co, 2017)

Patterson, Ian, *Guernica and Total War* (Harvard University Press, 2007)

Perarnau, Martí, *Pep Confidential* (Arena Sport, 2014)

Perarnau, Martí, *Pep Guardiola: The Evolution* (Arena Sport, 2016)

Porta, Frederic, *Kubala! The Hero Who Changed Barça's History* (Ediciones Saldonar, 2012)

Preston Paul, *The Destruction of Guernica* (William Collins, 2017)

Reina, Pepe, *Pepe: My Autobiography* (Trinity Mirror Sport Media, 2011)

Robson, Bobby and Hayward, Paul, *Farewell but not Goodbye* (Hodder & Stoughton, 2005)

Smith, Rory, *Mister* (Simon & Schuster, 2016)

Soriano, Ferran, *La pelota no entra por azar* (Granica, 2013)

Thomas, Gordon and Morgan-Witts, Max, *Guernica: The Crucible of World War II* (Open Road, 2014)

Tusell, Javier, *Spain: From Dictatorship to Democracy* (Blackwell Publishing, 2007)

Venables, Terry, *Born to Manage* (Simon & Schuster, 2014)

Winter, Henry, *Fifty Years of Hurt* (Bantam Press, 2016)

Newspaper Articles/PHD/Podcast

Balague, Guillem, *Jose Antonio Reyes interview* (Observer, 8 August 2004)

Carlin, John, *Pep Guardiola: football's most wanted* (Financial Times, 18 January 2013)

Campbell, Denis, *Marcelino just wants to play again* (Guardian, 5 May 2002)

Diehl, Jorg, *Practising Blitzkrieg in the Basque country* (Spiegel Online, 26 April 2007)

Ducker, James, *How Barça came to Stoke City in Mark Hughes revolution* (The Times, 12 December 2015)

Editorial, The Guardian, *In praise of Guernica* (Guardian, 26 March 2009)

Hawkey, Ian, *Herrera plans to give Spurs the elbow* (Sunday Times, 11 December 2016)

Hunter, Graham, *Steve Archibald podcast* (Grahamhunter.tv, December 2016)

Hytner, David, *Watford's Quique Flores: Journalism made me a better manager* (Guardian, 22 April 2016)

Jahangir, Rumeana, *Spanish Civil War: The child refugees Britain did not want* (BBC, 17 July 2016)

James, Stuart, *Meet the man who discovered Gareth Bale*, (Observer, 17 May 2014)

Lawton, Matt, *Aitor Karanka interview* (Daily Mail, 23 January 2015)

Jenson, Pete, *Juande Ramos interview* (Daily Mail, 14 February 2014)

Liedtke, Boris Nikolaj, *International Relations between the US and Spain 1945-53* (PHD, London School of Economics and Political Sciences, ProQuest LLC, 2014)

Lowe, Sid, *Jose Antonio Reyes comes in from the cold to be Sevilla's saviour again* (Guardian, 19 November 2012)

Lowe, Sid, *Ramos reminds the world of his class* (Guardian, 20 February 2009)

Montague, James, *Manchester City's new owners put national pride before profit* (Guardian, 1 September 2008)

Rankin, Nicholas, *Guernica, seventy years on*, (Times Literary Supplement, 4 July 2007)

Sinca, Genis, *Oriol Tort: The soul of Barça's La Masia* (lameva. barcelona.cat, No date provided)

Smith, Rory, *Pepe Mel ready to write new chapter at West Bromwich* (The Times, 16 January 2014)

Steer, George, *The tragedy of Guernica* (The Times, 27 April 1937)

Talbot, Simon, *Reyes – the small-town boy born to be king* (Guardian, 30 January 2004)

Taylor, Matthew, *Through the net* (When Saturday Comes, February 2000)

Trautmann, Bert, *From Nazi paratrooper to hero of Manchester City* (Guardian, 10 April 2010)

Walker, Michael, *Boro all in it together* (Independent, 6 February 2015)

Williams, Richard, *The story of the fabulous Robledo boys* (Independent, 20 May 1999)

INDEX